Land Property Rights and Natural Resource Use

DEVELOPMENT ECONOMICS AND POLICY

Series edited by Franz Heidhues, Joachim von Braun and Manfred Zeller

Vol. 61

PETER LANG

Frankfurt am Main · Berlin · Bern · Bruxelles · New York · Oxford · Wien

Land Property Rights and Natural Resource Use

An Analysis
of Household Behavior
in Rural China

Stephan Piotrowski

PETER LANG
Internationaler Verlag der Wissenschaften

Bibliographic Information published by the Deutsche Nationalbibliothek
The Deutsche Nationalbibliothek lists this publication in the Deutsche Nationalbibliografie; detailed bibliographic data is available in the internet at <http://www.d-nb.de>.

Zugl.: Hohenheim, Univ., Diss., 2008

D 100
ISSN 0948-1338
ISBN 978-3-631-59143-7

© Peter Lang GmbH
Internationaler Verlag der Wissenschaften
Frankfurt am Main 2009
All rights reserved.

Printed in Germany 1 2 3 4 5   7

www.peterlang.de

Preface

With the reform processes in the former socialist countries, the allocative consequences of various forms of land ownership have received widespread attention in the economic literature. The paths to ownership reform that transforming countries have taken differ significantly, ranging from complete privatization of land ownership, e.g. in Russia and the Eastern European countries to rigid state ownership of all land, e.g. in Uzbekistan. In this continuum of ownership systems and tenure reforms, China stands out for its unique two-tier system of collective land ownership and private use rights in rural areas, and a system of state ownership in urban areas. Private land use rights are marketable, which has provided for a narrow land rental market in recent years.

China thus makes an interesting case to analyse how efficient this system is in achieving land productivity increases and sustainable resource use in spite of absent full private ownership. This is the focus of this volume of the series *Development Economics and Policy*. It begins with a presentation of current rural land policies in China and discusses some of the pressing issues which the tenure system could not adequately resolve. Among these are the linkages between tenure security and land related investments, the role of farmers' use rights for the access to credit and the discrimination of women in the land allocation process.

These important issues are analysed in this study by making use of two primary data sets. The first consists of a comprehensive rural household survey from the North China Plain, the main study area of the International Research Training Group "Sustainable Resource Use in North China". The second data set is a representative village leader survey in one of the counties from the household survey region.

In the econometric analysis, the study focuses on the production function approach and estimates a stochastic frontier production function at the household level as well as a deterministic production function at the village level. The marginal value product of land as estimated from the village-level production function is then compared with average village-level land rental prices in order to assess the allocative efficiency of the land rental market.

The research concludes that the mechanisms to transfer rural land use rights in China currently suffer from numerous imperfections. The rental market is clearly driven by the supply of land from off-farm oriented households and the demand of relatively few households which rent in land in the study area but do not appear to be more efficient than the lessors. The land rental market therefore falls short of its potential to increase land use efficiency. Nevertheless, land rental prices show a positive correlation with the estimated marginal value product of land which shows that rental prices are at least based on the productive value of land.

Recommendations to improve the functioning of land rental markets include the establishment of institutions which serve as brokers, or mediators, between potential lessors and lessees. Further reforms in the ownership and tenure structure towards privatization in order to facilitate an enlargement of farm sizes are not encouraged in China since rural households depend on a minimum of land as a means for social security. Although the Chinese land tenure system may not be efficient, it largely avoids the problem of landless peasants; mainly where peasants are illegally deprived of their land use rights can landlessness be observed as a significant problem.

Prof. Dr. Franz Heidhues *Prof. Dr. Manfred Zeller*
University of Hohenheim *University of Hohenheim*
Stuttgart *Stuttgart*

Prof. Dr. Joachim von Braun
International Food Policy Research Institute (IFPRI),
Washington D.C.

Acknowledgements

With a few words I would like to reflect on my doctoral studies at the University of Hohenheim. First and foremost I would like to express my profound gratitude to Prof. Dr. Franz Heidhues who accepted me as his doctoral student and generously supported and guided me throughout the past three and a half years.

Since I had spent the largest part of my student life at the University of Hohenheim, I was very happy to return to my alma mater in 2004. In the first weeks I had had a very good start with the help of Prof. Dr. Gertrud Buchenrieder who willingly introduced to me the topic of my prospective Ph.D. thesis and the basics of managing life as a doctoral student. For all her efforts I am extremely thankful. Furthermore, Prof. Dr. Manfred Zeller and Prof. Dr. Reiner Doluschitz on the German side and Prof. Dr. Wu Laping and Prof. Dr. Ke Binsheng on the Chinese side were always open to any of my requests and needs.

Apart from the academic achievements, the cordial relationship with my fellow doctoral students from the University of Hohenheim and China Agricultural University was what upheld my motivation even in slightly difficult times. I have unforgettable memories of jolly evenings with my dear colleagues Jia Xiangping, Clemens Breisinger, Ira Matuschke, Roland Barning, Martin Henseler, Malte Hillebrand, Jenny Kopsch, Christian Böber, Tina Beuchelt, Yoshiko Saigenji, Gabriela Alcaraz, Camille Saint-Macary, Wang Jiao and Ma Ji and many, many others. Special thanks deserve Alwin Keil for his patience in answering all my methodological questions and Ira Matuschke for commenting on parts of the thesis. Gudrun Contag, Cornelia Schumacher and Diana Ebersberger gave invaluable administrative support. Frank Bode and Barbara Bichler introduced to me the basics of GIS. I am indebted to Li Lan for her very good work in inputting the statistical data from Quzhou County. What's more, she cheered me up many times with her positive mood. Countless students from China Agricultural University got involved in our project by working as interviewers and made the extensive surveys we have conducted possible in the first place. Of these, Yang Xin and Gao Chuan stand out due to their utmost commitment and support.

All the fruitful academic and personal exchange and development within the Research Training Group would have been impossible without the generous financial support by the Deutsche Forschungsgemeinschaft (DFG) and the Ministry of Education of the People's Republic of China.

I am grateful to my parents for all their year-long tangible and intangible support and encouragement. Last but not least, I thank my girlfriend Nanne for sharing with me some spare time far away from University life.

Table of Contents

List of Tables xi
List of Figures xiii
Abbreviations and acronyms xv
Summary xvii
Zusammenfassung xxi
1   Introduction..1
   1.1   Problem statement 1
   1.2   Objectives 2
   1.3   Outline...3
2   Land rental markets in developing countries 5
3   Agriculture in the North China Plain 9
   3.1   Natural conditions and economic development 9
   3.2   Factor markets, product markets and natural resource management ..10
      3.2.1   Factor markets...12
         3.2.1.1   Land...12
         3.2.1.2   Labor 14
         3.2.1.3   Fertilizer...16
         3.2.1.4   Water 17
         3.2.1.5   Other capital inputs..18
         3.2.1.6   Information..19
      3.2.2   Product markets...19
4   Rural land policies in China 25
   4.1   Rural land property rights: theoretical background 25
   4.2   Formulation and implementation of rural land policies in China...........27
      4.2.1   The village in China's administrative and political hierarchy........27
      4.2.2   The legal framework defining rural land property rights...............30
   4.3   Unresolved issues...37
      4.3.1   Land reallocations and tenure insecurity 37
      4.3.2   Land rights and social security 38
      4.3.3   Land rights and gender inequality......................................39
      4.3.4   Land rights and credit access 40
5   Data collection 43
   5.1   Household data 43
   5.2   Village data 44
6   Methodological approaches used for the data analysis....................47
   6.1   Inequality Measurement...47
   6.2   Efficiency Analysis 49
      6.2.1   Technical Efficiency 50
      6.2.2   Allocative Efficiency 52
      6.2.3   Economic Efficiency...53
      6.2.4   Efficiency studies of Chinese agriculture 54
      6.2.5   Estimating agricultural production functions 56
   6.3   Spatial analysis of village data 58

6.4   Further econometric techniques used for the data analysis...............60
   6.4.1   Binary dependent variables 60
   6.4.2   Censored regressions and selection bias...............................61
7   Descriptive Analysis 63
  7.1   Household level...64
   7.1.1   Household composition 64
   7.1.2   Household agricultural production 67
    7.1.2.1   Land endowment and land use 68
    7.1.2.2   Input use in crop production 70
    7.1.2.3   Profitability of agricultural production...................................75
   7.1.3   Land use rights 77
   7.1.4   Household non-agricultural income sources..............................82
   7.1.5   Household income and decomposition of inequality.....................83
  7.2   Village level..86
   7.2.1   Summary of village level studies in rural China 86
   7.2.2   Data base for the village-level analysis 88
   7.2.3   Agricultural production 93
   7.2.4   Socio-demographic analysis...101
   7.2.5   Off-farm employment and inequality...103
   7.2.6   Land transfers and land use rights 106
8   Econometric Results...111
  8.1   Land endowment and land fragmentation.................................112
   8.1.1   Household level 112
   8.1.2   Village level...116
  8.2   Determinants of input use 118
   8.2.1   Household level 119
   8.2.2   Village level...120
  8.3   Determinants of land use right restrictions 122
   8.3.1   Household level 122
   8.3.2   Village level...123
  8.4   Determinants of the participation in land transfers..................125
   8.4.1   Household level 125
   8.4.2   Village level...127
  8.5   Results of the production function models 128
   8.5.1   Household level 128
   8.5.2   Village level...133
  8.6   Allocative efficiency in the land rental market 137
9   Main results, policy recommendations and suggestions for further
   research..141
  9.1   Main results..141
  9.2   Policy recommendations 143
  9.3   Suggestions for further research...145
References 147
Appendix...165

List of Tables

Table 3.1 Average labor demand per *mu* in crop production (2004)............14
Table 3.2 Technical constraints to improved grain yield..............................19
Table 4.1 Rights and obligations associated with different tenure types......32
Table 4.2 Farmers' land use rights: the formal legal framework..................36
Table 5.1 Household surveys: sampling design..43
Table 5.2 County and provincial-level economic indicators (2005).............44
Table 6.1 Production function studies on Chinese agriculture 55
Table 6.2 Example for a spatial weights matrix..59
Table 7.1 Household composition: Summary statistics................................65
Table 7.2 Farm man-day equivalents as a combination of occupation
           and gender 66
Table 7.3 Occupation of family members by gender....................................67
Table 7.4 Education of family members 67
Table 7.5 Household land endowment and land use 69
Table 7.6 Nitrogen fertilizer application by crops and counties...................71
Table 7.7 Reasons for and against application of organic fertilizer.............71
Table 7.8 Perception of water quantity and quality decline 72
Table 7.9 Use of agricultural machinery...73
Table 7.10 Labor demand by main crops..73
Table 7.11 Labor surplus by provinces...74
Table 7.12 Hired labor in crop production 75
Table 7.13 Profitability of agricultural production by provinces 76
Table 7.14 Profitability of wheat production by provinces 77
Table 7.15 Stated opinions on land reallocations...78
Table 7.16 Land reallocations in survey villages..79
Table 7.17 Incidence of land use right certificates 79
Table 7.18 Reasons for not participating in the land rental market................80
Table 7.19 Incidence of land rental transactions: comparison of own survey
           results with Schwarzwalder et al. (2002)......................................81
Table 7.20 Off-farm employment by survey counties......................................83
Table 7.21 Typical off-farm wages by counties 84
Table 7.22 Composition of income of sample households 84
Table 7.23 Decomposition of inequality in income and land endowment........85
Table 7.24 Inequality in land endowment (Gini coefficients) 86
Table 7.25 Village-level summary statistics (September 2007).......................90
Table 7.26 Quzhou Statistical Yearbook: Summary statistics (2006).............91
Table 7.27 Decomposition of changes in average wheat production 95
Table 7.28 Correlations of production costs between villages 98
Table 7.29 Village-level questionnaire (September 2007): Direct production
           costs for wheat, maize and cotton 98
Table 7.30 Fertilizer consumption in Quzhou County.....................................99
Table 7.31 Nitrogen excretion from organic fertilizer sources in China.........100
Table 7.32 Producer prices of agricultural products in Quzhou County 100

Table 7.33 Calculation of net income per capita 101
Table 7.34 Demographic variables by townships 103
Table 7.35 Correlation between cropping patterns and off-farm
          employment 104
Table 7.36 Correlation between the village location and socioeconomic
          variables 104
Table 7.37 Inequality decomposition in Quzhou County 105
Table 7.38 Gini coefficients in Quzhou County by townships....................106
Table 8.1 Determinants of land endowment and fragmentation:
          Summary statistics 113
Table 8.2 Determinants of household land endowment and fragmentation
          (OLS)...114
Table 8.3 Categorization of plot qualities: Summary statistics 115
Table 8.4 Categorization of plot qualities (Multinomial logistic regression).115
Table 8.5 Determinants of plots per household and average plot size:
          Summary statistics 116
Table 8.6 Determinants of plots per household and average plot size:
          Findings for Quzhou County (OLS) 117
Table 8.7 Regression analysis on the impact of village location (OLS).......118
Table 8.8 Determinants of nitrogen fertilizer use in winter wheat:
          Summary statistics 120
Table 8.9 Determinants of nitrogen fertilizer use in winter wheat (OLS).....120
Table 8.10 Determinants of wheat production costs: Summary statistics 121
Table 8.11 Determinants of wheat production costs (OLS).......................122
Table 8.12 Determinants of credit applications: Summary statistics 124
Table 8.13 Determinants of credit applications (Logistic regression)...........124
Table 8.14 Land right restrictions (Logistic regressions).........................125
Table 8.15 Determinants of land market participation (Logistic regression)..126
Table 8.16 Determinants of land market activity at the village level
          (tobit model)..127
Table 8.17 Variables used in the stochastic frontier models at the
          household level..129
Table 8.18 Maximum likelihood estimates of the stochastic frontier
          functions for winter wheat and GVAO (Cobb-Douglas).............130
Table 8.19 Maximum likelihood estimates of the parameters in the
          inefficiency model for winter wheat and GVAO 132
Table 8.20 Mean efficiency scores by provinces...................................132
Table 8.21 Likelihood ratio tests of hypotheses related to the specification
          of the stochastic frontier models at the household level............133
Table 8.22 Variables used in the deterministic production function for
          Quzhou County..134
Table 8.23 Deterministic production function for Quzhou County (Cobb-
          Douglas) 136
Table 8.24 Land rental prices (Heckman two-step procedure)...................139

List of Figures

Figure 1.1 IRTG research structure and data flow................................1
Figure 3.1 Direct production costs for winter wheat, summer maize and
cotton in 2004 11
Figure 3.2 Population and labor force in rural areas...........................15
Figure 3.3 Development of fertilizer consumption in agriculture.............17
Figure 3.4 Development of area sown to grain and cotton (Hebei, Henan
and Shandong)...21
Figure 3.5 Output price indices (1986-2003) 22
Figure 4.1 Transformation of rural administrative institutions................28
Figure 5.1 Quzhou County...45
Figure 6.1 Technical, allocative and economic efficiency......................54
Figure 7.1 Average temperature and precipitation in Quzhou County,
1980-2006 92
Figure 7.2 Development of sown area and yields in Quzhou County,
1996-2006 94
Figure 7.3 Fertilizer consumption and agricultural machinery use in
Quzhou County...96
Figure 7.4 Development of male labor force in Quzhou County.............102
Figure 7.5 Between which groups land transfers take place 107

Abbreviations and acronyms

AI	Allocative inefficiency score
AVP	Average value product
Bt	Bacillus thuringiensis
CCP	Chinese Communist Party
CD	Cobb-Douglas
CV	Coefficient of variation
DEA	Data Envelopment Analysis
EIA	Effectively irrigated area
FAR	First Order Autoregressive Model
GDP	Gross domestic product
GIS	Geographic Information System
GVAO	Gross value of agricultural product
HH	Sample household
HRS	Household Responsibility System
IMR	Inverse Mill's ratio
IRTG	International Research Training Group
LAL	Land Administration Law
LLCRA	Law on Land Contract in Rural Areas
MC	Marginal cost
MCI	Multiple cropping index
MDE	Man-day equivalent
MLD	Mean logarithmic deviation
MPL	Marginal productivity of labor
MRTS	Marginal rate of technical substitution
MVP	Marginal value product
NCCR	National compilation of costs and revenues of agricultural products
NCP	North China Plain
NIE	New Institutional Economics
NPL	Nonperforming loans
OLS	Ordinary Least Squares
PRC	People's Republic of China
QAB	Quzhou Agricultural Bureau
QSB	Quzhou Statistical Bureau
QSY	Quzhou Statistical Yearbook
RCC	Rural Credit Cooperative
RCF	Rural cooperative foundations
SAR	Spatial Autoregressive Model
SFA	Stochastic Frontier Analysis
SHYF	Stable high-yield fields
SI	Simpson Index
TE	Technical efficiency
TFP	Total Factor Productivity

TVE	Township and Village Enterprise
TFS	Two-Farmland System
US	United States
VA	Villagers' Assembly
VC	Villagers' Committee
VIF	Variance Inflation Factor
VRA	Village Representative Assembly
WTO	World Trade Organization
WUA	Water User Association

1 Yuan (¥) = 0.13 US$ (Sept. 2006)
1 *mu* (Chinese square measure) = 0.0067 hectares

Summary

Agricultural land in China is collectively owned. Farm households are entitled to an equal share of the village land to which they have usufruct rights. Under certain conditions they also have the right to transfer the use rights to other households. A narrow land rental market has developed, but agriculture in China is still characterized by extremely small, fragmented household farms. Most agricultural households earn side-line income from local off-farm employment, especially in collective enterprises at the level of villages and townships or through temporary migration of individual household members. However, only few households are willing to forego their land use rights, which are contingent on the permanent cultivation of the soil, and move out of agriculture. Land constitutes the central means for social security and this situation hinders a structural change towards larger, more competitive full-time farms.

From the viewpoint of economic theory, land rental markets are important because they allocate this scarce resource to the most productive uses. Well-functioning land rental markets are therefore crucial to the development of sustainable agriculture. With this background, it was the objective of this dissertation to analyze the emerging land rental market with regard to which farm households currently participate in this market and which constraints exist for an expansion of the transfer of land use rights through rental arrangements.

The main primary dataset for this study is a survey of 337 agricultural households in 20 villages in Hebei, Henan and Shandong Province in the North China Plain. This survey was carried out in 2005 by two subprojects of the International Research Training Group "Sustainable Resource Use in North China". For one of the survey counties, Quzhou County in Hebei Province, statistical yearbooks for the period 1996-2006 were collected. These yearbooks contain demographic and production oriented data at the village level. A complementary survey of village leaders was conducted in September 2007, covering 90% of the villages in this county.

About 5% of all households rent in any land additional to the plots allocated by the village, though only very small parcels. Moreover, land transfers tend to be restricted to single villages. The share of income derived from agriculture is lowest in Shandong Province, which goes along with a significantly more active land rental market. This confirms that the rural land rental market in the study area is currently mainly driven by the off-farm labor market, i.e. the intention of off-farm oriented households to move out of agriculture. This leads to the question, which households remain predominantly in agriculture and which households specialize in off-farm employment. The descriptive analysis of the household data shows that mainly younger, better educated, male family members work outside of agriculture. Furthermore, the statistical data for Quzhou County shows a slight but continuous decline of the share of male labor within the villages, which suggests that male workers increasingly leave the rural areas in search for non-agricultural employment opportunities.

Apart from various standard approaches, the emphasis of the econometric analysis is on methodologies for analyzing efficiency in agricultural production. A stochastic frontier production function estimated with the household-level data for winter wheat and the gross value of agricultural output produced by a household suggests that households with a higher share of their labor force working in agriculture are characterized by lower technical efficiency. This is in line with the result that such households apply more mineral fertilizer. Since overuse of chemical fertilizer is a serious environmental and economic problem in the study area, this is a worrying result. Apparently, management capabilities in agriculture and the off-farm labor market are positively correlated. These results allow the conclusion that on the whole also the potentially more capable, i.e. the more efficient farmers, leave agriculture, while mainly the older, less educated population continues farming. The land rental market does therefore not necessarily transfer the land to more efficient producers.

Adverse effects of land fragmentation on resource use and technical efficiency can not be clearly identified in this study. Nevertheless, farmers clearly favor larger plots closer to their homesteads. However, whether this is related to differences in soil properties or simply to ease of cultivation is uncertain. Also a negative effect of tenure insecurity could not be substantiated. Not all villages included in the household survey adhere to the legal stipulation of keeping land allocation stable for at least 30 years and to refrain from reallocations. However, these reallocations, which are essentially based upon the household size, guarantee egalitarian access to land. This explains why a majority of the surveyed households consents to the practice of reallocations. Also the use of organic fertilizer in crop production seems to be mainly determined by the availability of manure from own livestock and not by relative tenure security.

Reallocations are less frequent in Quzhou County than in the other counties included in the household survey. Only 30 of the 306 surveyed villages reported to have conducted any reallocation after 1992. As the most important factor determining the decision to conduct a reallocation, this study identifies land scarcity in a village, which confirms previous studies. This can be explained by the notion that the less land is available, the more important is egalitarian access to this factor.

The Quzhou case study also identifies a fundamental constraint of the land rental market, namely the prohibition to rent out land to persons outside the village community. In 20% of the villages such a prohibition exists. Such a practice can be justified by recalling that land is collectively owned by the village and not privately owned by the farmers. Also for the decision to restrict land transfers to members of the village community, land scarcity plays an important role.

A unique contribution of this study is the combination of different data sources for the Quzhou County case study. A georeferenced map of the county, which shows all villages as data points, was used jointly with the statistical and survey data to assess their spatial distribution. A deterministic village-level agricultural production function was estimated using a Spatial Autoregressive Model since the data showed strong spatial autocorrelation. The marginal value product of land as estimated from this function was then compared with average land rental prices. Land rental prices paid and received by farmers are shown to be positively correlated with the marginal value product, which implies that rental prices are in fact market prices and not arbitrarily set by village administrations. However, rental fees are consistently below the estimated marginal value product. Probably, returns from renting-out can therefore not adequately substitute for own cultivation.

Policy suggestions to improve rural land allocation include the establishment of local agencies which encourage farmers to engage in land use transfers, the promotion of inter-village land rentals and the support for voluntary exchanges of plots among households. This study describes various interesting tenure arrangements which have emerged from local experimentation with different policies. The relevance of well-functioning institutions highlights the importance of conducting the kind of micro-level research as done for this study in order to identify successful local institutional arrangements.

Zusammenfassung

Agrarland befindet sich in China im Kollektiveigentum. Landwirtschaftlichen Haushalten stehen Nießbrauchrechte eines gleichen Anteils der landwirtschaftlichen Fläche in einem Dorf zu. Unter bestimmten Bedingungen sind sie berechtigt, ihre Nutzungsrechte an andere Haushalte zu übertragen. Dadurch hat sich in begrenztem Umfang ein Landpachtmarkt entwickelt, doch Landwirtschaft in China ist noch immer durch extrem kleine, fragmentierte bäuerliche Betriebe geprägt. Die meisten landwirtschaftlichen Haushalte verdienen neben der Landwirtschaft zusätzliches Einkommen durch lokale Erwerbsquellen, vor allem in Kollektivbetrieben auf Dorf- und Gemeindeebene, oder durch zeitweise Migration einzelner Familienmitglieder. Nur wenige Haushalte sind jedoch bereit auf ihre Landnutzungsrechte, die an die Bewirtschaftung des Bodens gebunden sind, zu verzichten und vollständig aus der Landwirtschaft abzuwandern. Land stellt das zentrale Mittel zur sozialen Sicherung dar und diese Situation verhindert einen Strukturwandel hin zu größeren, wettbewerbsfähigen Vollerwerbsbetrieben.

Aus Sicht der ökonomischen Theorie sind Landpachtmärkte wichtig da sie diese knappe Ressource der produktivsten Nutzung zuführen. Gut funktionierende Landpachtmärkte sind daher entscheidend für die Entwicklung nachhaltiger Landwirtschaft. Vor diesem Hintergrund ist es das Ziel dieser Arbeit gewesen, den sich entwickelnden Landpachtmarkt dahingehend zu untersuchen, welche Bauern derzeit am Pachtmarkt teilnehmen und welche Beschränkungen es für eine Ausweitung der Übertragung von Landnutzungsrechten durch Pacht gibt. Hierfür wurde im Jahr 2005 in Zusammenarbeit mit anderen Teilprojekten des Internationalen Graduierten-kollegs „Sustainable Resource Use in North China" eine Befragung von 337 landwirtschaftlichen Haushalten 20 Dörfern in den Provinzen Hebei, Henan und Shandong in der Nordchinesischen Tiefebene durchgeführt. Für einen der untersuchten Landkreise, Quzhou in der Provinz Hebei, standen statistische Jahrbücher für die Jahre 1996-2006 zur Verfügung. Diese Jahrbücher enthalten demographische und produktionsorientierte Daten auf Dorfebene. Eine ergänzende Befragung der Dorfverwaltungen, die 90% der Dörfer in diesem Landkreis erfasste, wurde im September 2007 durchgeführt.

Etwa 5% der Haushalte pachten neben dem vom Dorf zugeteilten Land zusätzliche Flächen, allerdings nur sehr kleine Parzellen. Landnutzungsübertragungen sind zudem meist auf ein Dorf beschränkt. Der Anteil des aus der Landwirtschaft erwirtschafteten Einkommens ist in der Provinz Shandong am geringsten, was mit einem sehr viel aktiveren Landpachtmarkt einhergeht. Dies bestätigt dass der Landpachtmarkt in der Untersuchungsregion zurzeit im Wesentlichen durch die Entwicklung des nichtlandwirtschaftlichen Arbeitsmarktes bestimmt wird, d.h. durch das Bestreben eines Teils der Haushalte aus der Landwirtschaft abzuwandern. Dies führt zu der Frage, welche Haushalte primär in der Landwirtschaft verbleiben und welche Haushalte sich auf außerlandwirtschaftliche Erwerbsquellen spezialisieren. Die deskriptive

Analyse der Haushaltsbefragung zeigt, dass überwiegend jüngere, besser ausgebildete, männliche Familienmitglieder außerhalb der Landwirtschaft arbeiten. Darüber hinaus zeigen die statistischen Daten des Landkreises Quzhou dass der Anteil männlicher Arbeitskräfte in den Dörfern kontinuierlich abgenommen hat, was nahe legt, dass männliche Arbeiter auf der Suche nach alternativen Erwerbsquellen verstärkt die ländlichen Gebiete verlassen.

Neben verschiedenen gebräuchlichen Verfahren liegt der Schwerpunkt der ökonometrischen Auswertung auf Methoden zur Analyse der Produktions-effizienz in der Landwirtschaft. Eine anhand der Daten aus der Haushalts-befragung geschätzte stochastische Produktionsfunktion für Winterweizen und den gesamten landwirtschaftlichen Produktionswert eines Haushaltes legt nahe, dass Haushalte mit einem höheren Anteil an ausschließlich in der Landwirtschaft tätigen Mitgliedern durch geringere technische Effizienz gekennzeichnet sind. Dies bestätigt auch das Ergebnis, dass diese Haushalte mehr mineralischen Stickstoffdünger einsetzen. Überdüngung und die resultierende Nitratbelastung des Grundwassers ist in den letzten Jahren in der Region zu einem wesentlichen Umweltproblem geworden. Es scheint daher, dass Managementfähigkeiten im nichtlandwirtschaftlichen Arbeitsmarkt mit denen in der Landwirtschaft positiv korrelieren, was den Schluss zulässt, dass derzeit tendenziell auch die fähigeren, d.h. effizienteren, Bauern abwandern, während Landwirtschaft hauptsächlich von der älteren, schlechter ausgebildeten Bevölkerung betrieben wird. Der Landpachtmarkt führt daher nicht unbedingt zu einer effizienteren Landallokation.

Negative Auswirkungen der Landfragmentierung auf technische Effizienz und Ressourcennutzung konnten in dieser Arbeit nicht eindeutig identifiziert werden. Die befragten Bauern werten jedoch kleinere, weiter von ihrem Haus entfernte Parzellen als von minderwertigerer Qualität gekennzeichnet. Ob dies allerdings auf Bodeneigenschaften oder Erschwernis bei der Bewirtschaftung zurückzuführen ist, konnte nicht geklärt werden. Auch negative Auswirkungen der durch regelmäßige Umverteilungen bedingten Landrechtsunsicherheit lassen sich nicht nachweisen. Nicht alle Dörfer aus der Haushaltsbefragung halten sich an die gesetzliche Vorgabe, die Landverteilung für mindestens 30 Jahre stabil zu halten und auf Umverteilungen zu verzichten. Diese Umverteilungen, die sich im Wesentlichen nach der Haushaltsgröße richten, garantieren jedoch einen egalitären Zugang zum Land. Dies erklärt, warum eine Mehrheit der Bauern diese Landumverteilungen befürwortet. Auch der Einsatz organischen Düngers in der pflanzlichen Produktion scheint haupt-sächlich abhängig zu sein von dessen Verfügbarkeit durch eigene Tierhaltung und nicht von der durch periodische Umverteilungen induzierten Landrechts-unsicherheit.

Landumverteilungen sind sehr viel seltener in Quzhou. Nur 30 der 306 befragten Dörfer gaben an, eine Umverteilung nach 1992 durchgeführt zu haben. Als wichtigster Faktor für die Wahrscheinlichkeit einer Landum-verteilung lässt sich Landknappheit ausmachen, wie auch vorherige Arbeiten bestätigen. Dies lässt sich damit begründen, dass ein egalitärer Zugang zum Boden umso wichtiger wird, je knapper dieser Faktor ist.

Die Fallstudie in Quzhou betrachtet auch eine wesentliche Beschränkung des Landpachtmarktes, nämlich das Verbot, Land an Personen außerhalb der Dorfgemeinschaft zu verpachten. In 20% der Dörfer gibt es eine solche Beschränkung. Zunächst lässt sich eine solche Beschränkung damit rechtfertigen, dass sich das Land im Kollektivbesitz der Dorfgemeinschaft befindet und nicht im Privatbesitz einzelner Bauern. Auch im Fall dieser Beschränkung spielt Landknappheit eine wichtige Rolle.

Ein wesentlicher Beitrag der vorliegenden Arbeit ist in der Verknüpfung verschiedener Datenquellen für die Fallstudie in Quzhou zu sehen. Eine georeferenzierte Karte des untersuchten Kreises, welche die einzelnen Dörfer als Datenpunkte zeigt, wurde herangezogen um die räumliche Verteilung der Daten aus der Dorfbefragung und den statistischen Jahrbüchern zu untersuchen. Eine deterministische landwirtschaftliche Produktionsfunktion auf Dorfebene wurde unter Verwendung eines Erweiterten Autoregressiven Modells geschätzt, da anhand der Karte starke räumliche Abhängigkeiten festgestellt wurden. Das aus der Produktionsfunktion geschätzte Wertgrenzprodukt des Landes wurde dann mit den durchschnittlichen Landpachtpreisen verglichen und festgestellt, dass diese in der Regel unter dem Wertgrenzprodukt liegen. Wahrscheinlich sind derzeit gezahlte Pachtpreise daher oft nicht ausreichend, um einen Anreiz für das Verpachten von Land darzustellen.

Politikempfehlungen zur Verbesserung der Landallokation beinhalten die Einführung lokaler Organisationen die Bauern bei der Entscheidung ihre Landnutzungsrechte zu verpachten unterstützen, die Förderung dorfüberschreitender Verpachtungen und des freiwilligen Austausches fragmentierter Parzellen im Sinne einer Flurbereinigung. Die vorliegende Arbeit beschreibt einige interessante Landverteilungs- und nutzungsregelungen die oft aus Experimenten auf lokaler Ebene hervorgegangen sind. Die Relevanz gut funktionierender Institutionen verdeutlicht die Bedeutung, Forschung wie für die vorliegende Arbeit durchzuführen, da nur so erfolgreiche lokale Institutionen identifiziert werden können.

1 Introduction

1.1 Problem statement

Farm households in the North China Plain (NCP) are practicing intensive agriculture that is characterized by high and unsustainable inputs of mineral fertilizer and plant protection chemicals. This has resulted in serious pollution of soil and water resources. The main research hypothesis of the International Research Training Group (IRTG) "Sustainable Resource Use in North China" is that adjustments in cropping systems and management practices provide potential for sustainable resource protection on a high yield level (IRTG 2003). This study is part of the interdisciplinary IRTG, which combines subprojects (SP) from different disciplines (soil sciences, plant nutrition, landscape ecology, physics, crop production, plant breeding, agricultural economics, agricultural informatics and rural development policy), most of which used different modeling approaches, in the pursuit of identifying, measuring and modeling material flows in intensive agricultural production systems in the North China Plain.

Figure 1.1 sketches the research structure and data flow of the IRTG. 11 subprojects have been grouped into the superordinate groups Material Flows/ Pollution Analysis, Cropping Systems and Farm Level, Regional and Sectoral Assessment. The research for this study has been part of subproject 3.3 "Land and Water Property Rights, Natural Resource Management and Rural Credit Access".

Figure 1.1   IRTG research structure and data flow

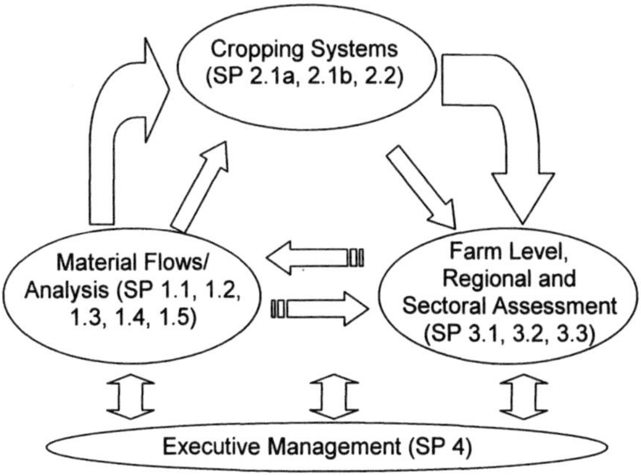

Source: Adapted from IRTG (2003).

Agriculture in China faces declining arable land, stagnating yields, worsening environmental conditions and the challenge of a deepening integration into the world market (Zhou and Tian, 2005). Agricultural producers adapt their cropping patterns increasingly to changing prices and comparative advantages, which makes the central government even more concerned about the country's grain security. Policy makers are concerned about maintaining farmers' "enthusiasm for grain production" (China Daily 2004). This policy goal and the above mentioned problems stand against the challenge of sharing the fruits of the thriving Chinese economy with the rural population. Apart from the income gap between urban and rural areas in China, there is also evidence of increasing inequality within rural areas stemming from unequal access to local off-farm employment and migration (Wan and Zhou, 2005).

While Institutional and market reforms since the late 1970s had boosted agricultural production by granting individual farm households extensive use rights, the potential of these reforms has been fully exploited according to most studies (Carter et al., 2003). As the downside of the Household Responsibility System (HRS), small, fragmented plots have emerged as a consequence of the policy to grant every rural household use rights to a share of the village land. As a consequence, few households are able to generate sufficient income solely from agricultural production and most depend on additional off-farm income sources. From the little land they cultivate, households attempt to maximize output by applying high, inefficient amounts of natural and industrial inputs, leading to resource degradation. Farmers willing to expand production are constrained in their access to land and capital. The lack of access to capital can be explained by imperfections of the rural credit market (Jia, 2007). The importance of access to land and the reasons for imperfections of the rural land market are explored in this thesis.

1.2 Objectives

There is a wide consensus that privatization of rural land ownership is not needed in order to break the deadlock of scattered land holdings and inefficient resource use. Research has shown that full privatization, implying the right to buy and sell land, is not a necessary requirement for efficiency gains in a situation of clear and enforceable user rights (Lohmar et al., 2002). Privatization of land ownership also still faces strong social and political opposition in China (Guo, 2003; Wang, 2005). In fact, maintaining collective land ownership can be seen as the attempt to maintain the framework of state socialism within a situation of widespread economic reforms towards liberalization (Guo, 2003).

Additionally, Kung (1995) identifies two conditions that need to be met for the emergence of private property rights to land: population pressure and resulting land scarcity and an increase in the value of land. While the first condition is clearly met, the author casts doubts on the fulfillment of the second requirement (Kung, 1995, p. 85). Therefore, a change to private ownership of agricultural land is unlikely and the present condition of collective ownership and private use rights to agricultural land can be regarded as a salient feature of Chinese agriculture also in the near future (Kung, 2002a). For this reason, the creation of innovative, viable institutions within the current legal framework is likely to be the most promising approach to tackle the aforementioned problems. Since the land allocation mechanism is, among other things, at the core of the problems in rural China, this study aims to better understand the principles and incentives of different local actors and eventually the mechanisms that lead to an improvement of land allocation. More specifically, the main research question is whether such local institutions can be shown to improve efficiency in agricultural production.

While the central government enacted laws for the administration of rural land, the villages and townships, as the representatives of the "collective" and therefore legal owners of rural land, have in practice some freedom to decide on land allocation rules. Moreover, the village is the basic decision making unit in many other aspects, such as the collection of fees from households and the development of local collective enterprises, which have been a main driving force of rural industrialization (Pei, 1998). The main part of this study therefore focuses on the situation at the village level rather than the individual household.

1.3 Outline

Chapter 2 gives an overview over the theory of agricultural factor and product markets in developing countries with the focus on land markets. With this background, chapter 3 discusses the specific situation of the rural economy in the research area, the North China Plain, in more detail. In order to better understand the present situation, chapter 4 gives an overview over the theory of rural land property rights and traces the development of land policies back to the beginning of the economic reforms in the late 1970s. It highlights how land policies in China struggled to uphold a balance between egalitarian principles and market mechanisms.

Chapter 5 introduces the household and village data sets used in this study and presents descriptive results with regard to household production and consumption and the characteristics of rural land allocation. Many studies observed a distinct heterogeneity of land property rights in rural China. This heterogeneity and the differentiating factors between households and villages are further explored in this chapter.

Chapter 6 explicates the methodologies used in the econometric data analysis. Apart from various econometric techniques for estimating models to answer the research questions concerning the rural land market, the emphasis in this chapter is on methodologies for analyzing production efficiency. Several studies on the efficiency of Chinese agriculture have been conducted, of which chapter 6 also gives an overview. Descriptive results are presented in chapter 7, followed by econometric evidence in chapter 8. The focus is here on the question which of those land tenure arrangements observed and described in chapter 4 are associated with higher production efficiency at the household or village level and what other determinants of production efficiency can be identified. In the concluding chapter 9, policy recommendations and suggestions for further research are formulated.

2 Land rental markets in developing countries

Economists attach great importance to a functioning land rental market for improving productivity and equity by transferring land to more productive users (Deininger, 2003). In more theoretical terms, land rental markets lead to an equalization of the marginal value product of land across households which increases allocative efficiency. Furthermore, a land rental market allows for specialization in either agriculture or off-farm employment and increases the incentives to undertake land related investments, provided that the benefits from such investments can be reaped through higher rental payments (Feng, 2006, p. 3).

In a situation where markets are suspected to be highly distorted, market price information is often not suitable for assessing the actual values of factors and products because decisions are made in line with unobserved, endogenous shadow prices. The concept of shadow prices is therefore also central to the theory of supply and demand behavior of agricultural households in developing countries, where markets are often incomplete or missing. Without market distortions, a profit-maximizing household equates the marginal value product (MVP) of a factor and the marginal cost (MC) of a product to their respective market prices. If markets function well, the MVPs and MCs should therefore equalize across households and market prices should equal to the households' shadow prices.

In a distorted market, shadow prices might differ from the observed market prices and households then attempt to equate their MVPs and MCs to these unobserved shadow prices. Due to this theoretical equality, the MVPs derived from an agricultural production function can be interpreted as the factors' shadow prices.

Shadow prices are determined within the household as a function of preferences, technology, fixed inputs and market prices (Skoufias, 1994). As an example, because of the lack of alternative mechanisms, arable land in China exerts an important social safety net function which increases its shadow price for potential lessors and this is most likely not accounted for in observed land market prices (see Conning and Robinson, 2007). If renting out land increases the risk of losing the use right, the decision to specialize in off-farm work is connected with a considerable disutility (Skoufias, 1994, p. 215).

Carter and Yao (2002) call these "retribution costs" incurred when renting out land and also consider search costs in view of the narrow rental market for those renting in land (p. 705). The conditions for the three possible land rental regimes (renting in, renting out and autarky) can then be defined as follows:

$$MVP = r + c^i \qquad (1)$$

$$MVP = r - c^o \qquad (2)$$

$$r - c^o < MVP < r + c^i,$$ (3)

where r is the observed rental price for land and c^i and c^o are, respectively, the unit costs incurred due to market imperfections which alter the market price into the shadow prices $r + c^i$ and $r - c^o$. Households facing a shadow price below their marginal value product for land (MVP) will desire to rent in land until both equalize (1). Likewise, households facing a shadow price above their MVP will equalize both by renting out land (2). Finally, non-participants in the land rental market are characterized by an MVP that is below the shadow price for renting in, but above the shadow price for renting out (3).

Institutional failures therefore drive a wedge between land shadow prices of potential lessors and lessees and these gaps cause land transfers between agricultural households to be less than economically efficient. The gap between market prices and estimated shadow prices endogenous to households can be used to derive the degree of market distortions (Ali et al., 1993; Wang et al., 1996).

Agricultural households also base their decisions on shadow prices when their production decisions cannot be assumed to be separated from consumption decisions. The basic household model is recursive, i.e. household production and consumption decisions are assumed to be separable. The linkage between consumption and production decisions is postulated to be only one-sided, i.e. the former are determined by the profit generated by production (hence, this paradigm is referred to as the profit effect). Production decisions are assumed to be independent of consumption and labor supply decisions (Singh et al., 1986, p. 7). In many cases, this assumption cannot be maintained. According to Singh et al. (1986, p. 48), nonseparability applies in cases where supply and demand prices differ for the same good and in face of incomplete markets caused by incentive problems or risk. The first situation may be observed in the case of staple crops produced by the household: the price received from selling them in the market might be lower than the cost of purchasing the staple crops. Then, some or all of the produce will be consumed by the household and consumption influences production. The second case applies to the situation of retribution costs when renting out land.

Incomplete markets imply that current endowment with factors determines production decisions. In this sense, nonseparability can be seen as endowment dependence in production (Carter and Yao, 2002). Land and labor markets allow households to break this endowment dependence and to freely choose their profit-maximizing levels of inputs, which then leads to an efficient allocation of resources. Bowlus and Sicular (2003) find that the nonseparability caused by incomplete labor markets in rural China can be associated with labor surplus and shortage coexisting at the same time, even within one county. Since It is believed that labor surplus will induce households to farm their land more intensively, equalization of the marginal value product of labor across households and villages can also have important implications for the sustainability of land use (Bowlus and Sicular, 2003). Carter and Yao (2002) describe how to test for separability when it is suspected that some, but not all households are affected by the market failures causing non-separability. In the case of completely missing land and labor markets, there is no market wage or market price for land and hence households cannot equate the marginal product of labor or land to the respective market prices or endogenous shadow prices. In those cases, households equate their demand for factors with their current endowment and therefore production decisions also become non-separable. Carter and Yao (2002) show that land transfer rights can break this endowment dependence in production. In the present study, the focus is therefore on the distortions caused by insecure or incomplete land transfer markets and how more complete and secure land use rights can improve production efficiency.

3 Agriculture in the North China Plain

This section briefly highlights the main characteristics of agriculture in China, and in the NCP in particular, before discussing the use of the most important natural and industrial inputs and the development of product market policies. Only 14% of China's total area of 9.5 million hectare is cultivable land, which results in a mere 0.106 ha of cultivated land per capita, compared to the world's average of 0.236 ha (Lin and Ho, 2003)[1].

Following from this, agriculture in China is mainly labor intensive and capital input is – apart from fertilizer – relatively low. With examples of other transition countries in mind, it could be expected, that in the course of economic development and integration into world markets, Chinese agriculture will need to move to more capital intensive, technology-driven, large-scale farms (Prosterman et al., 1998). On the other hand, it can be argued that China should focus on its comparative advantage in labor intensive crops (Schwarzwalder et al., 2002).

3.1 Natural conditions and economic development

The North China Plain mainly spans across Hebei, Henan and Shandong Province and parts of Beijing, Tianjin, Anhui and Jiangsu Province (see Appendix). With a size of 320.000 km², a population of 200 million people, a 50% share of total Chinese wheat production and 33% of Chinese maize production, respectively, the NCP is one of China's most important agricultural regions (Kendy et al., 2003). Apart from the traditional double cropping system of winter wheat and summer maize, cotton is an important cash crop in most parts of the region. To a lesser extent, some areas have also specialized in vegetable production. Since it is situated in the alluvial plains of the Yellow River it is a fertile region which faces, however, increasing pressure on its natural resources due to competition for land and water between agriculture, industries and the domestic sector.

Water and land resources are unevenly distributed in China. North China accounts for 60% of the land area but only 20% of the water resources. Since water demand of winter wheat and summer maize exceeds rainfall in the growing season by two to three times (Zhen and Routray, 2002), their cultivation depends on irrigation. Due to pollution or drying up of surface waters, farmers increasingly turn to groundwater irrigation. While wheat yields had increased steadily since the 1970s, they have stagnated at around 5 t/ha in recent years (Wu et al., 2006). Wu et al. (2006) simulate average potential wheat yields and wheat yields under limited water availability using a crop growth model and find that long-term potential wheat yields could be on average 8.2 t/ha. However, simulated yields under water stress only averaged

---

[1] The traditional Chinese unit for an area of land is *mu*, which equals 1/15 ha. This unit is used henceforth, since a conversion to ha would, due to the extremely small plot sizes, lead to small, uneven numbers.

the actual yield level of 5 t/ha. Furthermore, Wu et al. (2006) found the yield gap due to water shortage to be highest in the Northern part of the NCP, which is the main research area for the present study. The authors therefore see great potential for increasing yields by improving water supply or the use efficiency of existing water sources.

3.2 Factor markets, product markets and natural resource management

When trying to assess how well the scarce resources are used in agriculture in the NCP, one observes first and foremost a puzzlingly high share of chemical fertilizer costs in direct production costs. In particular, overuse of nitrogen fertilizer has become a serious threat to agricultural sustainability in the NCP. Figure 3.1 gives an overview over the cost structure for winter wheat, summer maize and cotton in Hebei, Shandong and Henan Province[2]. According to these figures, chemical fertilizer accounts for 40%-50% of direct production costs in winter wheat. These correspond well to Qiao et al. (2003, p. 1223) who mention a 40% share of fertilizer in farmers' cash outlays. Hu et al. (2004) compared the cost structure of Chinese and US wheat production in 1998 and included all other indirect production costs. In their comparison, chemical fertilizer made up 20% of the costs for Chinese producers and 11% for their US counterparts. However, they arrive at the interesting conclusion that North American wheat production has in fact no cost advantage over production in China due to higher land, labor and machinery costs (Hu et al., 2004, p. 1078).

While Shandong and Hebei show a similar cost level and structure, wheat production costs in Henan province are around 50 ¥/*mu* lower which can be mainly attributed to lower fertilizer costs and overall lower irrigation costs. Also the production costs for maize and cotton are significantly lower in Henan. Labor costs are not included in these tables as they are more difficult to assess since most of the labor employed on farm is family labor.

---

[2] For these three provinces, primary and secondary data were collected for this study, so the following analysis leaves out Jiangsu and Anhui Province, which are also part of the NCP.

Figure 3.1   Direct production costs for winter wheat, summer maize and cotton in 2004 (in ¥/mu)

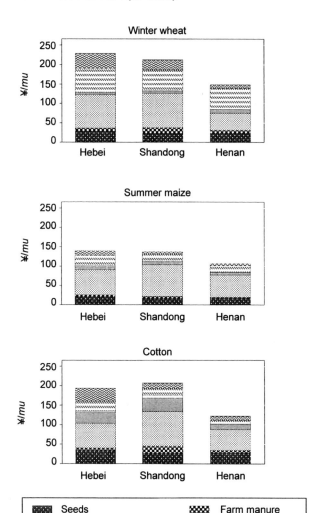

Source: National Bureau of Statistics of China (various years).

3.2.1 Factor markets

The following sections discuss in more detail the characteristics and key drivers of input use in Chinese agriculture, with emphasis on the particular conditions in the NCP, and the development of product markets.

3.2.1.1 Land

The HRS provided agricultural households with long-term use rights to a share of the village land. Compared to other developing countries, rural land in China is therefore allocated to households in a highly egalitarian way (Burgess, 2001). Due to the high population and the fact that few households are willing to give up their use rights, the average farm size is around 0.5 ha (7.5 *mu*) which are segmented into about 6 plots as a result of the pursuit to divide the village land equally also in terms of plot quality (Wu, 2005).

The basis for land allocation is either the total household size or the household's labor endowment. Nonetheless, there may be certain household and village characteristics that determine a household's land endowment apart from household size or labor endowment. Burgess (2001) found that other demographic characteristics such as age and number of children (households with more than two children are found to be punished in the land allocation process) also influence how much land is allotted to a household.

While the village leadership is usually the party giving out land use contracts and commanding over land distribution, the land remains collectively owned (see section 4 in this study) and it would be inadequate to describe the relation between peasants and village administration as a tenant-landlord relationship. In principle, farmers do not pay for their land use rights and with recent reforms also explicit taxation of agriculture has been removed (Heerink et al., 2006).

Kung (1995) notes that egalitarian land distribution need not a priori lead to land fragmentation as long as farmers can voluntarily exchange or transfer plots. However, it is evident that the egalitarian principle of the HRS has indeed led to small, scattered land holdings (Reisch and Vermeer, 1992). Land fragmentation is a multi-level phenomenon and can be measured by total farm size, number of plots per farm, distance between these plots and the homestead, average plot size or a combination of these aspects, such as the Simpson Index (Blarel et al., 1992; Tan, 2005). Such a combined measure is more appropriate, because any one of the aforementioned aspects may be counteracted by others, e.g. small farm sizes do not necessarily have to go along with the fragmentation of one household's plots.

Particularly land fragmentation in terms of total farm size is a salient feature of Chinese agriculture, with land holdings per household well below averages of other Asian countries. According to Fan and Chan-Kang (2005), average farm size in the early 1990s stood at 3.36 ha in Thailand, 1.55 ha in India, 1.37 ha in Japan, 1.23 ha in South Korea and 0.43 ha in China. Whether land fragmentation *per se* is detrimental is not unambiguous: in principle, land fragmentation prevents economies of scale, but fragmentation can also serve to spread risk.

Wu (2005) in fact detects an inverse relationship between farm size and land productivity coupled with a higher overall efficiency of larger farms. Keeping in mind that land productivity has been in the past more important for China than production efficiency, this may explain why the country has not witnessed a development towards larger farms so far. On the other hand, the inverse relationship may also be explained by systematic plot quality differences. Nguyen and Cheng (1996) claim that at the beginning of the HRS, land had been divided in such a way that good quality plots were subdivided into smaller plots while poor quality plots remained larger in size. As a consequence, the adverse effects of land fragmentation may be underestimated. For instance, Chen et al. (2003, p. 15) could not reject the hypothesis of decreasing returns to scale and also provide land quality differences between small and large farms as a possible explanation.

However, many unobservable factors influencing plot quality and the multi-level nature of "quality" itself makes it a difficult task to show this empirically (Tan, 2007). This complexity renders studies on the adverse effects of fragmentation questionable. It is also necessary to weigh the detrimental effects of fragmentation against the fact that universal access to land has been vitally important in the past for achieving food security (Burgess, 2001).

Overall, a review of the literature on this topic in China shows that criticism of land fragmentation prevails (see e.g. Tan, 2005). Chen et al. (2003, p. 16) found a negative impact of the number of plots a household cultivates on technical efficiency (see section 6.2.1 of this study). Fleisher and Liu (1992) showed that in their sample of 1200 farm households surveyed in 1987-1988, reducing the number of plots from the average of four to one would increase Total Factor Productivity (TFP) by 8%.

Tan (2005) found in her analysis of small rice farms in Jiangxi Province that non-farm employment and the land rental market also correlate with more consolidated land holdings. This is explained by the notion that lessees prefer to rent in land adjacent to their current plots.

To sum up, the literature review largely confirms the intuition that land fragmentation is detrimental to resource use efficiency, although this is sometimes difficult to show due to incomplete data. For instance, it is evident that independent of other possible impacts, large land areas in China are simply lost due to plot boundaries and tracks leading to the fields. The role of land property rights in causing, and possibly overcoming land fragmentation, is further dealt with in section 4 and the empirical part of this study.

3.2.1.2 Labor

Given a large labor surplus[3], most of the agricultural operations in the study region are done manually. This includes pesticide and fertilizer applications and harvesting. Table 3.1 provides a first impression of the labor demand for the main crops in the NCP, given current technology. The labor demand for wheat and maize shown in this table is much in line with Yang (1997), who reports a labor demand of 6 to 8 days/*mu* for wheat and around 10 days/*mu* for maize.

Table 3.1   Average labor demand per *mu* in crop production in days/*mu* (2004)

	Wheat	Maize	Cotton	Peanuts	Soybeans
Hebei	7.3	7.6	20.4	10.8	6.1
Henan	6.5	8.3	26.8	13.0	5.5
Shandong	8.3	8.8	26.6	13.8	6.2

Source: National Bureau of Statistics of China (various years).

From 1986 to 2003, the share of rural to total population and the share of the agricultural labor in total rural labor force declined annually by 0.4% and 1% respectively. In the same period, the share of total labor force in the rural population increased, however, by about 0.4% annually (see Figure 3.2). Although the growing off-farm labor market has already transferred large parts of the rural labor force out of agriculture, most studies conclude that there is still considerable surplus rural labor, according to Wu (2005) amounting to 50 to 100 million.

Given the increasing share of off-farm income in rural areas, the question arises which household members continue to do the farm work and how this impacts on agricultural productivity. Most studies conclude that the farm work is increasingly done by older laborers (Pang et al., 2004). Since de Brauw (2003, p. 19) finds that women do not participate less in off-farm work than men, he concludes that these are mainly older men. Zhang et al. (2006) argue in the same direction and find that a "feminization of agriculture" does not take place in China. However, this issue is not resolved unanimously since Li and Bruce (2005) indeed observed an increase in the share of female labor in agriculture.

---

[3] Agricultural labor intensity, defined as the number of agricultural workers per hectare of arable land, amounted in China to 3.3 in 2003 compared to the world's average of 0.87 and Asia's average of 2.04 (World Resources Institute, 2007).

Figure 3.2 Population and labor force in rural areas

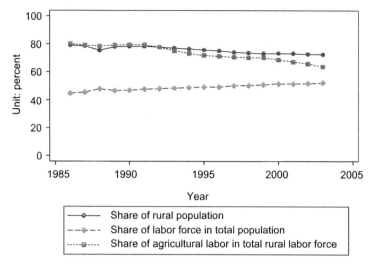

Source: Ministry of Agriculture (2004).

No consistent method to calculate rural labor surplus in China has been developed, which has been criticized by Chu et al. (2000). One obvious approach would be to compare how much labor is needed at a given technology with the actual labor employed. One problem with this approach is that one needs good estimates of the actual labor demand. A second problem is that part of the assumed labor surplus could also be caused by farmers overstating the hours worked on-farm (Kung and Lee, 2001). In any case, however, the output elasticity of labor can be expected to be very low in comparison to that of land (see e.g. Chen et al., 2003). Chu et al. (2000) made an attempt to estimate what they call net surplus labor at the village level by identifying those laborers among the employed workforce which may be dubbed "disguised unemployed". According to Chu et al. (2000), these are workers who are either technically inefficient, substitutable by other inputs in order to minimize costs or unproductive to the extent that their marginal product becomes zero or negative. Only the latter are referred to by Chu et al. (2000) as net surplus laborers.

In the case of labor surplus in agriculture, a utility maximizing household would be expected to reallocate its labor between agricultural production and off-farm work so that the marginal value product of labor in agriculture and the off-farm wage rate equalize (Singh et al., 1986, p. 19). If the markets function well, this would lead to an equalization of the marginal productivity of labor (MPL) between agricultural and non-agricultural sectors and hence to an overall increase in output without additional use of resources (Fleisher and

Yang, 2006, p. 17). However, labor allocation in rural China is characterized by different utility valuation between on-farm and off-farm work. While off-farm work is often better paid, employment is usually insecure and the risk of losing land use rights may pose an additional disincentive for working off the farm. In such a situation, the shadow price of on-farm work is endogenously determined within in the farm household (Singh et al., 1986, p. 307).

3.2.1.3 Fertilizer

Land reform in the early 1950s, i.e. the expropriation of landlords and distribution of land to peasants, had boosted production incentives of farmers and led to a rapid increase in the use of organic fertilizer (Wang et al., 1996, p. 285). Shortage of sources for organic fertilizer then led to the promotion of chemical fertilizer, which was initially produced in small, cheap plants but eventually surpassed the application of organic fertilizer in the 1960s (Löw, 2003, p. 59). The HRS further stimulated farmers' incentives to increase land productivity and thus increased chemical fertilizer consumption. However, the uncertainty to reap benefits from long-term soil improvements, induced by periodic plot reallocations, has been blamed for the relatively low level of organic fertilizer use in the past two decades. The importance of property rights in this context is contested, however (see section 4.3.1).

During the 1980s, China became the largest fertilizer importer and the second largest fertilizer consumer in the world (Ye and Rozelle, 1994). Typical fertilizer application rates are biased towards nitrogen and phosphate, while potash is in fact under used and further increases in crop productivity could be achieved by more balanced nutrient ratios, which would also reduce the groundwater contamination from nitrate (Wang et al., 1996, p. 295). Nitrate contamination of groundwater poses threats to the safety of drinking water (Chen et al., 2005).

In terms of actual nitrogen inputs through fertilization, Zhen et al. (2006) find in their survey of farmers in Shandong province an average input of 375 kg N in wheat, 240 kg N in maize and 360 kg N in cotton. These quantities were, respectively, 47%, 14% and 50% higher than the maximum recommended quantities. Not surprisingly given such high input rates, Wang et al. (1996) find a still positive but decreasing marginal productivity of fertilizer.

As a possible reason for the underutilization of potash, Löw (2003, p. 61) remarks that fertilizer consumption used to be mainly based on local supply and locally produced nitrogen fertilizer used to be more abundant. Domestic production of potash, on the other hand, is more costly and only increased during the last decade. Data from the China Statistical Yearbook (Figure 3.3) suggests that consumption of nitrogenous and phosphate fertilizer has in fact stagnated since 1998 while the use of compound and potash fertilizer is rising slowly, but steadily.

Figure 3.3   Development of fertilizer consumption in agriculture

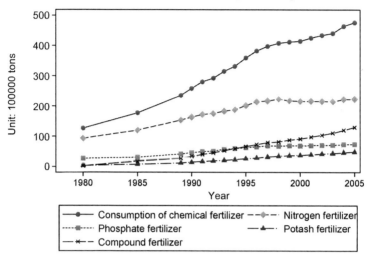

Source: National Bureau of Statistics of China (2006).

According to Qiao et al. (2003), the reform of input markets lags behind reforms in product markets. In the 1980s, fertilizer distribution was dominated by planned, administrative allocation and only in 1997 domestic trade by private dealers became fully allowed while international trade remained largely state controlled. Although liberalization of international trade did not occur, domestic farmers benefited from lower fertilizer prices. Qiao et al. (2003) then conclude that the domestic fertilizer market has become more integrated and expect that farmers should also be able to benefit from further liberalization in the course of China's WTO accession.

3.2.1.4 Water

Next to fertilizer overuse, water scarcity is the second main environmental problem connected with current cultivation practices in the study area. In many parts of the NCP, farmers have turned to groundwater irrigation due to scarcity and pollution of surface water. Competition between use of water for agriculture, industry or domestic uses has increased and Beijing has been given priority in water supply over the surrounding provinces (Holland, 2000). Since the 1970s, the phenomenon of the Yellow River drying up before reaching the ocean has drawn widespread attention to the problem (Kaneko et al., 2004, p. 232). Groundwater extraction is hardly regulated, i.e. farmers have open access to this resource, with all the negative implications of such a regime. In most cases, there is no explicit water pricing and farmers only pay for electricity or fuel to operate water pumps. Typically, single plots are flooded by pumping groundwater with plastic pipes from tube-wells to the fields. This technology leads to an application of water of about 60% in excess of the recommended level (Zhen et al., 2005, p. 513). In the case of surface water, the control of the quantity applied, and hence volumetric water pricing, is even more difficult.

While it is often advocated that higher pricing of irrigation water would automatically induce more efficient use of water (see e.g. Holland, 2000), Yang et al. (2003) show that water demand of farmers in surface water irrigated areas is inelastic to price changes. Raising prices would therefore depress farmers' incomes but not necessarily lead to lower water use unless farmers make significant adjustments in their cropping patterns. In groundwater irrigated areas the incentives are higher and accordingly, Yang et al. (2003) find a higher adoption of water-saving technologies in the groundwater irrigated district of Luancheng County (Hebei Province) as compared to the surface water irrigated districts included in their study.

Yang et al. (2003) call for a more comprehensive reform of water rights and institutions. Two basic types of institutional innovations for irrigation water management in rural China have been observed in several studies, namely Water User Associations (WUA) and the contracting out of tube-wells to service providers (Shah et al., 2004; Wang et al., 2003). In the latter case, the management of wells is contracted to single farmers responsible for operation and maintenance.

3.2.1.5 Other capital inputs

Other inputs needed in production include seeds, pesticides and machinery. As can be seen from Figure 3.1, their shares in production costs are comparably low. Recent policies including input subsidies are expected to increase mechanization and the use of high value seeds (Gale et al., 2005). While the effect of machinery subsidies is questionable since the small plot sizes do not seem to make increased machinery use profitable, Table 3.2 gives an idea of the importance of better seed varieties. It shows results of a 1992 survey of Chinese breeders and agronomists, asking about the technical reasons for gaps between highest crop yields on experimental field and actual average yields attained by farmers.

According to Figure 3.1, the share of pesticide costs in wheat and maize cultivation is almost negligible, but markedly higher in cotton. Zhen et al. (2005, p. 515) find in their study in Shandong Province that dosages of the cheap and readily available pesticides are two to three times higher than recommended. The problem of overuse therefore resembles that of fertilizer, with similarly hazardous outcomes for the environment and human health.

Table 3.2   Technical constraints to improved grain yield

	Wheat	Maize
Yield gap resulting from technical constraints (kg/*mu*)	600.0	767.0
Contributing factors (%):	100.0	100.0
1. Crop characteristics	52.5	49.0
2. Environmental conditions	32.3	35.2
3. Soil conditions	6.2	6.9
4. Pests, diseases, weeds	2.4	2.7
5. Weather conditions	6.6	5.2

Source: Adapted from Lin (2004, p. 50).

Cultivation of Bt-cotton is widespread, but contrary to the study of Qaim and Zilberman (2003) on the impact of Bt-cotton in India, Pemsl et al. (2005) found that many farmers in China did not reduce their pesticide use compared to conventional cotton. Pemsl et al. (2005) see institutional failures and the lack of knowledge of farmers as the main reasons for the inefficient use of the Bt-technology.

3.2.1.6 Information

Zhen et al. (2005) found in their 2001 survey of farmers in the NCP that only 30% had contact with extension workers and that those farmers who did were significantly more likely to follow input use recommendations than those who did not. Similarly, Liang et al. (2006) note that most farmers in their case study of Quzhou County (Hebei Province) never received any extension service and that input decisions are mainly based on information from neighbors, friends and relatives. Likewise, Zhen et al. (2006) find that farmers are neither aware of the current nutrient status of their plots nor of adequate application rates. Insufficient knowledge can therefore be seen as one reason for inappropriate fertilizer use. There is also anecdotal evidence of poor quality, tampered fertilizer packages with nutrient contents below the indicated level, adding to the uncertainty of farmers how much to apply.

Although it is to be expected that the misallocation of inputs in Chinese agriculture is also partly a consequence of insufficient or malfunctioning extension services, this issue has not received much attention. A frequently observed flaw of the current extension system is that extension employees earn sideline income by selling inputs to farmers, resulting in a severe conflict of interest. Generally, the extension system in China needs significant improvement (Zuo et al., 2005).

3.2.2 Product markets

As the second stage of China's agricultural reforms, after the institutional reforms of HRS, gradual market reforms only began in the mid 1980s (de Brauw et al., 2000, p. 1134). Their efficiency enhancing effect, understood as the responsiveness of farmers to price changes, has been shown by de Brauw et al. (2000) to be smaller than the effect of institutional reforms but increasing over time.

Past policy interventions in agricultural product markets have been largely motivated by the concern to maintain grain self-sufficiency. Since the early 1950s, grain marketing had been based on the farm gate procurement by state companies. The compulsory delivery of fixed grain quotas had been relaxed in 1985 by a system in which farm households were expected, but not forced to sell their grain to the state agencies. Many farmers were reluctant to do so and concomitant with other unfavorable conditions, grain production dropped by 7% in 1985. The government thus resumed control over grain purchases in 1986. In 1993 the government made a renewed attempt to deregulate the market by tying purchase prices of government agencies more closely to private market prices, liberalizing private markets and reducing mandatory grain deliveries. Farmers responded by selling more of their grain to private dealers which led to a surge in grain prices for urban consumers. The government renounced the reforms in 1995 and demanded provinces to ensure grain self-sufficiency by introducing the so-called governor's grain bag responsibility system (Buschena et al., 2005; Chen, 2007; Cheng and Tsang, 1994).

Only gradually, the state began to withdraw from its monopsony in grain markets, accelerated by China's accession to WTO. The compulsory grain procurement system has been abolished between 2000 and 2002 and grain purchase markets are now open to private traders (Chen, 2007). However, due to the semi-subsistence nature of typical Chinese household farms, about 60% of grain output is still consumed on-farm (Zhou and Tian, 2005, p. 21).

Following grain market liberalization, China's agricultural policy entered a new stage in 2004, when agricultural taxes were phased out and direct payments as well as subsidies for purchases of machinery and seeds were introduced. Direct payments, based on the farmers' taxed area (i.e. the total allocated land), grain sowing area or historical planting patterns followed the twin objectives of increasing rural incomes and grain output. Recently, the central government turned attention to a more comprehensive rural development program with the initiation of the "New Rural Campaign" in 2006 (Jia and Fock, 2007).

Grain quota obligations and agricultural taxation have been blamed to suppress both the demand and supply of land via the land rental market (Kung, 2002b, p. 396). Since these burdens have been suspended, the volume of land rental transactions might increase in the near future.

Furthermore, the abandonment of compulsory grain quotas allowed farmers to cultivate more profitable crops. In the NCP, area sown to wheat and maize is increasingly competing with cash crops, cotton in particular, and vegetables. Due to this change in incentives and partly also due to the conversion of farm land for other uses (Zhou and Tian, 2005, p. 230), the area sown to grain decreased rapidly since 1998. These effects have been different between provinces. Apparently, grain area in Hebei and Shandong Province dropped by about 15 Mill. *mu*, or 10%-20%, while it remained almost constant in Henan Province (Figure 3.4).

Figure 3.4   **Development of area sown to grain and cotton (Hebei, Henan and Shandong)**

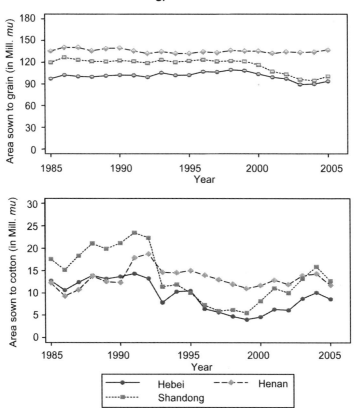

Sources: Hebei Province Statistical Bureau (2006), Henan Province Statistical Bureau (2006), Shandong Province Statistical Bureau (2006).

Following this development closely is crucial because grain self-sufficiency remains high on the political agenda. As Chen (2007, p. 15) notes, however, the central government did not return to the restrictive policies of the mid 1990s, and as producer prices increased again (Figure 3.5), grain production slowly began to recover, too.

Figure 3.5   Output price indices (1986-2003)

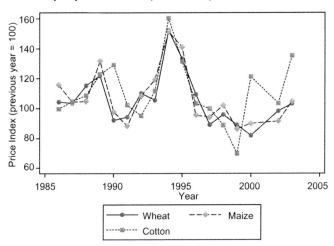

Source: Ministry of Agriculture (2004).

The coincidence of rising prices and favorable weather conditions in 2004 led to the question of what merit for stimulating grain production can be attributed to the direct payments, input subsidies and abolition of agricultural taxes. First studies on the impacts of these policy measures agree that they achieved the goal of income support, but not that of increasing grain production. Heerink et al. (2006) simulated the effects of tax abolition and direct payments for two villages in Jiangxi Province. Direct payments are paid in Jiangxi on the basis of taxed area, i.e. they are not directly linked to production. In the simulations by Heerink et al. (2006), farm households use the slightly increased incomes from the direct payments for other, more remunerative purposes than grain cultivation. The contradiction between the policy goals of increasing incomes and increasing low-return grain production had also been noted by Gale et al. (2005). Furthermore, Heerink et al. (2006) find that the effect on incomes from tax abolition was much larger than from direct payments.

The observation that farmers increasingly make cropping decisions according to relative prices between grain and commercial crops raises the question of whether price signals induce efficient decisions, i.e. how well domestic agricultural commodity markets are integrated. Integration of agricultural product markets in China has much improved (Rozelle et al., 1997), but Gustafsson and Shi (2002) still see a lack of communication facilities and labor mobility as barriers for further integration. Moreover, transaction costs can differ widely between villages (Heerink et al., 2006, p. 59).

While domestic grain trade traditionally used to be limited to the region of production, interregional trade increased since the 1980s. For instance, trade of wheat and rice between North and South China increased due to changing consumption patterns and demand from migrant workers (Zhou and Tian, 2005). As You (2006) shows for the period of 1980-1997, production patterns also shifted considerably. Overall, grain production moved to the Northern provinces, but area expansion of the main grain crops rice, wheat and maize differed between regions. Growth rate of rice was highest in the Northeast and parts of Henan and Shandong, while wheat area mainly expanded in Inner Mongolia and some of the Western provinces. Maize area increased considerably in southeast China, which You (2006) attributes to the increasing demand for feed.

In fact, future increases in grain demand are projected to come mainly from increased demand for feed due to increased consumption of animal products (Zhou and Tian, 2005). In view of this likely increase in feed demand, Liu and Luo (2004) argue that China should focus its policy of self-sufficiency only on foodgrain and allow increasing imports of feedgrain.

4 Rural land policies in China

The principle of equal distribution of land among the rural population has been a main feature of the Household Responsibility System (HRS) which established a new order after the People's Commune era. This egalitarianism is increasingly in opposition to the market economy which is developing in other sectors. In order to better understand the seemingly contradictory nature of rural land policies in China, this section reviews how current legislation developed and highlights implications for the use of natural resources in agriculture and unresolved issues in connection with property rights to rural land.

4.1 Rural land property rights: theoretical background

Before discussing rural land property rights in China, the following paragraphs outline the history of thought of the property rights approach in order to clarify these terms and their theoretical implications. Since the 1960s, a large body of literature in the field of New Institutional Economics (NIE) established that the design of property rights is important for understanding the allocation and use of resources because it determines the incentives of individuals and thus economic outcomes (Furubotn and Pejovich, 1972).

The connotation of property rights in NIE is broader than in a purely legal sense. As Eggertsson (1990) points out, the property rights concept also includes social norms and values. Evidently, such divergent views between law and economics can lead to some confusion about what property rights are (Cole and Grossmann, 2002). Following Bromley (2005, p. 44), the terms rights, property and property rights may be distinguished by saying that "rights allow an individual to *compel* the coercive power of the state to come to her assistance" while property is a *value* where the value consists of "the control over a benefit stream" which follows from acquiring a "piece of property". Finally, property rights "bring together legal concepts of *rights* and *duties* with settings and circumstances (including objects) capable of producing income". The essence of these definitions is that, first, rights have to be actually enforceable to deserve the term and, second, property does not refer to an object but to the value accruable from using an object.

Of the four property *regimes* identified by Bromley (1989) – state, private, common property and nonproperty – too often only the private property regime has been considered to provide the incentives necessary to warrant productivity increases, adoption of new technology and sustainable resource use. Especially the *common property regime* has been dismissed as inevitably leading to overexploitation and degradation of the resource base. This view had been strengthened by the seminal paper of Hardin (1968) and recently challenged e.g. by Ostrom et al. (1999) who argue that resources owned and managed by small to relatively large groups can indeed be used sustainably if certain conditions are met. Such conditions are more likely to be met if the users depend to a large extent on the resource for their livelihood, have some autonomy in setting access rules, trust other group members and share perceptions of how their actions affect other users and the resource base (Ostrom et al., 1999, p. 281).

Common property is distinctly different from an *open access regime*, as becomes clear from the following characterization of common property:

"The management group (the "owners") has the right to exclude nonmembers, and nonmembers have a duty to abide by exclusion. Individual members of the management group (the "co-owners") have both rights and duties with respect to use rates and maintenance of the thing owned." (Bromley, 1989, p. 872).

A common property regime therefore does not imply that no individual rights of the community members exist. To the contrary, individual rights and duties form an integral part of a successful common property regime (Bromley, 1989, p. 870).

The above statement attributes all group members the status of "co-owners". In practice, however, it is likely that individuals or a sub-group in the community will claim to be leaders and exercise ownership rights to common property. The extent to which group leaders are able to appropriate ownership rights will depend on the power structure in the community. Furthermore, the degree of power associated with exercising ownership rights is contingent on the definition of ownership.

Ownership entails different connotations in the two main western legal traditions, the civil law, originated from Roman law, and the Anglo-Saxon common law. In short, civil law sees ownership as an absolute and supreme right, i.e. as the right to "use and abuse one's own property" (Van Banning, 2002, p. 14). Common law, instead, is more familiar with the concept of ownership as a "bundle of rights" (Ho, 2001) .

In calling attention to those attributes associated with ownership that transcend different legal systems, Honoré (1961) lists an extensive "bundle of rights and duties" that together constitute ownership. These include the right to possess, use, and manage property and the right to obtain income from it. Furthermore, ownership entails the right to the capital, meaning the right to dispose of the capital value of the property as desired, the right to security, transmissibility (i.e. the right of inheritance), absence of term, the duty to prevent harm, the liability to execution (i.e. the right of mortgage) and the residuary character, meaning that upon the expiration of rights of other stakeholders (e.g. lessors) all property rights reside again with the original owner (Honoré, 1961, p. 107).

In the more absolute sense, the right of ownership to an asset is only limited by what is explicitly stated in laws. This means in turn that ownership rights are most often *attenuated*, i.e. laws prohibit certain actions of an owner in relation to the asset (Furubotn and Pejovich, 1974, p. 4). Furubotn and Pejovich (1974) condense the bundle of rights listed above and identify three elements which together constitute ownership: the right to use (*usus*), the right to appropriate returns (*usus fructus*) and the right to "change the asset's form and/or substance (*abusus*)", under which the freedom to transfer all or some rights in the asset is subsumed. The person or group claiming all three elements would be considered to hold ownership, independent of the legal system, while others may only have the right to use or appropriate returns. The difference between the terms *use rights* and *usufruct rights*, which are often used interchangeably, becomes clear from the definition above. Furthermore, the distinction is important because in the civil law tradition only usufruct rights are recognized as real rights (*jus in rem*, in German *dingliches Recht*) as opposed to personal rights (*jus in personam* or *relatives Recht*). A real right implies an actual right to an object itself, which can be defended against anyone in court, whereas a personal right only defines a relation between certain persons (Baur et al., 1999; Wang, 2005).

4.2 Formulation and implementation of rural land policies in China

Rural land in China is by law "collectively owned", while individual households have long-term use rights to equal shares of the village land. This system of collective ownership and private use rights is known as the two-tier land system (Chin, 2005).

Following the above classification of property regimes, rural land in China can be characterized as common property with the village (or village representatives) being the "management group" and individuals in the village being the "co-owners". However, following the definition of ownership as the absolute and supreme right, Ho (2001) concludes that ultimately the *state* holds ownership over rural land. Although this is nowhere explicitly mentioned, this opinion is supported by the stipulation in the Constitution of the PRC that the state may requisition collectively owned land "in the public interest" (PRC, 2004a, Art. 10). State ownership is therefore, according to Ho (2001), superior to collective ownership, which is merely derived from implicit state ownership. Accounts of hasty expropriations of farmers' land for non-agricultural purposes assert that the state indeed claims ultimate ownership (Cai, 2003).

These coherences and conflicts that have arisen from the ambiguous legal status of rural land are illustrated in the following two sections which first describe the nature of the Chinese village and then sketch the legal framework of rural land property rights in China.

4.2.1 The village in China's administrative and political hierarchy

In the early 1980s, the People's Communes disintegrated and their three-level hierarchy was transformed as indicated in Figure 4.1. The term administrative village today refers to a village with own formal institutions which may govern a territory that consists of one or several natural villages (Zhu and Jiang, 1993, pp. 443). The production team, equivalent to today's natural village, had in fact been recognized as the basic unit of the Communes and thus as the legal owner of the land within its vicinity (Ho, 2001, p. 405).

This status has been largely weakened and vested in the administrative village (see section 4.2.2) which is in charge of implementing higher level policies and is therefore the most important unit for understanding the impacts that such policies have on land use decisions of individual farmers. A number of studies deal with the specific power relations between the central government, provincial, prefecture, county and township governments and village administrations. These studies conclude that power relations and rent-seeking lead to distorted outcomes of national policies (Hsing, 2006; Zhang and Carter, 1997; Zhou and Yang, 2004). In the case of land rights this has led to significant heterogeneity between villages. In order to understand how this heterogeneity ensued, the following paragraphs evaluate the position of the administrative village within China's political and administrative system.

Figure 4.1   Transformation of rural administrative institutions

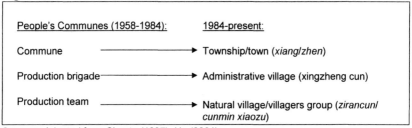

Sources: Adapted from Choate (1997), Ho (2001).

People's congresses and people's governments constitute the legislature and executive at the national level (National People's Congress and State Council) and at the levels of provinces, municipalities, counties, cities, municipal districts, townships and towns. Towns (*zhen*) and townships (*xiang*), which replaced the People's Communes, are the lowest levels in this political hierarchy. Town and township governments may therefore be characterized as "power brokers" between the state and the villages (Hsing, 2006).

The distinction between towns or, more specifically, "officially designated towns", and townships is important insofar as "officially designated towns" (*jianzhi zhen*) constitute the lowest level of the *urban* administrative hierarchy, even though agriculture may still be the main income source and the difference to townships may not be apparent at first sight (Chan, 1994). Comparatively urban centers in the countryside are called "small towns" and four categories of small towns are described in the literature (Zweig, 1992, p. 338): county seats, county-towns, township seats and rural market towns. Only county seats and county-towns are designated towns. Since 1992 more townships became designated towns which resulted in a somewhat more rural character of *zhen* (Taubmann, 1997). One objective of this establishment of designated towns within rural areas was to create spill-over effects by having "the town leading (administering) the development in the countryside" (Chan, 1994).

There exist different ways of describing the nature of *zhen* as compared to *xiang*. *Zhen* may be characterized as "an administrative division under a county with a jurisdiction over an area with a relatively high level of industrial and commercial development, a relatively dense population and fairly complete public facilities" (Yang, 2004, p. 263). Townships may request the status of a *zhen* if they have less than 20.000 inhabitants with at least 10% nonagrarian inhabitants or more than 20.000 inhabitants with at least 10% nonagrarian population living in the seat of the township administration. The term nonagrarian here refers to persons with urban registration status independent of their actual occupation (Fan et al., 2006). The importance of the household registration system (*hukou*) is further illustrated in section 4.3.2.

In the past, there has been a sharp distinction between designated towns and settlements without this status. Residents of designated towns were eligible for certain amenities such as state-subsidized grain (Zweig, 1992). At least until the end of the 1980s, county seats, town and township seats had differential access to funds and income opportunities. *Zhen* were allowed to collect certain taxes and received more assistance from the county. On the other hand, *zhen* were also more dependent on the county and the county government may have exerted more power to implement its policies and development strategies in *zhen* (Zweig, 1992). It is therefore likely that *zhen* and *xiang* have followed different development paths. Therefore, this dichotomy is emphasized in the following data analysis.[4]

In most cases, the town or township seat is at the same time the main, and often the only market place for peasants to exchange their products and buy agricultural inputs (Chung, 2004). There has been considerable administrative control over the development of these market places and peasants from more remote villages probably have faced some obstacles to enter the central market. Apart from the differences between *zhen* and *xiang* it is therefore hypothesized that pronounced differences can be found between the development of villages close to the town or township seats and those further away.

Village affairs are administered by Villagers' Committees (VCs, *cunmin wei yuan hui*) which are "mass organizations of self-management at the grass-roots level" (PRC, 2004a) and local cadres of the Chinese Communist Party (CCP), both of which are typically closely intertwined. Often, leaders of both groups are the same persons (Zhu and Jiang, 1993, p. 444). VCs are assigned the responsibility to "administer the affairs concerning the land and other property owned collectively by the peasants of the village and disseminate

---

[4] In the following text, towns and townships are only distinguished where this is relevant. When this is not the case, the term township is used for simplicity.

knowledge among the villagers about rational utilization of the natural resources and protection and improvement of the ecological environment" (Article 5, PRC, 1998).

While the VC is elected by the villagers, the members of the local Party branch are appointed by their superiors (Guo and Bernstein, 2004). VCs report to Villagers' Assemblies (VA) or Village Representative Assemblies (VRA), which are composed of representatives of groups of households. According to Choate (1997), the VRA is thus the highest administrative authority in a village.

The extent to which this kind of local self-government can be seen as "grass root autonomy" is controversial. On the one hand, the end of the People's Communes has indeed been accompanied by a separation of villages from official government administration (Zhou and Yang, 2004, p. 6). This has spurred the villages' proactive development of social services and non-agricultural employment and can also be thought of as the main reason for the diverse land tenure arrangements that can be observed today (Zhu and Jiang, 1993, p. 441). Nee and Su (1990) found that village autonomy *vis à vis* the township government is higher as compared to the situation during the Commune era. Township governments today find it harder to "gain compliance with village leaders" (Nee and Su, 1990, p. 20). The limited resources of township governments are often not sufficient to adequately perform their functions, namely implementing policies of higher levels and integrating the villagers' interests (Yang, 2004, pp. 250). On the other hand, of the various local institutions it is often the village secretary of the CCP who actually implements such policies at the village level (Vermeer, 2004, p. 127). Zhao (2006) observed that concomitant to the proliferation of village self-government, township governments have again strengthened their administrative control and also Yang (2004) points out that the state, via town and township governments, still exerts great influence on villages' decisions.[5]

4.2.2 The legal framework defining rural land property rights

When the People's Communes were dismantled in the late 1970s, households were initially granted short term use-right contracts with the defunct production teams continuing to be the collective owners of the village land. In 1981, the HRS became officially sanctioned (Lin, 1992, p. 37). In 1984, these short annual contracts were officially extended to a period of 15 years. In a further step towards stabilizing land tenure, a central government directive declared in 1993 that after expiration of the initial 15-year contracts, new contracts be issued with a duration of 30 years (Kung and Liu, 1997).

---

[5] The extent of this influence becomes apparent in the statement by Feng Xu (1998, quoted in Ho, 2001, p. 409): "'If the Villagers' Committee is entrusted by all villagers, it is eligible to be the owner of land', however, 'in reality the Villagers' Committee has become an extension of the political power of the township/town, [...] as a result of which collective ownership of farmers is often difficult to realize and farmers cannot enjoy the rights and interests of the collective.'"

It is interesting to note that the HRS evolved by spontaneous experimentation in a few villages and that its main aspects only became formalized in the 1986 Land Administration Law (LAL), the 1988 Organic Law of the Villagers' Committees and the 2002 Law on Land Contract in Rural Areas (LLCRA; PRC, 2004b). Further legal documents relevant to this study include the 1986 General Principles of Civil Law, the 1993 Agriculture Law, the 1995 Guarentee Law and the 2007 Property Law.

While the 1982 Constitution had asserted collective ownership of rural land (PRC, 2004a, Art. 10), it did not specify which administrative unit (county, township, administrative or natural village) shall in practice exercise ownership rights. The LAL only clarified that "collectively owned land that lawfully belongs to rural collectives shall be operated and managed by village collective economic organizations or village committees" (PRC, 2000b, Art. 10). With this statement, ownership rights of the natural village were somewhat weakened and shifted more towards the administrative village, but no clear devolution of ownership was prescribed.[6]

Mainly in response to mandatory grain quota deliveries, plots allocated to farmers were divided into several categories, each with particular rights and obligations connected to them which varied between villages (Lohmar, 2006). Table 4.1 gives an overview over these tenure categories. In some cases, common translations of the Chinese terms to English vary, which makes differentiation of tenure types in the literature cumbersome.

The main distinction between these categories – that between plots on which grain for the quota had to be produced and for which taxes had to be paid and those without such obligations – became redundant with the abolishment of grain quotas from 2002 onwards and agricultural taxes in 2004. According to Pieke (2005), since the mid-1990s zoning rules as part of integrated land use plans designated single plots to specific purposes. The LLCRA (Art. 14 (2)) states that the party giving out land contracts, i.e. in most cases the village, has to carry out land use plans (*tudi liyong zong gui hua*) which have been worked out by township governments in accordance with the LAL (Art. 17). Pieke (2005) argues that today land use plans effectively provide an alternative instrument of control over the development of rural areas after the abolishment of compulsory grain deliveries.

---

[6] The dilemma inherent in this indefiniteness becomes manifest in the following quotation: "The owner of a collective has been proposed to be 'its founding members or investors', 'the collective itself', or 'all members of the collective jointly'. The ambiguity of the identity of owners has caused a lack of ownership supervision of the management and disposition of collective assets" (Huang, 2004, p. 211, citing Wang Liming, 2001).

Table 4.1   Rights and obligations associated with different tenure types

Chinese term	Common English translation	Definition, rights and obligations
Ziren tian	• Responsibility land	• Allocated to households on the basis of family members or number of laborers • Conditional on the delivery of a grain quota
Kouliang tian	• Ration land • Self-sufficiency land • Consumption land	• For household subsistence needs • Usually not subject to grain quotas and taxes
Jidong di	• Flexible land • Mobile land • Reserve land	• Rented out by the village to households for a fee, often in a bidding process • Land used to accommodate for reallocations and contingencies • If reserve land is rented out to households it also is referred to as contract land (*chengbao tian*)
Chengbao tian	• Contract land	• Contracted to households in an open bidding within the Two field system • Auctioned off or allocated by village leaders for a fee
Huang di	• Unused land • Waste land	• Land of very poor quality that is auctioned off to households
Ziliu di	• Private plots	• Small, backyard plots for growing vegetables etc. for meeting subsistence needs • Very stable use rights

Sources: Lohmar (2006), Rozelle et al. (2005), Chen and Brown (2001), Li et al. (2000, p. 6).

The second important difference between these types of land, namely whether the plots are allocated on an egalitarian basis or rented out to the highest bidder, needs more explanation. Occasionally, the term contract land is used in the context of the so-called Two-Farmland System (TFS), which sought to overcome land fragmentation caused by HRS. In this system, the principle of egalitarian distribution of all village land was given up and land was divided into subsistence land, which was equally allocated, and contract land to which farmers could acquire the cultivation right through bidding. The TFS had been introduced in the late 1980s in Shandong Province and spread to neighboring provinces. While its success in overcoming land fragmentation earned its support by the government, problems soon arose due to excessively high contract fees charged by local officials. This led to the renunciation of TFS in 1998 (Chen and Brown, 2001). However, according to the extensive survey by Zhu et al. (2006), around 15% of all villages continued to practice the TFS in 2005.

The term contract (*chengbao*) as used in the 2002 LLCRA carries a different meaning, namely that of a basic right of farmers to an equal land share by stating that this law aims to stabilize and improve the "two-tier management system that combines centralized and decentralized management on the basis of household contractual management, granting to the peasants long-term and guaranteed land-use right" (Art. 1). In principle, these contractual use rights should be extended to households free of charge.

Furthermore, the LLCRA reiterates that arable land shall be contracted out to households for a period of 30 years (Article 20). Unlike arable land, village land "not suited to household contract", such as barren mountains, gullies, hills and beaches may be contracted out through bid invitation, auction etc. (Article 45). So called private plots (see Table 4.1) constitute a very small share of the total village land. However, since use rights to these plots have been very stable compared to the other tenure types, some studies compared input use between private plots and allocated plots in order to make a case for long-term tenure security. This is further discussed in section 4.3.1.

All members of a *collective economic organization* (i.e. a village) shall enjoy equal rights to undertake arable land contracts within their own village (Article 5). The contracts shall be decided upon by a contract working team, elected by the Villagers' Assembly. The possibility to unilaterally revoke the contracts in order to reestablish responsibility land or ration land or modify the rights of the contractor in any other way is explicitly ruled out (Article 35).

If, within the contract period, readjustments of the contracted land have to be made (e.g. due to significant changes in household sizes and new inhabitants), only reserve land, reclaimed land or land voluntarily returned by individual contractors shall be used for readjustments (Article 28). The possibility of retaining part of the village land as reserve land, which may be contracted out by the collective for a fee, is limited. The LLCRA states in Article 63 that reserve land (*jidong di*) shall not constitute more than 5% of the village arable land and that villages which have not kept reserve land in the past may not set aside new reserve land in the future. However, in the study of Schwarzwalder et al. (2002) only half of the villages keeping reserve land were found to stay within this limit although the policy of restricting reserve land to 5% had been advocated by the central government as early as 1997. The incidence of reserve land differs greatly between different parts of China, ranging from 51% and 45.77% of the villages in North/Northwestern China and the coast to 11.9% and 20.87% in Central and Southwestern China (Deininger et al., 2006).

Using reserve land for readjustments may have the effect of increasing tenure security over the remaining, non-reserve land, since households holding contracts to non-reserve plots may feel assured that their use rights will not be infringed upon within the contract period (Chen and Brown, 2001, p. 283). Furthermore, Lin and Zhang (2006) report that the function of reserve land as explained by village leaders is, apart from retaining land for readjustments, also income generation for the village collective. This is contradicted, though, by Alpermann (2001), who found in his study of eleven villages, that reserve land is mainly kept as a means to give plots to land-scarce families (p. 60). According to Li and Xi (2006), this also involves married women who had not yet received land shares in their husbands' villages. Reserve land may therefore also help to secure women's land rights.

In effect, keeping reserve land may be regarded as a way of providing a second land rental market in which the village collective represents the supply side (Tan, 2005, p. 31).

Apart from these provisions, the LLCRA allows households to transfer their use rights acquired through contracts by subcontracting (*zhuan bao*), leasing (*chu zu*), exchanging (*hu huan*) transferring (*zhuan rang*) and "other means" (Article 32). Some of these terms are not consistently used throughout China. In particular the difference between *zhuan bao* and *zhuang rang* appears to be not clearly defined (Brandt et al., 2002). According to (Deininger et al., 2006, p. 5), *zhuang rang*, as opposed to *zhuan bao*, implies that the original contract rights of the lessor are terminated and permanently transferred to the lessee. The terms *zhuan bao* and *chu zu* come closest to the conventional notion of land renting.

All land use transfers are bound to the restriction that the transferee shall be capable of agricultural operations and may not use the land for non-agricultural purposes (Art. 33, LLCRA). While Article 33 does not explicitly limit the transfer of land use rights to inhabitants of the village in question, it does state that "under equal conditions, members of the collective economic organization shall enjoy priority". Furthermore, if land is *contracted* out by the village to non-members of the collective, two third of the villagers must consent to it (LAL, Art. 15).

Contrary to different claims (e.g. by Huang, 2004, p. 217), the LLCRA does not clearly provide for the inheritance of use rights to arable land. The wording of the relevant article is as follows: "The benefits derived from the contract which are due to the contractor shall be inherited in accordance with the provisions of the Succession Law. In case a contractor for forestland is dead, his/her successor may, within the term of contract, continue to undertake the contract" (LLCRA, Art. 32). This wording suggests that except for forest land, the right to inheritance only includes the *benefits derived from the contract*, but not the contract itself. This is the interpretation followed by Li (2003, p. 62). The logic behind this stipulation is, according to Li (2003), that contracts to arable land are issued in the name of a household, not an individual person. In the event of a death of one household member, the contract shall therefore remain unchanged.

Concerning the question which factors lead to an exclusion of non-villagers, the literature is scarce. As one of the only sources on this matter, Kung (2000) finds the uncertainty to sufficiently meet grain quota deliveries to be one possible reason for local officials to impose such restrictions. Although grain quotas have been abolished and can therefore not be used as a variable explaining rental restrictions, it is hypothesized in this study that villages that are highly dependent on their land resources will be more inclined to exclude non-villagers from accessing these resources via land renting.

Empirical studies find that 5% to 10% of households participate in the nascent rental market for rural land use rights (Deininger and Jin, 2005; Lohmar et al., 2001). Transfers outside the village are rare. Reasons given by

Lohmar et al. (2001, p. 9) include lower transaction costs within the village and the fear of dispossession in subsequent reallocations. The low extent of market-mediated land transfers seems to call for institutions to encourage and facilitate such transfers by reducing transaction costs for farm households. As one suggestion in this direction, it has been proposed to establish a "land bank" as a national policy bank with the specific purpose of encouraging land transfers and thereby finally ensuring "farmers' enthusiasm for planting grain crops" (China Daily, 2005). In such a land bank, farmers willing to rent out their land could deposit their land use rights at a high interest rate, while those willing to expand production could obtain land use rights at a low lending rate. Such a framework could decrease the wedge between supply and demand prices for land use rights (as described in section 2) and build up farmers' trust in the land rental market. Zhang et al. (2004) found land trusts, a variant of the proposed land bank, to be in fact active in Zhejiang Province. Such land trusts are described as local institutions acting as brokers between lessors and lessees, disseminating information on supply and demand for land, helping to negotiate and write contracts and mediating disputes.

Until very recently, China lacked a comprehensive property law. The 1986 General Principles of Civil Law served as a place holder in which ownership was defined as "the owner's right in accordance with law to possess, use, benefit from and dispose of his own property" (Gray and Zheng, 1989, Art. 71). According to Epstein (1989, p. 178) as well as Wang (2005, p. 64), the 'General Principles' follow with this notion of supreme ownership clearly the tradition of Roman civil law.

In the meantime, the Property Law had been drafted, has been adopted in March 2007 and came into effect on October 1st 2007. During the drafting stage, legal scholars suggested that in order to further clarify the nature of farmers' land use rights, they should be categorized as real rights (*wuquan*) instead of personal rights (*zhaiquan*). According to Ho (2005, p. 81), the interpretation of the use rights as real rights would allow a better protection of the farmers' interests, including unimpaired transfer of contract rights. With the promulgation of the new Property Law, this step has indeed been made. The law categorizes the right to land contractual management as a usufructuary right (Art. 125). The definition of a usufructuary right as the right to "possess, utilize, and obtain profits from the real and movable properties owned by others" (Art. 117) conforms to that outlined in section 4.1.

Table 4.2 summarizes the main formal legal stipulations pertaining to farmers' land use rights as discussed above.

Table 4.2   Farmers' land use rights: the formal legal framework

Year	Law	Main stipulations
1982	Constitution	• Confirmation of the two-tier system of collective ownership and household contract rights to arable land (Art. 8 and Art. 10) • Collectively owned land may be requisitioned by the state in the public interest (Art. 10)
1986	General Principles of Civil Law	• Notion of ownership as an absolute right (Art. 71) • Assertion of legal protection of contracted land (Art. 80)
1988	Organic Law of the Villagers' Committees	• Villagers' Committees as primary organizations of village self-government (Art. 2) • Village CCP organizations as the "leading nucleus" (Art. 3)
1993	Agriculture Law	• Obligation to pay agricultural taxes and fees for collective purposes (Art. 69 and Art. 73) • If land is requisitioned from farmers, a compensation shall be paid (Art. 71)
1995	Guarantee Law	• Use rights to waste land may be mortgaged (Art. 34) • No mortgage of use rights to arable land (Art. 37)
1998	Land Administration Law	• Ownership rights to collective land shifted towards administrative village (Art. 10) • Local people's governments draw up land use plans (Art. 17)
2002	Law on Land Contract in Rural Areas	• Contract duration of 30 years (Art. 20) • Villages may retain at most 5% of the arable land as reserve land (Art. 63) • This land may be used for readjustments (Art. 28) • Households may transfer their land use rights through various means (Art. 32) • Villages carry out land use plans set up by local people's governments (Art. 14)
2007	Property Law	• Clarification of use rights as usufructuary rights

Source: Own presentation.

To conclude, the seemingly vague and ambiguous formulations inherent in many Chinese laws pose a considerable challenge for their correct interpretation. Von Senger (1996, p. 173) identifies three explanations for the inaccurate use of language in Chinese laws. First, it allows for a flexible interpretation adapted to changing situations. Second, it was intended to make laws also understandable for the "masses", and hence using simple language was preferred. Chinese laws are meant to be 'educative' (Cao, 2001, p. 240). Third, Chinese lawmakers may take some background knowledge for granted and therefore do not deem it necessary to define every detail. Of these explanations, the intention to keep interpretation "flexible" is probably the most important. As Ho (2001) put it, this "deliberate ambiguity" is what "makes the system tick". In this context, it is also advisable to conclude with Bromley (2005, p. 55), that one should not "fetishize land ownership" and rather try to understand the full institutional framework and whether it provides sufficient incentives for a sustainable resource use.

4.3 Unresolved issues

While the two-tier system of collective ownership and private use rights is today firmly established, there are a number of unresolved issues related to farmers' property rights to land. Four of these issues, which have attracted most attention by researchers, are discussed in the following sections.

4.3.1 Land reallocations and tenure insecurity

Many studies have shown that not all villages adhere to the policy of granting households stable use rights for 30 years. Jacoby et al. (2002) identify three motivations for reallocations: maintaining egalitarian land distribution, substituting the land rental market and putting pressure on households to deliver quotas and taxes. As discussed above, the last reason has become redundant with recent policy changes. The practice of frequent reallocations in response to changes in household sizes or composition is generally believed to introduce tenure insecurity (see e.g. Lohmar et al., 2001). Possible consequences of this insecurity to be able to cultivate the same plots in the future range from less investment in land quality improvements to labor market distortions (see section 4.3.2). Reallocations have also been suspected to encourage births because of the rule to allocate land on a per capita basis (Zhu and Jiang, 1993, p. 456). Furthermore, children and tenure security may be substitutes to guarantee old age security. However, Kung (2006), in a study of a county in Guizhou Province in which the government introduced long-term use rights in the 1980s in order to assess their effect on birth rates, could not find strong evidence for this proposition.

Two types of reallocations are usually distinguished: those in which only plots of few households are reallocated (partial or small) and those which affect all village land (full or large reallocation). Kung (2000) found in a survey of 80 villages that partial reallocations dominate and that reallocations are more frequent in villages with tight land endowments and less off-farm employment.

Denouncing egalitarian land distribution in favor of tenure security may have unintended negative effects. Li et al. (2006, p. 16) suspect that the less egalitarian land allocation as a consequence of more stable tenure is a main reason for the increasing rural inequality. In fact, the policy to refrain from reallocations for a period of 30 years can be argued to *deprive* farmers of the right to an equal share of the village land. This explains why long-term contracts are often not preferred by households (Kung and Liu, 1997). On the other hand inequality in land endowment does not have to imply income inequality if land scarce households have access to off-farm employment. Providing off-farm opportunities may therefore strengthen the support for long-term land use contracts (Kung and Liu, 1997, p. 54).

Although the nexus between tenure security and investments in land is often taken as common knowledge, literature review of the topic in China gives somewhat mixed results. The diverging results may partly be caused by methodological problems, e.g. which indicators to use for tenure security and land investments. Most often, the application of organic fertilizer is regarded as an investment in land which farmers would allegedly only consider in a situation of relatively secure tenure (Jacoby et al., 2002). Arguably, this indicator is usually chosen because of the absence of any other observable type of land investment (i.e. plot boundaries, wells, drainages, and other fixed constructions). However, it still may not be a good indicator. Kung and Cai (2000) conclude that fertilizing practices by Chinese farmers are determined by other factors than tenure security. They argue that households with good off-farm opportunities, facing high opportunity costs when working in agriculture, substitute their labor for chemical fertilizer and engage less in the labor intensive use of manure. Contrary to that, Brandt et al. (2002, p. 91) found higher yields, higher use of organic fertilizers and an overall higher input intensity on private plots than on responsibility plots. The authors explain this result with the fact that the use period for private plots tended to be much longer. However, private plots also tended to be smaller and input intensity on such plots may be in general higher. Causality is therefore not straightforward.

The length of time that a household has held use rights to a plot in the past could be used a proxy for tenure security. However, as Jacoby et al. (2002) point out, such a measure is not straightforward. First, tenure security and plot investments may be determined simultaneously. Investments made in the past may improve tenure security and tenure security may in turn stimulate investments. Second, it is not clear whether long-term use indicates a very secure tenure status or whether it may to the contrary increase the probability of expropriation. In order to derive whether the time passed since the last reallocation increases the risk of expropriation, Jacoby et al. (2002) estimate a duration model, in which the hazard function represents the probability of losing a plot, given that it has already been cultivated for a several years.

4.3.2 Land rights and social security

If markets function perfectly, the optimal strategy for farm households would be to allocate their labor in such a way that the marginal value product of household labor in agriculture equals that in off-farm work. In many cases, however, households are constrained in their off-farm labor supply, i.e. off-farm supply elasticity is low (Hertel and Fan, 2006). One reason is that land exerts an important function as a social safety net for farm households. It is uncommon to give up farming completely because of the disutility connected with the loss of land use rights (to engage in farming is a necessary requirement for claiming use rights to arable land). The land tenure system therefore raises the opportunity costs of leaving agriculture. Even allocating only part of the labor to off-farm activities may introduce additional opportunity costs if land endowment can be modeled as a function of labor presence on-farm (Hertel and Fan, 2006).

However, the dividing line for granting land use rights is usually simply the household registration status (*hukou*). Individuals are either registered as urban or rural. Being registered as urban provides access to the urban social security system, but is also connected with a loss of rural land use rights. Therefore, households that completely give up farming to enter the urban labor market have significant difficulties to return to farming if they fail in their non-farm employment. Consequently, the household registration system has been a successful instrument to keep the rural population in the countryside. Even if most family members are engaged in off-farm work, some – mainly elder – household members will typically continue farming in order to keep the household's land use rights.

The *hukou* system had been initiated in the 1950s in an attempt to regulate population movement and influx into cities in particular (Cheng and Selden, 1994). The discrimination against the rural population is rooted in the early strategy of the PRC of first developing the urban based heavy industry. The result was a polarization of "capital in urban areas and labor in rural areas" (Fleisher and Yang, 2006). In recent years, control over population movement loosened and it has become much easier for rural dwellers to change their *hukou* status (Fleisher and Yang, 2006, p. 12).

Apart from land use rights, support by own children constitutes an obvious means to ensure old age security. As Zhao and Wen (1999) argue, in traditional China, the prospect of inheriting land has served as an important bargaining instrument for rural elderly to ensure this support by their children. With the village collective retaining land ownership, this bargaining power is lost.

4.3.3 Land rights and gender inequality

A number of studies explore the extent of gender discrimination in the process of administrative land allocation. The cultural disruption and reorientation during the reform period have led to a resurgence of social norms and values, amongst others virilocal marriages (i.e. married women move to their husbands' villages) and patrilineal inheritance. In concurrence with the freezing of reallocations and increasing population pressure on land, married women would therefore lose their land shares in their maiden villages while land endowments could not be adjusted in their husbands' households to reflect the additional person in the family. Maintaining land reallocations can therefore be seen a means to secure women's land use rights (Lin and Zhang, 2006, p. 638). The expectation that young women would soon leave their parents' households may even entail that in the land allocation process, girls receive less land shares in the first place, according to Li and Bruce (2005, p. 314) 50% to 70% of the shares boys would get. Additionally, there are numerous accounts that land rights of widowed or divorced women are infringed, owing to patrilineal inheritance of land use rights (Li and Xi, 2006; Li and Bruce, 2005; Lin and Zhang, 2006).

Despite these findings, the LLCRA states: "In undertaking land contracts in rural areas, women shall enjoy equal rights with men. The legitimate rights and interests of women shall be protected in contract. No organizations or individuals may deprive their rights to land contractual management, which they are entitled to, or infringe upon such right." (Art. 6). As is typical for Chinese laws, this formulation is on the one hand straightforward in its objective, but on the other hand does not provide any reference as to what consequences should follow from noncompliance and how it should be enforced.

As a response to the low enforceability of their land use rights, an increasing number of unmarried women appears to turn to migratory labor (Lin and Zhang, 2006, p. 638). In line with the studies quoted in section 4.3.2, Zhang et al. (2004) also find that women do not participate less in off-farm work and that, more importantly, in cases where women do most of the farm work, productivity does not decrease. To the contrary, they find that farming efficiency of female-headed households is actually higher. In that case, curtailing land use rights of women may actually have a negative impact on land productivity.

4.3.4 Land rights and credit access

In view of the fact that farmers in rural China hardly have any other assets to use as a security, the right to offer their land use rights as collateral could potentially be an important means to increase their access to credit. However, the 1995 Guarantee Law prohibited the mortgaging of land use rights to arable land (PRC, 2000a, Art. 37). According to Zhu et al. (2006) an earlier draft of the new Property Law allowed the mortgaging of land use rights under certain conditions, but such a provision is not contained anymore in its final version. The right to offer land use rights as collateral for acquiring credit therefore remains excluded from the bundle of rights currently held by farmers. The political concern about allowing mortgage of land use rights centers around the fear that this could drive farmers into landlessness.

However, there is also disagreement about how important it would be for farmers to have this right. Kung and Liu (1997) showed that most farmers do not deem it important to have the right to use their use rights as collateral. First, they do not see themselves as the legal owners of the land they cultivate and, second, the lack of lending institutions is their primary constraint and the mere right to offer land use rights as collateral would not change this situation. The primary formal lending institutions in rural China are the Rural Credit Cooperatives (RCCs) which were established in the 1950s with the aim to protect farmers against usury (Cheng, 2006, p. 26). From the very beginning, RCCs had been under strong influence of local CCP cadres. In the reform period, RCCs were placed under the administration of the Agricultural Bank of China (ABC), to which they had to transfer a large share of their deposits. This reduced the amount of funds available for loans. Furthermore, unsustainable interest rate policies led to great financial losses. Financial reforms in the mid-1990s sought to separate profit-oriented commercial banks and policy oriented banks. RCCs were separated again from the ABC and put under the control of the central bank. RCCs became the main source of credit in rural China and also began microfinance activities. However, supply of rural credit as a proportion of deposits in fact decreased after the reforms due to a diversion of credit to urban areas, increasing nonperforming loans (NPLs) and the success of deposit-only Postal Savings (Cheng and Xu, 2004, p. 152). Informal lending institutions, called rural cooperative foundations (RCF) had appeared in the mid-1980s but were closed down again until the end of the 1990s.

RCCs remained financially unsustainable, which led to wider reforms in 2003-2004. These relieved RCCs of the financial burden of NPLs, gave them more freedom in choosing appropriate ownership structures and allowed more flexible interest rates. Whether these reforms were sufficient to ensure financial independence and an increase in agriculture related lending activities is uncertain, however (Cheng, 2006; Jia and Guo, 2007).

5 Data collection

Two types of primary data, at the household and at the village level, were used for this study. The following two sections describe the data collection process and provide background information of the survey sites.

5.1 Household data

Primary data collection began in May 2005 with a large household survey conducted jointly with subproject 3.1 (see Figure 1.1). This survey was conducted in 20 villages in three provinces (Henan, Hebei and Shandong). The 5 counties in which these villages are situated (Quzhou, Liangshan, Huimin, Yanjin and Kaifeng) have good relations to the China Agricultural University, which made them easily accessible also for foreign researchers. The demographic variables shown in Table 5.1 are based on information given by village leaders. All villages are predominantly agricultural, but regional differences exist. Villages in Shandong Province appear to have a consistently lower share of agricultural households, while villages in Henan are almost exclusively agricultural, with one exception.

Table 5.1   Household surveys: sampling design

Province	County	Township	Village	Population	Households	Agricultural households (%)	1st sample (HHs)	2nd sample (HHs)
Hebei	Quzhou (QZ)	1	1	780	188	90	17	-
			2	1373	334	100	18	-
		2	3	1580	340	98	17	40
			4	960	196	80	17	-
Shandong	Liangshan (LS)	3	5	1964	520	100	17	-
			6	1443	430	98	17	-
		4	7	550	148	84	13	40
			8	655	109	96	19	-
	Huimin (HM)	5	9	620	200	95	17	-
			10	1221	330	85	16	-
		6	11	937	224	98	18	40
			12	930	246	98	16	-
Henan	Kaifeng (KF)	7	13	1100	263	100	17	40
			14	2200	540	98	17	-
		8	15	1800	500	60	18	-
			16	1530	390	100	15	-
	Yanjin (YJ)	9	17	970	225	100	17	-
			18	1114	330	100	17	-
		10	19	1353	300	100	17	-
			20	570	131	100	17	40

Source: IRTG (2005).

The villages were selected purposely in order to meet the different research interests for both participating subprojects. In each village around 17 households were randomly selected for interviews. The total sample size is

337 households. The five selected counties (abbreviated in the following as in Table 5.1) reflect the diverse socioeconomic conditions found in the NCP, as Table 5.2 shows on the basis of economic indicators from provincial yearbooks. Liangshan and Huimin County are situated in the rather prosperous Shandong Province and Yanjin and Kaifeng County in the inland, less developed Henan Province. Quzhou County in Hebei Province takes a middle position, geographically and economically.

Table 5.2   County and provincial-level economic indicators (2005)

	QZ	LS	HM	YJ	KF	Hebei	Henan	Shandong
Average wage of staff and workers (¥/year)	10484	-	-	7446	7801	14707	14282	16614
Per capita GDP (¥/year)	8465	9492	10458	7629	7176	14782	11346	20096
Rural household per capita net income (¥/year)	3552	3681	3667	3265	2674	3482	2871	3931

Note: Average wages were not available for counties in Shandong Province.
Sources: Hebei Province Statistical Bureau (2006), Henan Province Statistical Bureau (2006), Shandong Province Statistical Bureau (2006).

The questionnaire contained extensive modules on the farm household structure, agricultural and non-agricultural production, land use rights and credit access. Due to the already voluminous questionnaire, plot level input and output data in this survey was limited. In order to better take into account the importance attributed to plot level input use and productivity differences (Tan, 2005), a second household sample was drawn in September 2005. From the 20 villages of the initial household survey, one of each county was selected in which a sample of 40 households each was randomly chosen for interviews, which resulted in an additional sample size of 200 households (see Table 5.1). Unfortunately, it was not possible to reach the same households as from the first survey for this purpose.

5.2 Village data

In each of the villages from the household surveys, interviews with village leaders were conducted as well. These focused on village infrastructure, farmers' land and water use rights and the implementation of agricultural policies outlined in section 3.2.2. However, due to the small sample size of 20 villages, no inference can be made about the underlying causes for variation between the villages in terms of tenure arrangements and economic development. This necessitated a larger village-level survey. Comprehensive data has been available for one of the survey counties, Quzhou County in Hebei Province. These comprise the county statistical yearbooks (QSY) for 11 consecutive years (1996 to 2006), which provide data on population development, yields and relative shares of the most important crops and livestock for all villages, climate data (temperature and precipitation), a soil classification and a GIS-based map. Given this data availability and good research conditions due to the local Agricultural Experimental Station, which is affiliated to China Agricultural University, it was decided to conduct a representative village-level survey in this county.

Figure 5.1   Quzhou County

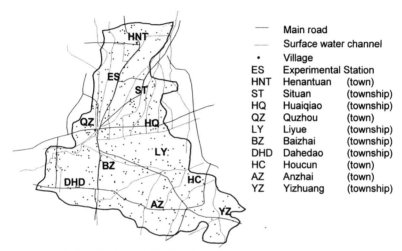

—	Main road	
....	Surface water channel	
•	Village	
ES	Experimental Station	
HNT	Henantuan	(town)
ST	Situan	(township)
HQ	Huaiqiao	(township)
QZ	Quzhou	(town)
LY	Liyue	(township)
BZ	Baizhai	(township)
DHD	Dahedao	(township)
HC	Houcun	(town)
AZ	Anzhai	(town)
YZ	Yizhuang	(township)

Source: Own design developed in ArcGIS® based on a county map.

Quzhou County consists of 6 townships, 4 towns and 342 administrative villages and is regarded as typical for the NCP.[7] Main crops cultivated are winter wheat, summer maize, cotton and vegetables. Until the 1980s, 40% of the land in Quzhou, mostly the northern townships, was heavily salt-affected. Gradually, soil quality has been improved by draining the salt using large amounts of fresh groundwater from deep wells (Chen et al., 2006). This practice has caused groundwater tables to decline and increased the dependence of agriculture on groundwater irrigation (Hu et al., 2005). According to the study of Kong et al. (2003), arable land decreased in the period from 1973 to 2000 by 0.026% annually, mainly due to construction activities. In the same period, land productivity increased 7 times.

---

[7] As Kung (2002b) notes, administrative villages in North China, in particular in Hebei Province, tend to coincide with natural villages. Quzhou County therefore consists only of administrative villages.

6 Methodological approaches used for the data analysis

6.1 Inequality Measurement

Inequality in rural China is an issue of increasing importance. It is closely related to the functioning of land and labor markets, since transfers of both factors between households may have profound effects on inequality. On the other hand the egalitarian distribution of land may partly explain why transfers of this factor are so limited. This study therefore seeks to measure inequality in the data sets used and detect possible impacts of the land transfer market. The household- and village-level data allow analyzing the level of inequality present within and between Quzhou and the other four survey counties. Generalization is limited due to the purposive selection. The following paragraphs introduce concepts of inequality and give examples of studies on rural inequality in China.

Common inequality indices are the Gini coefficient, the Theil index, the squared coefficient of variation (CV), i.e. the standard deviation divided by the mean of a variable, and the mean logarithmic deviation (MLD) index. All these indices except the Gini coefficient are decomposable by subgroups. Indices that satisfy this condition are known as belonging to the generalized entropy class (Chakravarty, 2001). Yu et al. (2007) calculate the Theil index and the MLD of income and decompose these indices in order to calculate the shares of income inequality attributable to different levels of aggregation. In their study, overall income inequality is decomposed into inequality within and between townships, counties and provinces. Intra-village inequality was not included in the study of Yu et al. (2007). They find that about ¾ of total inequality can be attributed to inter-township inequality and only ¼ to intra-township inequality. Of the inequality due to inter-township differences, the largest part (70%) is further accounted to inter-county as opposed to intra-county inequality. Similar to the approach of Yu et al. (2007), inequality in the household data could be decomposed into village, township, county and province contributions. In the case of the village-level data from Quzhou County, it can be assessed whether inequality is mainly caused by within- or between-township effects.

The Theil index can be expressed as

$$T = \sum_{v=1}^{n} \frac{y_v}{Y} * \log\left[\left(\frac{y_v}{Y} \right) \Big/ \left(\frac{1}{n} \right) \right], \tag{4}$$

where n is the total number of observations, y_v is the income of observation v and Y is the total income in the population. The part that is due to between-group effects can be calculated as

$$T^b = \sum_{i=1}^{m} \frac{Y_i}{Y} * \log\left[\left(\frac{Y_i}{Y}\right) \Big/ \left(\frac{n_i}{n}\right)\right], \tag{5}$$

where Y_i is the total income of the population n_i in group i. The part of the overall index attributable to effects within groups is the

$$T^w = \sum_{i=1}^{m} \frac{Y_i}{Y} * \sum_{v=1}^{n} \frac{y_{iv}}{Y_i} * \log\left[\left(\frac{y_{iv}}{Y_i}\right) \Big/ \left(\frac{1}{n_i}\right)\right], \tag{6}$$

which is the sum of the Theil indices in each group, weighted with the income share of each group. The MLD is defined by Yu et al. (2007) as

$$MLD = \frac{1}{n}\sum_{v=1}^{n}\log\left(\frac{U_Y}{y_v}\right), \tag{7}$$

where, in the case of income inequality, U_Y is mean income and n and y_v are defined as above. The decomposition of the MLD is similar to that of the Theil index.

The part of the coefficient of variation due to within-group inequality is obtained by weighting the CV of subgroup k (CV_k) as follows (Jenkins, 1999):

$$CV_w = \sum_{k=1}^{K}\left(\frac{p_k}{P}\right)^{-1} * \frac{S_k}{S} * CV_k, \tag{8}$$

where p_k is the number of observations in group k, P is the total number of observations, S_k is total income in group k and S is total income in the population. The between-group inequality is then obtained as the difference between overall inequality and the calculated within-group inequality.

Income inequality can not only be decomposed by groups, but also by income sources. Following Shorrocks (1982), the proportionate contribution of the income component f to total inequality can be expressed as follows:

$$s(f) = r(f, inc) * \frac{\sigma(f)}{\sigma(inc)}, \tag{9}$$

where $r(f, inc)$ is the correlation between the income component f and total income (inc) and $\sigma(f)$ and $\sigma(inc)$ are the standard deviations of component f

and total income, respectively. These shares add up to unity and the decomposition rule is independent of the inequality index used (Jenkins, 1999). Morduch and Sicular (2002) decompose income inequality in a household sample from 16 villages in a rural county in Shandong Province and use a regression-based approach to explain the sources of inequality. They find that in most cases the results on the sources of inequality are sensitive to the decomposition rules, but that the village location had a large inequality increasing effect in all decompositions. According to Morduch and Sicular (2002, p. 101), factors associated with the location of a village include geographic diversity in land and water availability, distance to markets, local leadership and different paths of economic development.

Rozelle (1994) decomposed the Gini coefficient by income source and analyzed inequality trends over time. He concludes that in the early years of economic reform, policies targeting agriculture have led to a reduction of income inequality, while those targeting rural industries have had an income inequality enhancing effect. This is attributed to administrative barriers which prevented interregional trade, implying that areas in which rural industries were less developed were not able to benefit from industrial growth in other areas.

Gustafsson and Shi (2002) used household samples in 18 provinces from 1988 and 1995 and decomposed the MLD and the Theil index into intra-county and inter-county contributions. Income inequality is found to have increased between the two years. Furthermore, the results confirm the spatial character of inequality as argued by Rozelle (1994). About half of the income inequality in 1995 is attributed by Gustafsson and Shi (2002) to inter-county inequality. This inter-county inequality is in turn mainly caused by inter-province inequality.

Contradicting the notion of rural industries to increase inequality, de Janvry et al. (2005) find for the case of Hubei Province that participation in rural non-farm activities, which mainly involves working in Township and Village Enterprises, decreases inequality. They argue that rural non-farm employment opportunities effectively transfer poorer, less productive households out of agriculture, while the more productive households decide to continue farming.

6.2 Efficiency Analysis

To some extent, it may be argued that equality and efficiency are contradicting policy goals. The current land tenure system allegedly prevents land to be transferred to the most efficient users. Yet, increasing resource use efficiency has been shown to be of no less importance than reducing income inequality in rural China. A comparison of both inequality and inefficiency at the household and village level could provide more insights into how both policy goals are interrelated. To establish the basis for this kind of analysis, the following sections discuss efficiency concepts and results of efficiency studies related to Chinese agriculture.

6.2.1 Technical Efficiency

Production efficiency can be broken down into allocative and technical efficiency (Coelli et al., 2005). Technical efficiency can be measured by examining a producer's relative performance on a production function. A producer operating on the production frontier is said to be technically efficient (Coelli et al., 2005). Technical efficiency can be expressed as output-oriented or input-oriented, where output-oriented efficiency measures the ability to maximize output with given inputs and input-oriented efficiency the ability to minimize inputs to attain a given amount of output.

Instead of using a production function, the production technology can also be represented by a profit function, which enables the estimation of profit efficiency. The use of the profit function may be more appropriate than the production function in the case of farm households who are heterogeneous in the prices they face and their factor endowments (Wang et al., 1996, p. 147). Estimating the different dimensions of production efficiency simultaneously in a profit function system enables more efficient estimates than in a production function framework (Rahman, 2003). In a profit function, profit is expressed as a function of output prices, input prices and quantities of fixed inputs. It follows that quantities of variable inputs are not needed for the estimation. Input demand and output supply are derived indirectly by applying Hotelling's Lemma and Shepard's Lemma (Chambers, 1988). Shephard's lemma allows deriving the demand for each input as the derivative of the cost function with respect to the input price:

$$x_i = \frac{\partial C(w,y)}{w_i}, \tag{10}$$

where $C(\cdot)$ is the cost function, w is a vector of input prices and y a given level of output.

Hotelling's Lemma states that the output supply of a certain good is equal to the derivative of the profit function with respect to the good's price:

$$y(p) = \frac{\partial \pi(p)}{\partial p}. \tag{11}$$

Two main approaches to efficiency analysis, the deterministic Data Envelopment Analysis (DEA) and the Stochastic Frontier Analysis (SFA) have been developed. Recently, the methodologies have been extended to the estimation of environmental efficiency, i.e. the ability of producers to minimize the production of undesirable output or use of undesirable inputs for emissions from chemical fertilizer (Fernandez et al., 2002; Reinhard et al., 1999; Reinhard et al., 2000).

In this study, the stochastic approach is preferred due to the nature of the survey data. The stochastic frontier production function, originally proposed by Aigner et al. (1977) and Meeusen and van den Broeck (1977) models technical inefficiency (TE_i) as a strictly non-negative error component (u_i), which reduces output. The general form of the equations can be written as:

$$\ln q_i = \mathbf{x}'_i \beta + v_i - u_i \qquad (12)$$

$$TE_i = \exp(-u_i), \qquad (13)$$

where q_i is output, $\mathbf{x}_i$ is a vector of inputs, β is the coefficient vector, v_i is the random error component, assumed to be independently and identically distributed as N (0, σ_v^2), and u_i is the non-negative inefficiency component, which can be modeled as having either a half-normal, exponential or truncated-normal distribution. Because this inefficiency component is not normally distributed, it would be inconsistent to take its estimated value as the dependant variable in a second regression to identify the determinants of inefficiency. Instead, both estimation steps need to be integrated (Battese and Coelli, 1995). According to Battese and Coelli (1995) some variables may be included in the error components regression as well as in the regression explaining technical inefficiency.

The total variance in the stochastic frontier production model, σ^2, can be divided into the variance attributed to the random error, σ_v^2, and the variance attributed to technical inefficiency, σ_u^2. The estimate of the ratio between both variance components, γ, can be tested to be zero by performing a likelihood ratio test. The general likelihood ratio test statistic λ is defined as:

$$\lambda = -2\ln\left[L(H_0)/L(H_1)\right] = -2\left[LL(H_0) - LL(H_1)\right], \qquad (14)$$

where $L(H_0)$ and $L(H_1)$ are the likelihoods when imposing the null hypothesis H_0 and the alternative hypothesis H_1, respectively, and $LL(H_0)$ and $LL(H_1)$ are their logarithms. Critical values for this test can be obtained from Kodde and Palm (1986). If the null hypothesis that $\gamma = \sigma_u^2/\sigma^2$ is zero can not be rejected, it must be concluded that no technical inefficiency is present in the model.

The software FRONTIER 4.1 (Coelli, 1996) is used to estimate the stochastic production function (with the error components model) and the determinants of inefficiency (with the technical efficiency effects model).

6.2.2 Allocative Efficiency

Production factors are said to be allocated efficiently if their marginal value products equal their marginal costs, which is equivalent to saying that production factors are chosen in such a way that a given quantity of output is produced at minimum cost (Schmidt and Lovell, 1979). If the MVP exceeds marginal costs, additional profit is generated from using more of an input. If the MVP is below marginal costs, less of the factor should be used in order to maximize profit (Colman and Young, 1989, pp. 19). In the simplifying example of one output and two variable inputs, the cost minimal input combination is achieved where the marginal rate of technical substitution (MRTS, i.e. the slope of the isoquant) equals the factor price ratio (Doll and Orazem, 1984, p. 113).

Allocative efficiency is also referred to as price efficiency when the equality of marginal costs with the market prices is examined. Price inefficiency is present when the marginal costs for producers differ from market prices, i.e. when producers base their decisions on shadow prices rather than observed market prices. The comparison of actual cost shares with estimated shadow cost shares of single inputs can be used to assess the degree of misallocation: an input can be said to be overused if its actual cost share exceeds its estimated shadow cost share and vice versa. Overall allocative efficiency is then the ratio between shadow cost and actual cost of production (Fan, 2000, p. 6). Fan (2000) estimated allocative efficiency of rice farmers in Jiangsu Province and found the relatively poor farmers in the North to be more allocatively efficient which the author takes as a confirmation of the "poor but efficient" hypothesis (Fan, 2000, p. 10).

The observed cost shares of variable inputs in crop production suggest that allocative inefficiency, i.e. the failure to choose cost-minimizing input combinations, is in China in fact more relevant than technical inefficiency. This is hypothesized to hold for the use of chemical fertilizer in particular. The reform of input and output markets, necessary to facilitate a more efficient allocation of inputs, has been neglected by the Chinese government until the mid 1980s (Fan, 2000).

The analogue to the stochastic frontier production function for estimating allocative efficiency involves the estimation of a stochastic frontier cost function, which contains input prices as arguments (Schmidt and Lovell, 1979). However, good data on all input prices relevant in a production process are often not available. Because of this limitation, Benjamin and Brandt (2002) apply a different approach and compare the MRTS between land and labor across farms in order to test for allocative efficiency between both factors. Under the assumption that land input is fixed and wage rates are the same for all farmers, their MRTS between the two factors should also be the same. Any differences between the MRTS can then be said to indicate allocative inefficiency.

A number of empirical studies take a simplified approach to allocative efficiency by actually comparing the MVP of a factor, estimated from a production function, with its market price (Liefert et al., 2005; Suresh and Reddy, 2006; Vranken and Mathijs, 2001). Such calculations do not give an estimate of the overall allocative efficiency of a firm but only the allocative efficiency with regard to one factor. However, given the available data, these less complex approaches are more suitable for the present study. Vranken and Mathijs (2001) compute the MVP of land for a sample of Hungarian farmers, compare these with rental prices paid or received by farmers active in the land rental market and construct allocative inefficiency scores (AI) with AI being the logarithm of the ratio between the MVP and the rental price. Therefore a positive AI indicates an MVP above the market rental rate and vice versa.

For the case of the emerging rural land rental market in China, it may already be interesting to confirm a positive relationship between the MVP of land and current land rental prices, which would indicate that land rental prices are in fact competitively determined.

6.2.3 Economic Efficiency

Overall economic efficiency or cost efficiency is defined as the product of technical and allocative efficiency. Technical, allocative and cost efficiency can be illustrated using the following graph. The point x^A shows a production process which is technically and allocatively inefficient. It is technically inefficient because it uses units of inputs x_1 and x_2 to produce y^a which exceed the lower boundary of the isoquant $L(y^a)$. It is also allocatively inefficient, because the technically efficient input combination deviates from the cost minimal combination of x_1 and x_2 at point x^E where the MRTS between both factors equals their price ratio. The total deviation of x^A from x^E is then a measure of cost inefficiency.

Figure 6.1   Technical, allocative and economic efficiency

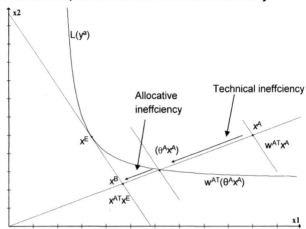

Source: Adapted from Kumbhakar and Lovell (2000).

6.2.4 Efficiency studies of Chinese agriculture

A number of studies have been conducted on technical efficiency of Chinese farm households (Carter and Estrin, 2001; Chen et al., 2003; Skoufias, 1994; Tian and Wan, 2000). In their study of Chinese provincial-level agricultural production data from the 1980s and 1990s, Carter and Estrin (2001) associate structural reforms directly with technical efficiency and market reforms with allocative efficiency. From their results can be concluded that fragmented landholdings caused technical inefficiency in the sense that the investigated provinces failed to produce the maximum attainable output with given inputs. Incomplete markets and misleading incentives, such as grain self-sufficiency policies, resulted in inefficient allocation of resources.

Tian and Wan (2000, p. 161) suspect the land tenure system to be detrimental to technical efficiency, but their data only allowed to include land per capita endowment, the ratio of irrigated area to total arable land and the multiple cropping index (MCI) as variables pertaining to land tenure in their estimation. The results they obtained for technical efficiencies of wheat and maize cultivation in Hebei, Henan and Shandong are reproduced in Table 6.1 together with other production function studies. Interestingly, it seems that while production costs in Henan Province tend to be lower, technical efficiency is also lower compared to Shandong and Hebei.

Table 6.1   Production function studies on Chinese agriculture

	Land	Labor	Fertilizer	Capital	Machinery	Returns to scale	TE
	— Partial production elasticities						
Chen et al. (2003)	0.68	0.04	0.06	0.13	-	0.90	0.85
Fleisher and Liu (1992)	0.70	0.20	0.09	0.06	-	1.05	-
Tian and Wan (1993)	0.67	0.06	0.06	-	-	-	-
Wan and Cheng (2001), wheat	0.67	-0.21	-	0.30	-	1.0	-
Chen and Huffman (2006)	0.16	0.24	0.24	-	0.25	0.89	0.80
Tian and Wan (2000)[1]							
Wheat, Hebei	-	0.06	0.30	0.15	-	-	0.94
Wheat, Henan	-					-	0.91
Wheat, Shandong	-					-	0.94
Maize, Hebei	-	0.07	0.04	0.17	-	-	0.94
Maize, Henan	-					-	0.87
Maize, Shandong	-					-	0.92

Note: If no technical efficiency (TE) estimate is reported, the study used a deterministic production function.
[1] Tian and Wan (2000) only report technical efficiency scores differentiated by provinces. The reported partial production elacticities are average elasticities across their sample of provinces.

Wang et al. (1996) estimated a stochastic shadow-profit frontier function for Chinese agricultural households. In their study, the relation between market prices and shadow prices is characterized by the price efficiency parameters θ. These θ's are modeled by the authors as a function of a household's labor-to-land ratio and education of its labor force in order to examine the influence of these variables on the household's response to market distortions (Wang et al., 1996, p. 149). Their main finding is that land scarcity and population density in the coastal provinces of China drives farmers to overuse inputs, thus reducing their profit efficiency.

A wide range of studies has employed the stochastic frontier production function approach to estimate technical efficiency of household agricultural production in other developing countries. Admassie (1994) found farms in Ethiopia using chemical fertilizer to display higher TE, since fertilizer is, contrary to China, still underused. Interestingly, in this study, there were no significant differences in TE between large and small farms. Keil (2004) analyzed technical efficiency of irrigated rice and cocoa cultivation in Indonesia and found availability of off-farm income to be efficiency reducing while specialization in the cultivation of the specific crops had an efficiency enhancing effect.

6.2.5 Estimating agricultural production functions

In this study, the production function approach to estimating technical efficiency is applied. The most commonly used agricultural production function is the Cobb-Douglas (CD) function, which can be written in the context of a stochastic frontier model as follows (Coelli, 1996, p. 20, adapted):

$$\ln Y = \beta_0 + \beta_1 \ln(x_1) + \beta_2 \ln(x_2) + ... + (v_i - u_i). \tag{15}$$

Other, more flexible functions include the generalized quadratic or translog function, which incorporate interactions between the factors of production. Likelihood ratio tests can be used to assert whether the translog specification should be preferred to the CD specification (Keil, 2004).

Partial output elasticities of production factors can be derived from the estimation of an agricultural production function. The marginal value product (MVP) of a factor can be calculated as the product of the output elasticity and the average value product:

$$\frac{\partial y}{\partial x} p = \left(\frac{\partial y}{\partial x} \frac{x}{y} \right) \left(\frac{y}{x} p \right). \tag{16}$$

As stated above, an efficient allocation of resources requires an equalization of a factor's MVP with its price. For the case of land, a gap between its MVP and typical land rental fees may provide evidence for price inefficiency. In order to make such a comparison, an estimate of the partial production elasticity, or output elasticity, is needed. In case of the CD-function, parameter estimates can be directly interpreted as output elasticities, while additional calculations have to be made to derive these from the estimates of the translog function (Chen et al., 2003; Fleisher and Liu, 1992; Wan and Cheng, 2001). While output elasticities in the CD-function are constant for all input levels, those elasticities derived from the translog function are observation specific (Greene, 2003).

For the hypothesis of constant returns to scale to hold, partial production elasticities for those production factors which can be effectively controlled by the farmer should add up to 1. An F-test, with the null hypothesis that the coefficients add up to unity, can be performed to test this hypothesis (Greene, 2003, p. 103).

The choice of variables used in a production function depends largely on the available data and different set-ups are possible. Empirical studies have either estimated crop-specific functions or functions taking the aggregated gross value of agricultural output as the dependent variable. For the estimation of crop-specific functions, exact input data is often missing, which may require making behavioral assumptions and estimating crop specific input allocation from the aggregate data (Just et al., 1990; Zhang and Fan, 2001).

In case of a function which aggregates total production on an area of land, either the total arable land or the sown area can be used as the land input variable. However, the sown area, which increases when multiple crops are grown in one season, is likely to be endogenous and correlated with the error term (Benjamin, 1995, p. 56). Instead of total production, Tian and Wan (2000) take production per *mu* as the dependent variable and therefore do not incorporate land as an input in the production function. Consequently, this approach does not provide an estimate of the partial production elasticity of land.

Land is a heterogeneous input and much information would be lost if land quality was not accounted for in a production function. In most cases, land quality is not directly observable and some proxy is used instead. The following paragraphs discuss the suitability of different indicators of land quality used in the literature.

The proportion of irrigated land in a village may be used as an indicator for land quality (Rozelle and Li, 1998). Such figures are available from statistics but should be interpreted with caution. Chinese statistics use various terms for irrigated area figures which may have very different meanings. Nickum (2003) distinguishes two main categories of irrigated area measures: the more theoretical command area and the area actually receiving irrigation in a given year. Command area data is naturally less precise but easier to obtain. Chinese statistics differentiate the command area into "effectively irrigated area" (EIA) and "stable high-yield fields" (SHYF). EIA is further subdivided into the categories bunded fields (*shuitian*) and irrigated dry land (*shuijiao di*). The QSY only reports the latter which is defined as "dryland that has a water source and irrigation facilities and which can be irrigated normally under the conditions prevailing in an ordinary year." (Nickum, 2003, p. 251).

Alternatively, land quality may be captured by a simple ordinal ranking ('low, medium, high'), as done by Benjamin and Brandt (2002). Benjamin and Brandt (2002) test for an inverse relationship between farm size and productivity and find that such a relationship can be entirely explained by omitted land quality differences. This implies that land of larger farms is systematically of lower quality, which is in line with the results of Nguyen and Cheng (1996) reported above.

Production functions can not only be estimated for households, but also for more aggregated production units. Chen and Huffman (2006) estimated a county-level stochastic frontier production function using a dataset containing production and socioeconomic variables for 2159 Chinese counties. The authors used the Gross Value of Agricultural Output (GVAO) as the dependent variable and labor (measured by number of agricultural laborers per hectare and year), sown area, machinery and fertilizer as inputs. Usage of geomembrane (i.e. plastic sheets used primarily as cover in cotton, vegetable and fruit production) was found to have a positive effect on technical efficiency (TE). The relation between population density and TE was characterized by an inverse-U shape: Chen and Huffman (2006) argue that higher population is related to higher soil fertility, better infrastructure and access to information. Extremely high population density, however, would imply land fragmentation and hence have a negative effect on TE. Chen and Huffman (2006, p. 159) note that land tenure and education could also be determinants of TE but could not incorporate such variables in their estimation.

6.3 Spatial analysis of village data

In many instances, it is reasonable to assume a positive correlation of data on observational units which are distributed in space if units are adjacent or close-by. This hypothesis applies to the village-level data from Quzhou County, where close by villages are likely to display some degree of similarity. At the same time, the data is likely to be spatially heterogeneous in the sense that some regions or clusters of villages may be distinctly different from other regions. In both cases, spatial autocorrelation is present. Spatial autocorrelation can be detected by computing the Moran's I test statistic. This statistic shows the degree of linear correlation between the observed variable y in one unit and a weighted average of the values of y in its neighboring units (Moran, 1948). The first step in order to compute Moran's I is therefore to define which units are to be considered neighbors. Since the data set for Quzhou County only contains point data, not polygons, it is not possible to use village borders for this purpose. Alternatively, points located within a certain distance to each other could justifiably be called neighbors (Anselin, 1988, p. 18). The choice of the distance radius is arbitrary, which is, however, also true for definitions of neighborhood when borders are known. For example, a choice has to be made between first-degree or second-degree neighborhood etc. Therefore, the approach of choosing a certain radius is applied in this study. In the case of Quzhou, it turned out that when using a radius of 3 km, every data point representing a village is on average assigned 11.4 neighbors. While this seems a bit high, using a smaller radius would have left some of the villages without any "neighbors".

The next step is to construct a binary neighborhood or spatial weights matrix in which a 1 signifies that two villages are neighbors. The diagonal of the matrix contains zeros. This is shown in Table 6.2 for an example of 6 villages. In this example, villages B, D and E are neighbors of village A.

Table 6.2   Example for a spatial weights matrix

	A	B	C	D	E	F
A	0	1	0	1	1	0
B	1	0	0	0	1	1
C	0	0	0	1	0	0
D	1	0	1	0	0	0
E	1	1	0	0	0	1
F	0	1	0	0	1	0

Source: Adapted from Bichler (2007)

In order to assign equal weights to the variable values in neighboring villages, the matrix is standardized by setting the row sums equal to unity. In other words, the values for each neighboring village are divided by the total number of neighbors. This standardized matrix is then multiplied with a vector of the values of a variable y, which results in a vector of the weighted average values of y of all neighbors for each village. In the example of village A, the variable values of its neighbors would be weighted with ⅓.

The test statistic Moran's I is given by

$$I = \frac{\sum_{i}^{N}\sum_{j}^{N} w_{ij}(Y_i - \overline{Y})(Y_j - \overline{Y})}{\sum_{i}^{N}\sum_{j}^{N} w_{ij}\sum_{i}^{N}(Y_i - \overline{Y})^2 / N}, \tag{17}$$

where w_{ij} are the elements of the spatial weights matrix, Y_i and Y_j are the values of variable y in villages i and j and $\overline{Y}$ is its average value over all villages. From this representation it becomes clear that Moran's I can be interpreted as a correlation coefficient which takes on values between -1.0 (indicating dispersion) and +1.0 (indicating complete clustering).

Under the null hypothesis that no spatial autocorrelation is present, the expected value of I is given by

$$E(I) = -1/(N - 1). \tag{18}$$

If I is larger than its expected value, positive correlation between neighboring villages can be said to exist. A test statistic to evaluate the significance of this correlation is given by z-values (see e.g. Cliff and Ord, 1973):

$$z_i = \frac{I - E(I)}{sd(I)}, \tag{19}$$

where $sd(l)$ is the standard deviation of l (Pisati, 2001). If spatial autocorrelation exists, OLS-regressions may give misleading results. Two situations occur in practice. First, the dependent variable in one location may be affected by its values in nearby locations. In this case, estimated coefficients will be biased. Second, the error term in one location may be correlated with error terms in neighboring locations, due to omitted variables that are spatially correlated. In such a case, coefficients will be unbiased but inefficient, implying that F- and t-tests would be misleading (Minot et al., 2006). As alternative models in the presence of either form of autocorrelation, the spatial lag dependence model and the spatial error dependence model have been developed (Anselin, 1988).

Furthermore, the First Order Autoregressive Model (FAR) and the Spatial Autoregressive Model (SAR) can be distinguished. The former only incorporates the vector of the average values of neighboring units as an explanatory variable. The model produces an estimated coefficient ρ, which shows the change in the dependent variable of unit i resulting from a 1% change in the average deviation from the mean in the neighboring units (Bichler, 2007, p. 89). The Spatial Autoregressive Model makes use of further explanatory variables.

An application of spatial econometrics very similar to the intended purpose in this study is Chen and Huffman (2006), who use the FAR-model to analyze spatial dependence of county-level agricultural production data from China. They find spatial dependence of technical efficiency between neighboring counties and attribute this mainly to technology spillover.

6.4 Further econometric techniques used for the data analysis

In many estimation problems, OLS-regressions would provide biased or inefficient estimates and different techniques are required. Some of these techniques, which will be used in the data analysis, are briefly described with examples from studies related to land tenure.

6.4.1 Binary dependent variables

If the dependent variable is of binary nature, estimated coefficients indicate the probability of an event occurring. In the logit model, the response probability is expressed by the logistic function evaluated at a linear function of the explanatory variables, while the probit model uses the standard normal cumulative density function (Wooldridge, 2006). Both models are fitted by maximum likelihood estimation and are widely used.

In logistic regression, the estimated coefficients represent the logarithm of the odds ratio for a unit change in a regressor, which is the ratio of the probability of an event occurring and the probability of it not occurring (Long, 1997, p. 113):

$$\Omega = \frac{Pr(y = 1 \mid x)}{1 - Pr(y = 1 \mid x)}. \tag{20}$$

The interpretation of the estimated coefficients in a logit or probit model can be simplified by either reporting the odds ratios instead of their logarithms or calculating the marginal effects of the explanatory variables on the probability p_i of an event occurring (Long, 1997, p. 139). Marginal effects and predicted probabilities from the logit and probit model are almost identical. The z-statistics in the output are approximations to t-statistics. There are various measures of the goodness of fit of the model and more than one should be used and results compared.

Multinomial logit is an extension of the logit model in which the dependent variable consists of more than two categories. One of the categories is designated as the base category to which the probability of the other outcomes is compared. In this study, households were asked to ordinally rank the quality of their cultivated plots into the categories 'below average', 'average' and 'above average'. To estimate the effects of regressors on the probability of a plot falling into either category, a multinomial logit model can be fitted. Feng (2006) used a multinomial probit model to estimate effects on the probability of households choosing between different land and labor market participation alternatives.

6.4.2 Censored regressions and selection bias

When values of the dependent variable are limited to a lower or upper bound for a number of observations on the independent variables, the data is said to be censored (Long, 1997). As an example from the land rental market, it may be that plots transferred in the market are of a certain minimum size. Some households may be willing to rent in land, but only less than the minimum size offered. These households will be recorded as non-participants in the market although they may be heterogeneous in their propensity to participate in the market. Some of such non-participants may have characteristics which make them seek participation in the land rental market, but they may be constrained, e.g. due to high transaction costs (Deininger and Jin, 2007). Recording all such households as zero-observations and using OLS on the subsample of uncensored observations would thus result in biased estimates (Dougherty, 2002). The tobit model, which combines a probit model with OLS regression analysis, corrects for this bias. In this model, the observed dependent variable y is expressed in terms of an unobserved latent variable y*, which satisfies the classical linear model assumptions and equals the observed variable for all uncensored observations (Wooldridge, 2006, p. 596). For example, Kung (2002b) estimated a tobit model to explain the amount of land rented in Chinese villages.

In cases where the chance of an observation falling into the censored or uncensored category is believed to depend on other underlying variables, a two-step estimation process which adjusts for sample selection bias may be required. In the Heckman two-step procedure, the inclusion in the uncensored category is estimated in the first stage, followed by a regression model parallel to the tobit model (Dougherty, 2002). As an example, excluding all non-participants in the land rental market from an estimation of the amount of land rented in causes the sample to be non-random when the decision to participate depends on some unobserved characteristics. By using the Heckman two-step selection model, the estimated probability to rent in land can be included in the estimation of the amount of land rented in (Feng, 2006, pp. 29).

Formally, the selection bias is caused by the correlation of the error terms in the two equations explaining participation in the land rental market and the amount of land rented in. First, let B_i^* be a latent (unobservable) variable which depends on a number of independent variables Q_{ji}. This variable takes on a value > 0 if a land rental market exists and ≤ 0 otherwise:

$$B_i^* = \delta_1 + \sum \delta_j Q_{ji} + \varepsilon_i. \tag{21}$$

Second, the amount of land rented in (Y_i^*) depends on a different set of independent variables and is only observed if $B_i^* > 0$:

$$Y_i^* = \beta_1 + \sum \beta_j X_{ji} + u_i. \tag{22}$$

Therefore, the expected value of the error term u_i is equal to

$$E\left(u_i \middle| B_i^* > 0\right) = E\left(u_i \middle| \varepsilon_i > -\delta_1 - \sum \delta_j Q_{ji}\right). \tag{23}$$

Hence, the error term u_i will be correlated with the error term ε_i from the first equation (adapted from Dougherty, 2002, p. 297).

7 Descriptive Analysis

The descriptive data analysis is divided into two main sections: the analysis at the household level (7.1) in which the data of the first and second household survey are analyzed and the analysis at the village level (7.2) which mainly deals with the village data from Quzhou County.

The analysis mainly involves standard mean comparison tests. Independent samples or two-samples t-tests compare the mean of one variable between two groups or categories (Hamilton, 2004, p. 143). The hypothesis of equal variances between groups is tested by evaluating Levene's statistic (Field, 2005, p. 98). A large and significant Levene's test statistic indicates different variances in the samples. The computation of the t-value depended on the result of this test. In cases where the assumption of a normal sampling distribution cannot be maintained and where the variables are measured on an ordinal or nominal scale, the nonparametric Mann-Whitney U-test is applied to find differences between the groups (Healey, 1999, p. 259). Normality of interval-scaled variables was examined using a χ^2 test statistic which combines tests of skewness and kurtosis (Hamilton, 2004, p. 127).

For comparisons of means between multiple groups, Analysis of Variance (ANOVA) was used because conducting multiple t-tests in these cases would increase the probability of a Type I error, i.e. the probability of rejecting the null hypothesis although it is true (Healey, 1999, p. 234). If the hypothesis of equal variances in subgroups is rejected by Levene's test, the Games-Howell test and otherwise the Hochberg GT2 test are used to identify the groups with significantly different means (Field, 2005, p. 341).

In case of non-normality, the non-parametric Kruskal-Wallis Test is used instead of ANOVA. If the Kruskal-Wallis Test finds significant differences between groups, it can then be followed by pair-wise Mann-Whitney U-tests (Field, 2005, p. 550). If this is done, however, the critical significance value in each Mann-Whitney U-test needs to be divided by the number of tests in order to avoid inflating the probability of a Type I error. For example, if 10 comparisons between groups are made, as it is the case when comparing each of the 5 survey counties with each other, the significance level at which the null hypothesis of no difference in means can be rejected drops from 0.05 to 0.005. The test therefore becomes very restrictive in rejecting the null hypothesis, which has the advantage, that only sizeable differences between means are tested to be significantly different.

Paired samples t-tests compare means of two variables within the same group of observations whereas one-sample t-tests test whether the sample mean $\bar{y}$ of a variable significantly differs from some hypothesized value (Hamilton, 2004, p. 143).

Correlations between interval scaled variables are evaluated using Pearson's correlation coefficient. The independence of the distributions of nominal or ordinal variables between different groups or categories was tested with Pearson's Chi-square test (Healey, 1999, pp. 280).

In mean comparison tests, means with different letters as superscripts have been tested as significantly different at the given error probability. Most of the analysis was done in Stata®, except the Analysis of Variance, which was done in SPSS® because Stata does not offer the appropriate Post-hoc tests in case of unequal variances.

7.1 Household level

Due to the structure of the household survey, variation in the data can be compared between households, villages, townships, counties and provinces. In the following subsections, most of the descriptive statistics are aggregated at the county level or at the provincial level. Since the subsequent village-level analysis focuses on Quzhou County, the situation of Quzhou relative to the other four counties will be occasionally highlighted in the following descriptive analysis.

7.1.1 Household composition

Table 7.1 summarizes the main household specific variables as collected in the first household survey, differentiated by counties. A common definition of a household is a group of individuals living together in the same residence for the whole or part of the year. Bowlus and Sicular (2003, p. 568) define as a household all individuals living in the same residence for one or more months of the year.

In the case of China, those family members living and earning income mainly outside the farmstead can contribute significantly to household income. Interviewees, which were in most cases the household heads, were therefore asked to differentiate between the total size of their family, the household size according to the definition above and the number of people to whom food is provided by the household. The last two figures differed slightly because some family members may live in the same village but in a different residence then the household to which the interviewee belonged. These appear to be in most cases young couples who moved out of their parents' house. As Table 7.1 shows, neither family size nor household size differs significantly between the five counties.

The assessment of the household labor force and the calculation of the household dependency ratio must be based on certain assumptions (see 3.2.1.2). For the calculation of household labor endowment, the survey grouped family members according to their availability for work in agricultural household production and other employment ("Occupation of family members", Table 7.1).

Table 7.1   Household composition: Summary statistics

	QZ	LS	HM	YJ	KF
N =	69	66	67	68	66
Household size					
Family size	4.3[a]	4.3[a]	4.1[a]	4.5[a]	4.5[a]
Household size	3.7[a]	3.5[a]	3.6[a]	4.0[a]	4.1[a]
MDE (Family members)	3.1[a]	3.0[a]	3.0[a]	3.0[a]	2.9[a]
MDE (Farm labor)	2.0[ac]	1.7[bd]	1.7[bc]	2.1[acd]	2.2[a]
Occupation of family members (%)					
Not working at all	6.5[a]	7.9[ab]	13.3[b]	8.3[ab]	8.8[ab]
Going to school	15.8[a]	19.5[a]	14.3[a]	15.4[a]	18.2[a]
Full time on-farm	57.3[ac]	50.8[bc]	47.2[bc]	58.7[ac]	63.7[a]
Only on-farm when needed	9.4[b]	12.7[b]	13.8[b]	12.5[b]	1.5[a]
Full-time off-farm	10.9[ab]	9.1[ab]	11.3[a]	5.2[b]	7.8[ab]
Household dependency ratio	0.47[a]	0.46[a]	0.34[a]	0.49[a]	0.53[a]
Age and gender					
Age of household members (years)	38.3[ab]	39.9[ab]	40.2[a]	34.3[b]	34.9[ab]
Age of family labor force (years)	40.2[a]	42.2[a]	40.1[a]	38.4[a]	40.2[a]
Age of farm labor (years)	42.7[ab]	44.4[a]	43.2[ab]	39.5[b]	42.5[ab]
Female share in family labor force (%)	46.8[a]	45.8[a]	44.1[a]	49.4[a]	48.8[a]
Female share in farm labor (%)	48.1[a]	47.7[a]	47.5[a]	50.4[a]	48.6[a]
Education					
Average years of education of family labor force	6.7[abcd]	6.0[ac]	6.8[bd]	7.5[b]	6.2[cd]
Average years of education of farm labor force	6.4[abc]	5.7[ac]	6.4[ac]	7.5[b]	5.8[ac]

Notes: Different letters as superscripts denote that means are significantly different at the 0.5% level of error probability based on the Kruskal-Wallis Test followed by Mann-Whitney U-tests (all variables were significantly non-normal based on a joint skewness/ kurtosis test). MDE = Man-day equivalents (see text).
Source: IRTG (2005).

It is common to define the dependency ratio as the ratio of non-working age household members to working-age household members (Dinh, 2005). Using this definition, Bowlus and Sicular (2003) find for their sample of Chinese households a ratio of 0.3, which is somewhat lower than the ratio of 0.46 as found in our survey, in which household members below 18 and above 65 years are counted as dependents.

Assigning weights on the labor force depending on their primary occupation, age and gender leads to an estimation of man-day equivalents (MDE), defined as "the amount of work (of a particular kind) that can be carried out by an adult male in an 8-hour work period" (ILCA, 1990). A common approach is to treat labor aged below 18 as children and labor between 18 and 65 years as working-age adults (Bowlus and Sicular, 2003, p. 568). Furthermore, Bowlus and Sicular (2003) use working efficiency weights of 0.79 for female adult labor and 0.5 for children relative to male adult labor. In their study, the weights for female labor were derived from county level wage data. Such gender-differentiated wage data was not available for the present study. Therefore in this study a weight of 0.75 for female adult labor is assumed.

By multiplying the farm labor MDE with the number of days a person typically works in a year, i.e. around 200 days (Yang, 2008), the total household labor supply in agriculture can be derived and compared with the labor demand of the production process. Acknowledging that this may involve the type of errors identified by Chu et al. (2000), labor surplus in this study will be defined as labor available for farm work above the demand in the production process.

Table 7.2   Farm man-day equivalents as a combination of occupation and gender

Gender	Male			Female		
Months working off-farm	0	<6	≥6	0	<6	≥6
"going to school"	0.25	-	-	0.25	-	-
"full-time on-farm"	1	0.75	0.5	0.75	0.5	0.25
"only on-farm when needed"	0.5	0.5	0.25	0.5	0.25	0.1
"working full-time off-farm"	-	-	-	-	-	-

Source: IRTG (2005).

While no significant differences in the means of the family labor force can be detected, the size of the farm labor is significantly lower in the two counties in Shandong Province (Table 7.1). This is mainly due to a lower share of family members working full-time on farm and higher shares working either part-time on-farm or full-time off-farm. This result is in line with the expectation that households in the prosperous, coastal province of Shandong are likely to have more opportunities for off-farm employment and be less dependent on agriculture.

The figures on the average age of the family labor force consider only those family members either working full-time on-farm, on-farm when needed or full-time off-farm. Compared to that, the average age of farm labor includes only those family members working either full-time on-farm or on-farm when needed. Family members mainly working in agriculture tend to be older than those mainly working off-farm, as is suggested by the higher age of farm labor in LS and HM County. On average, those family members working full-time on-farm are almost twice as old (43 years) as those working full-time off-farm (24 years).

Furthermore, the average share of female labor in the farm labor force, again defined as those family members working full-time on-farm or on-farm when needed) tends to be higher than the share when considering the total family labor force. This result suggests that indeed female family members participate less in off-farm employment and more in agriculture. This is further evidenced by a comparison of occupations differentiated by gender (Table 7.3).

Table 7.3   Occupation of family members by gender (%)

		Not working	Going to school	Full time on-farm	Only on-farm when needed	Full-time off-farm
Male	N = 739	10.7	18.5	44.8	14.7	11.2
Female	N = 653	9.2	16.5	63.1**	3.4**	7.8*

* (**) Pearson's Chi-square test significant at the 5% (1%) level of error probability.
Source: IRTG (2005).

Education of family members was assessed by a five-level ordinal scale corresponding to the highest education achieved. This scale is transformed into an interval scale by converting the levels into years of schooling (Table 7.4). Table 7.1 compared years of schooling of the total family labor force and the labor force mainly working in agriculture. The intuition that better educated family members will mainly engage in off-farm employment can clearly be confirmed. As can be seen from the last row in Table 7.4, the average years of schooling of family members aged 10 years and older is 6-7 years. Interestingly, years of schooling attained by household members in Yanjin County was significantly higher compared to Kaifeng and Liangshan County.

Table 7.4   Education of family members (%)

	QZ	LS	HM	YJ	KF
Illiterate	9.5[a]	14.3[a]	13.2[a]	8.3[a]	16.9[a]
Primary school	30.3[a]	37.7[a]	27.5[ab]	16.3[b]	25.5[ab]
Middle school	43.3[ab]	34.7[a]	44.3[ab]	58.2[b]	42.3[a]
High school	12.9[a]	8.3[a]	11.8[a]	14.6[a]	12.7[a]
College	1.5[a]	1.5[a]	2.6[a]	1.3[a]	1.8[a]
Missing values	2.7	3.6	0.8	1.4	0.8
Average years of schooling (in years)[1]	6.8[ab]	6.0[a]	6.6[ab]	7.4[b]	6.4[a]

[1]Illiteracy is assumed to be equivalent to 0 years of education. Education at the primary, middle, high school and college level is assumed to be equivalent to 5, 8, 11 and 15 years of education, respectively. Household members aged less than 10 years were excluded. Letters denote significantly different means at the 0.5% level based on the Kruskal-Wallis Test followed by Mann-Whitney U-tests.
Source: IRTG (2005).

7.1.2 Household agricultural production

All households (HHs) in the sample engage to some extent in agricultural production. Questions on household agricultural production related to the cultivation year 2003-2004. Section 7.1.2.1 describes characteristics of land endowment and land use of the survey HHs at the household and at the plot level. Section 7.1.2.2 then describes in more detail the use of the most important inputs in crop production apart from land. The last section then calculates net income from crop production and compares the result between the sample HHs.

7.1.2.1 Land endowment and land use

Table 7.5 gives an overview of land endowment at the household level and a number of plot level characteristics, differentiated by counties. The number of plots per HH refers to the plots that have been allocated to a household, i.e. they include plots rented out and exclude plots rented in. Accordingly, the land per capita is the total size of allocated farm land per family member.

Land fragmentation can be measured by the average plot size, the number of plots per household and a combined measure known as the Simpson Index (SI) which is defined as

$$SI = 1 - \frac{\sum_{i=1}^{n} a_i^2}{\left(\sum_{i=1}^{n} a_i\right)^2} \tag{24}$$

where n equals the number of plots and a_i is the size of plot i (Blarel et al., 1992; Tan, 2005). The SI lies between 0 and 1, with larger values indicating fragmentation. The average SI across households in the sample, also based on the number of allocated plots, is 0.51. Interestingly, the SI is much lower (0.31) in KF, which deserves further attention.

In total, the survey contains data on 1123 plots. On average, these have a size of 2.4 *mu* with plots being significantly larger in Henan Province. In the cultivation year 2003-2004, the five most important crops – in terms of the number of plots covered with these crops – were winter wheat (681 plots), summer maize (432), cotton (381), peanuts (164) and soybeans (39 plots). The remaining crops are quantitatively of minor importance. Villages have typically specialized in one or two other crops, mainly different types of vegetables and fruits. The pure double-cropping pattern of winter wheat followed by summer maize is practiced only on 27% of all plots, the highest percentage of which can be found in QZ (Table 7.5).

Perennial crops (trees, orchards, grapes) are only grown on 47 plots. As expected, such plots have been held by farmers for a significantly longer time (15 years) than the average of 9 years. Mean comparison tests of the number of plots, land per capita, SI and the average years plots have been cultivated confirm that significant differences between the five counties exist.

Regarding the tenure status of plots, interviewees were only asked whether a plot is contracted, rented from other farmers or rented from the village collectives. Other possible tenure arrangements such as that of reserve land as mentioned in section 4.2.2 was not included. Tan (2005) differentiated in her study plots rented from the collective and reserve land, but both tenure types are very similar.

Table 7.5   Household land endowment and land use

		QZ	LS	HM	YJ	KF
Household level	N =	69	66	67	68	66
Number of plots per household[1]		4.0[b]	3.7[b]	3.5[b]	2.1[c]	2.8[a]
Land per capita (*mu*)[1]		1.7[ab]	1.5[b]	1.7[bc]	2.0[ac]	2.2[a]
Simpson Index (SI)		0.6	0.6	0.6	0.3	0.5
Plot level	N =	279	247	256	150	191
Average size (*mu*)		1.8	1.7	1.8	4.3	3.3
Cropping patterns						
Wheat single-cropping (%)		7.2	8.5	6.3	5.3	12.6
Maize single-cropping (%)		1.1	0.8	0.0	0.0	5.8
Wheat – maize (%)		43.4	18.6	22.7	32.0	16.2
Cotton single (%)		43.7	15.0	40.6	1.3	1.0
Multiple cropping index (MCI)		1.6	2.5	1.8	2.8	1.7
Plots planted with wheat (%)		60.0	61.1	38.3	93.3	75.9
Rented plots (%)		0.02	0.02	0.10	0.03	0.05
Average land rental fee (¥/*mu*)		357.0	216.2	166.4	232.8	104.7
Potential wheat yield (kg/*mu*)		346.5	340.0	367.5	378.5	314.5
Average years of cultivation		11.1	13.6	6.4	7.7	5.7
Plot level, 2nd survey	N =	105	92	98	126	192
Subjective plot quality						
"below average" (%)		15.2	8.7	10.2	28.6	24.0
"average" (%)		66.7	52.2	71.4	41.3	58.3
"above average" (%)		18.1	39.1	18.4	30.2	17.7
Distance plot – house (m)		944.0	374.1	1027.3	433.2	1195.1
Distance plot – water source (m)		216.9	74.8	237.3	69.5	74.8

[1] Different letters as superscripts denote that means are significantly different at the 0.5% level of error probability based on the Kruskal-Wallis Test followed by Mann-Whitney U-tests. Source: IRTG (2005).

In order to obtain a simple estimate of plot quality, respondents were asked to state for each plot their perceived yield potential for winter wheat. However, this variable is problematic because it is likely to be endogenous to the farmers' cultivation practices. Moreover, as explained above, plot level information from the first household survey was limited and did not include actual input levels and yields. In order to gain more insight into plot level differences and possible effects of land fragmentation, a second sample of households was collected in September 2005. This sample of 200 households contains information on 613 plots. Some results from this survey are shown in Table 7.5 below the dashed line. In this survey, the approach taken to measure plot quality was to ask respondents whether they perceive their plots to be below, above or equal to average quality at the village level. Furthermore, data on plot level yields, distance of a plot to the farmstead and to the nearest water source were collected.[8]

7.1.2.2 Input use in crop production

The following paragraphs focus on the three most important inputs in crop production apart from land, namely labor, fertilizer and water. Apart from the use of these inputs, it is also interesting to explore which HHs make use of agricultural machinery since the land fragmentation has been blamed for the low level of mechanization in Chinese agriculture.

While plot-level analysis of input use, labor allocation and yields is inevitable to assess the impacts of land allocation, tenure status and land fragmentation, comprehensive and exact data is needed. Ideally, this would require actual observation of farmers over several growing seasons, which was not feasible for this study. Therefore, all input and output data is exclusively collected through farmers' recall.

Assessing the farm-level quantity of fertilizer input in terms of pure nitrogen content is difficult insofar as the actual amounts of nitrogen contained in the fertilizer products used by farmers are not known. Therefore, typical nitrogen contents in the fertilizers that farmers applied were imputed. Considering that fertilizer products in China are said to be often tampered (see section 3.2.1.6), assumptions about actual nitrogen contents may be faulty. Moreover, using the area sown with a crop as the basis against which to evaluate fertilizer input may be subject to errors, because the actual plant density is not known. Therefore Table 7.6 shows fertilizer input for wheat, maize and cotton per planted area (in kg N/ha to make comparisons with other countries easier) as well as per unit of output (in kg N/t of harvested crop), which may be a better indicator of fertilizer use efficiency.

In total, the survey contains observations on 2017 single fertilizer applications, i.e. each household reported on average around 6 fertilizer applications, most of which (5.4) were applications of nitrogenous fertilizers. The calculated average level of pure nitrogen input for winter wheat, as obtained in the survey, of 367 kg/ha is very close to the 375 kg/ha found in the study of Zhen et al. (2006) for a county in Shandong Province. For maize and cotton, Zhen et al. (2006) report a farmers' practice of 240 kg/ha and 360 kg/ha, respectively. For the case of maize, the average nitrogen input of 223 kg/ha from the IRTG survey matches this fairly well while it is much lower for cotton (194 kg/ha). At least for the case of wheat, Table 7.6 confirms the expectation from Figure 3.1 that agriculture in Henan Province tends to be less intensive than in Shandong and Hebei, given the average nitrogen input of 315 kg/ha in Henan compared to 386 kg/ha in Shandong and 437 kg/ha in Hebei.

---

[8] In this study, this data from the second household survey will only be used for the analysis of land fragmentation. If not explicitly stating otherwise, the text refers to the first household sample.

Table 7.6   Nitrogen fertilizer application by crops and counties

	N =	QZ		LS		HM		YJ		KF	
		kg N/ha	kg N/t output	kg N/ha	kg N/t output	kg N/ha	kg N/t output	kg N/ha	kg N/t output	kg N/ha	kg N/t output
Wheat	320	437	167	336	158	439	146	307	131	322	124
Maize	271	161	55	148	82	259	77	332	100	204	77
Cotton	159	164	99	114	106	258	196	227	237	146	223

Source: IRTG (2005).

49% of HHs apply organic fertilizer in the form of manure. Respondents were asked about the reasons for applying manure (Table 7.7). The dominating reason for using manure is simply the availability of manure from own livestock production (33.8%), followed by the recognition of its positive effects on soil quality (25.8%). Surprisingly, saving money due to lower costs than for chemical fertilizer does not play an important role (6.5%).

Table 7.7   Reasons for and against application of organic fertilizer

	QZ	LS	HM	YJ	KF
N =	65	64	67	66	65
% HH using any manure	50.7	65.2	59.7	67.6	44.8
Yes, because...					
Availability of livestock	15.9	25.8	55.2	29.4	40.3
Cheaper than chemical fertilizer	1.4	1.5	7.5	7.4	14.9
Improves soil quality	31.9	36.4	11.9	33.8	14.9
Other reasons	1.4	10.6	0.0	0.0	1.5
No, because...					
too time consuming	0.0	0.0	3.0	5.9	0.0
effect on yield takes long	0.0	0.0	0.0	1.5	0.0
not enough livestock available	47.8	31.8	34.3	22.1	44.8
other reasons	1.4	0.0	0.0	2.9	0.0
No valid response	0.0	3.0	3.0	0.0	10.4

Source: IRTG (2005).

Likewise, the dominating reason for not applying manure is the lack of sufficient sources from own livestock. Naturally, if no manure is available, the argument that the effect on yields takes too long, as put forth by proponents of a connection between the use of manure and tenure security, does not play any role.

Collecting data on water use for irrigation entails similar difficulties as described for the case of fertilizer. The actual quantity of water applied could not be directly provided by farmers and an estimation of actual water input in crop production based on the information that farmers could potentially give would have to include data on the types of wells and pumps used. Since this was not possible given the resource constraints, the approach taken in the first household survey was to assess the costs of irrigation. In an effort to increase the accuracy of the data, interviewees were asked about the number of irrigations, hours spent irrigating and costs per hour for pumping the water. The results in Table 7.14 below indicate that average irrigation costs for winter wheat in Shandong are quite close to those obtained from secondary data, while they are about three times higher in Henan and two times higher in Hebei. Land in Shandong Province is mainly irrigated by surface water, while agriculture in Henan and Hebei relies more heavily on groundwater. An underlying reason for the apparently higher costs may therefore be that hours spent irrigating are overstated when groundwater pumps are used, due to higher set-up time. However, irrigation costs as reported in the village-level survey in Quzhou County (section 7.2.3), where village leaders were asked directly about total average irrigation costs, are in the same range.

Problems related to water scarcity and pollution have been mentioned in section 3.2.1.4. In order to get an idea about the seriousness of the problem in the survey counties, households were asked about how severe they perceive decline in groundwater and surface water quality and quantity to be in their village (Table 7.8). The fact that the survey counties primarily use surface water or groundwater explains why answers mainly relate to either of the two sources. Concern about water quantity is clearly higher than about water quality. The highest percentage of farmers concerned about quality is found in Quzhou County, which is mainly due to high salt contents in groundwater (Hu et al., 2005).

Table 7.8   Perception of water quantity and quality decline

		Severe decline in surface water...		Severe decline in groundwater...	
	N =	...quantity (% of HHs)	...quality (% of HHs)	...quantity (% of HHs)	...quality (% of HHs)
QZ	69	0.00	0.00	24.64	18.84
LS	66	42.42	13.64	0.00	0.00
HM	67	40.30	10.45	0.00	2.99
YJ	68	10.29	5.88	32.35	11.76
KF	67	5.97	5.97	26.87	5.97

Source: IRTG (2005).

As mentioned in section 3, most of the farm work is done manually. Some of the machinery which is mainly needed for seasonal work is rented, while transportation vehicles are typically owned (Table 7.9). Mean comparison tests of the average plot size and farm size between households owning and not owning certain machinery imply that larger plot sizes and larger farm sizes matter for the decision to invest in such agricultural equipment. The policy objective of increasing mechanization in Chinese agriculture as indicated by the recent introduction of machinery subsidies (Heerink et al., 2006) may therefore not benefit very small and fragmented farms for which increased use of machinery is not practicable.

Table 7.9   Use of agricultural machinery

	% of households renting	% of households owning	Mean comparison of average plot size[a]	Mean comparison of farm size[a]
Wheat cutter	23.7	4.2	3.64**	4.75***
Corn thresher	10.0	2.1	-0.87	2.43*
Plough	0.9	14.2	0.47	1.99***
Two-wheel tractor	4.7	17.2	1.74**	2.45***
Three-wheel tractor	0.3	32.9	0.26	0.21
Four-wheel tractor	12.2	13.3	-1.01	0.05
Knapsack sprayer	0.9	0.0	-	-
Sowing machine	15.7	7.1	3.84***	4.30***
Irrigation pump	11.0	0.0	-	-

[a] Shows the mean difference of the average plot size and farm size between households owning this machine and those not owning it.
* (**) [***] Mann-Whitney U-test significant at the 10% (5%) [1%] level of error probability.
Source: IRTG (2005).

The survey asked about labor input in crop production measured in hours spent for different activities. These are ploughing, sowing, weeding, fertilization, irrigation and harvest. These data are converted to days of work, assuming an 8-hour workday. Given the difficulties of households to realistically state the amount of time spent working, several observations had to be dropped for this analysis. Labor time needed for pesticide applications was not included in the questionnaire because it was expected that pest management would be mainly confined to weeding. As well, labor needed in livestock production is not considered because livestock raising is done very extensively in the study area.

Table 7.10 shows average labor demand for the main activities across all counties. On average, the figures for maize, peanuts and soybeans match well with those shown in Table 3.1 but are somewhat too low for wheat and cotton.

Summing up labor demand for all crops, multiplying this figure with their respective acreages and comparing it with the labor available for agriculture (farm labor MDE as shown in Table 7.1) may allow conclusions as to which households appear to be particularly labor abundant or labor scarce.

Table 7.10   Labor demand by main crops (days/*mu*)

	Wheat	Maize	Cotton	Peanuts	Soybeans
Ploughing	0.59	0.38	0.33	0.76	0.03
Sowing	0.61	1.44	3.64	2.10	0.71
Weeding	0.89	1.03	1.29	1.41	2.54
Fertilizer	0.46	0.24	0.39	0.10	0.03
Irrigation	0.64	0.38	0.21	0.66	0.13
Harvest	2.05	4.05	11.79	5.81	1.44
Total labor days/*mu*	5.24	7.52	17.65	10.84	4.88

Source: IRTG (2005).

Table 7.11 shows the total days of work needed for the main crops as stated by interviewees across the five counties together with the total labor demand as derived from the *National compilation of costs and revenues of agricultural products* (NCCR, National Bureau of Statistics of China, various years). Under the assumption that all households in the sample use similar technology, a better estimate of labor surplus and labor scarcity may be obtained from calculating labor demand for crop production by taking the NCCR figures as the basis, rather then using respondents' recall data.

Labor surplus is expressed in Table 7.11 as the ratio between days of work in agriculture in excess of those indispensable in the production process ("Total days of work") and available labor ("Available labor days"), which is calculated by multiplying the farm labor MDE with 200, assuming 200 days of work per year. The labor surplus calculated from the survey data shows a much larger variation and appears to be too high, while the calculation from the NCCR data results in an average surplus of 60%. Compared to Chu et al. (2000), who report what they call gross labor surplus for Jiangsu Province of 49% in 1992, this estimate may still overstate the surplus.

Table 7.11   Labor surplus by provinces

	QZ	LS	HM	YJ	KF
N =	69	65	62	67	65
Total days of work (Survey)	53.7	88.1	154.6	67.5	205.3
Total days of work (NCCR)	114.3	144.9	175.1	173.0	171.6
Available labor days	439.9	366.2	391.9	451.5	496.9
% labor surplus (Survey)	86.0	75.6	57.1	85.8	60.3
% labor surplus (NCCR)	70.8	57.3	50.7	57.7	63.7

Sources: IRTG (2005), National Bureau of Statistics of China (various years).

The average calculated labor surplus using the NCCR-data is 71% for Quzhou, 61% for the counties in Henan Province and 54% for Shandong Province. The surplus in Quzhou is significantly higher compared to Henan and Shandong (at the 1.66% level based on the Mann-Whitney U-test), which suggests that HHs in this county have fewer opportunities to transfer their labor out of agriculture.

Despite the apparent labor surplus, most households make use of some form of hired labor, with marked differences between the three provinces. The use of hired labor could be seen as an important decision that indicates on the one hand separability and on the other hand a step towards commercialization. However, Table 7.12 shows that the use of hired labor is confined to ploughing, sowing and harvest work, which can be explained by the fact that these activities often involve the hiring of machinery services. While the survey data does not contain any more specific information about the type of hired labor, it is likely that this labor is needed for operating the machinery. If this is so, hiring of labor is not motivated by general labor scarcity but rather by the lack of own machinery and qualified personnel for operating it.

Table 7.12   Hired labor in crop production

	Hebei		Henan		Shandong	
	% of HH using any hired labor	% of work by hired labor	% HH using any hired labor	% of work by hired labor	% HH using any hired labor	% of work by hired labor
Ploughing	72.5	68.2	14.8	12.4	67.7	61.8
Sowing	85.5	62.0	16.3	9.1	81.2	21.9
Weeding	0.0	0.0	0.0	0.0	1.5	0.0
Fertilizer	2.9	0.2	1.5	1.5	0.8	0.5
Harvest	72.5	11.4	39.3	7.2	64.7	8.7
Total	94.2	15.0	45.2	4.5	94.7	9.1

Source: IRTG (2005).

The share of HHs hiring any labor is equally high in Quzhou and in the survey counties in Shandong Province. The high use of hired labor in Shandong Province may be explained by a more developed labor market as a result of more advanced economic development. However, this does not explain the equally high share of households using hired labor in Quzhou County.

HHs in the counties in Henan Province make much less use of hired labor. The relation between hiring labor and machinery services is supported by the finding that the incidence of HHs owning any of the agricultural machinery listed in Table 7.9 is highest in Henan (70.4%), followed by Quzhou (68.1%) and lowest in Shandong Province (54.9%). Apparently, many HHs in Henan Province do not need to hire labor for ploughing, sowing, and harvest work because they own most of the necessary machinery themselves.

7.1.2.3 Profitability of agricultural production

Summing up production of all crops valued with their average output prices allows deriving the gross value of agricultural output (GVAO) produced by a household. In doing so, one needs to keep in mind that typical agricultural households in China are semicommercial in the sense that around 50% of their agricultural production value is in fact used for own consumption (Carter and Zhong, 1999). The survey results are very much in line with this characterization and show that only 50% of winter wheat yield is sold to the market, while 20% of the households keep all their winter wheat yield for own consumption.

Comparisons of the GVAO, component costs and gross margins differentiated by provinces are shown in Table 7.13. This table leads to the interesting conclusion that agriculture in Henan Province is most profitable with a gross margin per arable land that is about 200 ¥/mu higher than in Shandong and Hebei. This observation is consistent with Figure 3.1, which suggested production costs for wheat, maize and cotton to be lowest in Henan.

Livestock production is only marginally considered in this study for two main reasons. First, livestock raising does not play an important role in household production in the study area and less data has been collected on livestock production. Second, it is not directly related to land use and land transfers, which is the main topic of this study.

Table 7.13   Profitability of agricultural production by provinces

		Hebei	Shandong	Henan
Household level (¥)	N =	69	129	134
	GVAO	6059.0	5746.0	9700.7
	Seed costs	445.1	511.3	688.0
	Manure	-	-	-
	Chemical fertilizer	1114.9	1147.6	1506.0
	Pesticides	291.6	262.2	289.1
	Draught animals	-	-	-
	Machinery	212.9	374.0	451.7
	Irrigation costs	679.4	256.9	486.2
	Others	93.0	118.4	158.5
	Salary for hired labor	290.8	267.8	187.0
	Land rent	46.8	60.0	87.4
	Sum of direct production costs	3174.4	2998.4	3853.8
	Gross margin	2884.5	2747.5	5846.8
Gross margin/land				
Sown area *(mu)*		11.5	11.7	19.2
Gross margin per sown area (¥/*mu*)		280.7	229.4	313.5
Arable land *(mu)*		7.4	6.6	9.6
Production costs per arable land		440.4	467.0	403.2
Gross margin per arable land (¥/*mu*)*		395.8[a]	425.3[a]	604.9[b]
*Gross margin per capita**		879.0[a]	829.5[a]	1615.3[b]

Note: From the total sample of 337 households, 5 observations are dropped due to extreme values. Only these 332 HHs are included in the table.
* Different letters as superscripts denote that means are significantly different at the 1.66% level of error probability based on pair-wise Mann-Whitney U-tests.
Source: IRTG (2005).

Labor costs include only costs for hired labor. One approach to include costs for family labor would be to use average wage rates, which were obtained in the village leader interviews, to calculate opportunity costs. However, it is very uncertain which household members would be qualified for the types of jobs shown in Table 7.21. Costs for family labor are therefore not further considered.

Since winter wheat is the quantitatively most important crop in the region, the calculation made above is repeated only for winter wheat in Table 7.14 and again compared with the data from the provincial statistics. While some of the figures match fairly well, costs for chemical fertilizer as reported in the survey are much higher across all three provinces. This leads to production costs for wheat that are about 100 ¥/*mu* higher than in the statistics. Still, the overall tendency of lower production costs in Henan Province compared to their neighbors in Shandong and Hebei, as suggested by Figure 3.1, can be confirmed. However, the gross margin for wheat in Henan Province is only significantly higher compared to Hebei Province.

Table 7.14   Profitability of wheat production by provinces

	Hebei		Shandong		Henan	
	provincial data	survey data	provincial data	survey data	provincial data	survey data
Production costs (¥/mu)		N = 65		N = 119		N = 133
Seeds	28.1	43.4	22.16	33.0	23.8	34.3
Farm manure	8.4	-	15.34	-	7.2	-
Chemical fertilizer	85.9	142.3	88.08	138.3	44.1	110.5
Pesticides	5.4	8.1	6.47	11.1	9.0	10.4
Draught animals	1.2	-	1.44	-	0.33	-
Machinery	61.1	37.3	53.11	58.9	54.4	55.4
Irrigation and Drainage	38.2	87.3	24.89	33.7	9.3	32.9
Others	0.3	-	0.4	-	0.0	-
Sum of direct costs	228.6	318.3	211.9	275.0	148.1	243.5
Average yield (kg/mu)		370.4		366.5		379.8
Average output price (¥/kg)		1.45		1.42		1.40
Gross margin (¥/mu)*		217.4[b]		252.0[ab]		287.9[a]

Note: Based on 317 HHs that provided complete data on wheat production costs.
* Different letters as superscripts denote that means are significantly different at the 5% level of error probability based on one-way ANOVA followed by the Hochberg GT2 test.
Sources: National Bureau of Statistics of China (various years), IRTG (2005).

7.1.3 Land use rights

Some of the responses of households to questions pertaining to their rights to agricultural land are highly subjective. Often, households do not have exact knowledge of their rights, also due to unclear legal settings. Rather, they often perceive to have certain rights and enjoy a certain level of tenure security. Deininger and Jin (2006, p. 11) found that knowledge about the exact stipulations made in the LLCRA is low on behalf of households as well as village leaders.

When asked about their opinions on land reallocations, 54% of HHs appear to consent to this practice because it guarantees equality among households. An overview of the stated opinions on land reallocations is given in Table 7.15. Respondents were allowed to give answers for and against reallocations, which is why the figures add up to more than 100%.

Table 7.15   Stated opinions on land reallocations

	% of HHs giving this answer		% of HHs giving this answer
Disapprove because…		*Approve because…*	
"It is better to use plots for a long time"	5.3	"reallocations provide equality"	54.1
"Village leader benefits from reallocations"	1.3	"gives land to those who need it"	12.2
"reallocations are unfair"	2.2	"reallocations are fair"	15.9
Other reasons	3.4	Other reasons	1.9
Don't know or no opinion	25.3		

Note: Based on 320 observations.
Source: IRTG (2005).

64% gave exclusively reasons in favor of reallocations, 10% completely disapproved, 25% had no opinion or did not know and only 1% gave both reasons for and against reallocations. Of those respondents who gave an answer to the question of when they expect the next village-wide reallocation (168), 21% expect such a reallocation to take place within the next 5 years, 20% expect it in more than 5 years, 4% expect no more large reallocation to take place and 54% do not know. This shows that the timing of reallocations is often uncertain. Those respondents who did not give any answer to this question most likely also did not know when to expect the next land reallocation in their village. Six of the 20 survey villages conform to the rule of conducting a large land reallocation only every 30 years while two villages stated to never conduct a large reallocation (Table 7.16) Of the five counties, land tenure appears to be most stable in QZ, with none of the 4 villages conducting small land adjustments.

63% of the households in the first survey claimed to possess land right certificates. Similar results were obtained by Deininger and Jin (2006), who found from a survey of 722 villages covering the 12 main agricultural provinces that in 83% of the villages, households possessed land certificates and that this number was only 67% in the North and Northwest and 93% in the South and Southwest. Reasons for the lower percentage of households holding certificates in the north were not given by Deininger and Jin (2006).

From the viewpoint of households, there appears to be no consensus as to which administrative level has the authority to issue such documents (Table 7.17), which is also in line with the fact that the subject of collective land ownership is not unambiguously defined in China Wang (2006). Some of the village leaders, however, also stated that households were handed out land right certificates many years ago and that some households might simply not remember that they have indeed such documents because they are of little importance to them.

Table 7.16   Land reallocations in survey villages

	QZ	LS	HM	YJ	KF
Large reallocations					
Every 5 years	-	1	-	2	3
Every 10 years	-	1	1	-	-
Every 13 years	1	-	-	-	-
Every 15 years	1	1	-	-	-
Every 20 years	-	-	-	1	-
Every 30 years	2	1	1	1	1
Never	-	-	2	-	-
Small reallocations					
Every year	-	2	1	1	1
Every 2 years	-	-	1	-	
Every 3 years	-	1	-	-	
Every 5 years	-	-	-	-	1
Every 6 years	-	1	-	-	
Never	4	-	2	3	2

Source: IRTG (2005).

Deininger and Jin (2006, p. 7) were able to circumvent this problem by collecting data on land titles from village records. In any case, the issuance of certificates only increases perceived tenure security if they are actually valid in the event of land disputes. Since such conditions cannot be expected to exist in China, Deininger and Jin (2006) conclude that merely issuing land certificates in China is currently not an effective means to protect farmers' land rights.

Table 7.17   Incidence of land use right certificates (% of HHs)

	N =	No title	Any title	Title issued by Village Committee	Title issued by township government	Title issued by county government or above	Title issued by others	Don't know
QZ	68	32.4	58.8	5.9	2.9	48.5	1.5	8.8
LS	65	55.4	40.0	4.6	13.8	21.5	0.0	4.6
HM	67	3.0	92.5	16.4	31.3	44.8	0.0	4.5
YJ	65	58.5	35.4	6.2	21.5	7.7	0.0	6.2
KF	65	12.3	86.2	9.2	76.9	0.0	0.0	1.5

Source: IRTG (2005).

Most studies find that the rural land rental market in China is not in equilibrium, i.e. that the marginal product of land does not equalize across households (see e.g. Lohmar et al., 2001). To some degree, households are rationed in their land market participation (Deininger and Jin, 2002).

Households were asked about the reasons for non-participation in the land rental market (Table 7.18). The main reason for the underdeveloped land transfer market appears to be the supply side, as implied by the high percentage (88.6%) of households who are not willing to rent out their land because they depend on all of the land they currently cultivate. This constrains households which appear to have a propensity to rent in land (43.9%). The fact that 18.8% of sample households do not rent in because of a lack of additional labor contradicts the common belief of labor surplus. As stated above, however, Bowlus and Sicular (2003) have shown that in the presence of incomplete markets, there may be areas of labor shortage and surplus within close proximity. Since 30.4% of HHs also stated that they do not need any more land, one reason for the narrow land rental market may also be the egalitarian land distribution, i.e. that there is no need for transferring land (Bowlus and Sicular, 2003, p. 571). None of the households in the survey stated that they fear to lose their use rights if they rented out any of their land although this is an often given explanation for the reluctance to rent out (Kung, 2002b, p. 296).

Table 7.18   Reasons for not participating in the land rental market

	% of households (N = 303)	QZ	LS	HM	YJ	KF
Reasons for not renting in:						
"Don't need more land"	30.4	45.5	19.4	44.0	11.3	33.3
"No land available"	43.9	24.2	29.0	62.0	56.5	52.4
"No money"	1.3	0.0	3.2	0.0	1.6	1.6
"Agriculture not profitable"	15.2	12.1	45.2	4.0	9.7	3.2
"No time to cultivate more"	4.6	1.5	11.3	2.0	6.5	1.6
"No additional labor"	18.8	18.2	30.6	4.0	25.8	12.7
"No right to rent in"	0.7	1.5	0.0	0.0	0.0	1.6
Other reasons	0.3	1.5	0.0	0.0	0.0	0.0
	% of households (N = 325)					
Reasons for not renting out:						
"Need all land myself"	88.6	87.0	79.0	96.8	84.8	95.5
"Nobody wants to rent"	6.8	0.0	29.0	1.7	3.0	1.5
Other reasons	4.6	13.0	0.0	0.0	7.6	1.5
"Might lose land"	0.0	0.0	0.0	0.0	0.0	0.0

Notes: Multiple answers possible. The number of observations consists of HHs not renting in or not renting out, less two HHs with missing answers.
Source: IRTG (2005).

Some controversy arises on the question whether land is currently actually transferred to users capable of using this factor more productively, i.e. with a higher marginal value product for land. As a counter-argument, one could postulate that those households with a higher marginal value product of land are able to use their labor even more productively outside of agriculture, i.e. that qualifications for farm and off-farm employment are positively correlated. If this was the case, agriculture would be mainly left to those without outstanding qualifications in neither agriculture nor off-farm work. At least for the situation in the early years of reform, this view is supported by Zhu and Jiang (1993, p. 456), who observed that those farmers with skills both in non-agriculture and agriculture were the first to engage in off-farm activities.

As stated above, de Janvry et al. (2005) find that those households that stay exclusively in agriculture have unobserved characteristics that make them more productive in agriculture and that thereby off-farm employment reduces rural income inequality instead of increasing it. Apparently, the allocative effect of the land rental market is an empirical question that cannot be answered beforehand.

Unfortunately, only 32 HHs (9.5%) stated to have currently rented in at least one plot. 17 of these reported to have rented plots from other farmers and 15 to have rented plots from the village collective. Only 10 households (3%) stated to have currently rented out any land. Since there are only few households in the sample that are active in the market, any conclusions on its effect are very limited. Interestingly, there are marked differences in the intensity of land transactions between the three provinces and these conform in their order with findings of Schwarzwalder et al. (2002, p. 201) as shown in Table 7.19. Rental activity is highest in the prosperous coastal province of Shandong which shows that overall economic development of a province is a good indicator for the intensity of land rental transactions. In fact, because of the close linkages between economic development and the land rental market, most studies on land rental activities concentrate on certain provinces, such as Zhejiang in South China (e.g. Wu, 2006; Zhang et al., 2004). In a comparison of 6 provinces, Kung (2002b, p. 402) found land rental activity in Hebei to be only 2% compared to 33% in Zhejiang Province and attributed this to differences in land endowment and off-farm income shares. Wu (2006) argued that the rural land rental market in Zhejiang Province is mainly driven by the desire of large parts of the labor force to leave agriculture and in fact found renting-in households to be slightly less productive than renting-out households.

Table 7.19   Incidence of land rental transactions: comparison of own survey results with Schwarzwalder et al. (2002)

| | % of households renting in | | % of households renting out | |
	IRTG (2005)	Schwarzwalder et al. (2002)	IRTG (2005)	Schwarzwalder et al. (2002)
Henan	5.9	12.0	0.7	8.4
Hebei	4.3	9.3	0.0	7.0
Shandong	15.8	21.4	6.8	18.6

7.1.4 Household non-agricultural income sources

As described above, non-agricultural employment is attributed great importance for transferring surplus labor out of agriculture, thereby allowing specialization and enlargement of farm sizes by those continuing agricultural production. Typically, however, HHs split their labor force between agricultural and non-agricultural employment. In order to adequately categorize HHs as being predominantly agriculturally or off-farm oriented, the following variables from the first household survey are used (Table 7.20).

This table shows that participation in off-farm employment differs significantly between counties. Participation is lowest in KF (29.8%) and if family members in this county earn any off-farm income, it is mainly derived from unskilled work (52%) outside the province, i.e. from migratory employment (67.9%). Participation in the two counties in Shandong Province is much higher (74.4%), which also goes along with higher wages. Moreover, more HHs in this province earn income from some kind of own small family business besides farming. This suggests strong regional differences between *distress-push* and *demand-pull* reasons for engaging in off-farm employment (Buchenrieder, 2005).

On average about 19% of family members earn some off-farm income. Of these, about two-third earn income within their respective prefecture (the administrative level between provinces and counties) and one-third outside the prefecture. It is expected, that remittances by migrated family members provide an important additional income, but precise information is not available from the survey.

In a separate section towards the end of the questionnaire, the survey asked respondents to list household income from these different sources. As can be seen from Table 7.20, agriculture constitutes the most important income source in all five counties, but in particular in the prosperous counties of Shandong Province a relatively large share of income is also derived from livestock production, small family businesses and local or seasonal off-farm employment. With more than ¾ of total income coming from crop production, the rural economy of Quzhou County is clearly the most agriculturally oriented in the sample.

Questions about income are sensitive and HHs may over- or understate their actual income. Since the validity of reported income from off-farm employment is very uncertain, a better variable to describe the off-farm orientation might be the ratio between the family labor working on-farm to the total family labor. This ratio (MDE farm labor/MDE family labor) will therefore be mainly used in the following to characterize HHs as more agriculturally or off-farm oriented.

Table 7.20 Off-farm employment by survey counties

	QZ	LS	HM	YJ	KF
N =	69	66	67	68	67
% of households having any member with off-farm employment ***	58.0	71.2	77.6	52.9	29.8
Of these, the following jobs are practiced (%):					
Construction worker	13.0	8.6	15.1	22.0	4.0
Cook	2.2	3.5	0.0	0.0	0.0
Craftsman	19.6	19.0	16.4	16.0	20.0
Office staff	2.2	3.5	5.5	6.0	8.0
Own family business	0.0	6.9	15.1	4.0	0.0
Salesman	15.2	0.0	1.4	2.0	0.0
Transportation service	6.5	3.5	4.1	4.0	4.0
Unskilled worker	8.7	20.7	28.8	38.0	52.0
Watchman	0.0	3.5	4.1	0.0	0.0
Worker in factory	6.5	13.8	2.7	4.0	4.0
Other	26.1	17.2	6.7	4.0	8.0
Employment within prefecture (%)	59.0	59.1	76.7	63.5	25.0
Employment outside prefecture (%)	19.7	21.2	8.2	15.4	7.1
Employment outside province (%)	21.3	19.7	15.1	17.3	67.9
MDE farm labor/MDE family labor	65.7	60.2	58.2	70.3	81.0
Average monthly off-farm wage (¥/month)	545.0	824.0	841.0	611.0	684.0
Income shares from different activities (%)					
crop farming	76.8	56.4	48.1	69.2	72.8
livestock production	5.4	5.6	18.0	9.1	8.0
small businesses	4.0	11.7	9.5	7.1	11.4
local off-farm employment	6.7	3.3	13.1	5.6	1.2
seasonal employment off-farm	3.2	21.3	9.7	7.1	5.6
pensions	0.3	0.0	1.1	0.5	0.0
alms	0.5	0.0	0.0	0.0	0.0
remittances	0.3	1.4	0.4	0.0	1.0

*** Pearson's Chi-square test significant at the 1% level of error probability.
Source: IRTG (2005).

7.1.5 Household income and decomposition of inequality

Household income can be broken down into net income from agriculture, income from non-agricultural employment and non-labor income, i.e. pensions, alms and remittances. As shown above, these latter three sources of income do not play an important role according to answers of interviewees.

Respondents were asked to estimate total household income themselves, which shows large variations between the five counties (Table 7.22). The stated income from farming can be compared with the gross margin as calculated from the very extensive preceding questions on household agricultural production. Such cross-checks are not possible for the figures concerning the remaining income sources. This caveat is important due to the sensitive nature of questions about income. Cross-checks of plausibility can only be made using typical off-farm wages which were collected in the survey of local leaders in the 20 villages (Table 7.21). In a few cases, village leaders were not able to give an estimate of wages, so that this table does not contain complete data for all three types of selected jobs in all villages.

Table 7.21   Typical off-farm wages by counties (¥/year)

	QZ	LS	HM	YJ	KF
Teacher	3375	5400	800	633	663
TVE worker	1133	5917	575	500	500
Office staff	1413	5800	575	320	500

Source: IRTG (2005).

The total calculated income in Table 7.22 adds up the calculated income from crop production and the stated income from livestock and off-farm activities. Income per capita, which averages 2614 ¥/year, is expressed in terms of the total household income divided by all household members. Additionally, income per family labor (MDE) is shown in Table 7.22. Overall, HHs seem to overstate their net income from farming, which is why income estimated by interviewees is in all counties higher than that obtained from using the total income from agriculture as calculated above. In 13 cases, calculated income even became negative.

The extent of income inequality in the sample can be further decomposed, using the different indices described in section 6.1. A problem arises for the observations with negative values of income per capita. These had to be recoded to arbitrarily low positive values since the equations involving logarithms would be otherwise not defined.

Table 7.22   Composition of income of sample households (¥/year)

	QZ	LS	HM	YJ	KF
N =	65	64	67	66	65
Av. net household income					
Estimated by interviewees	7275.1	8844.5	22735.4	12139.1	9748.2
Income from livestock	562.9	304.8	6441.8	1200.4	1075.0
Income from crop production (gross margin)	2884.5	1422.6	4012.2	6630.8	5062.9
Non-agricultural income	1346.4	4980.3	9424.2	3124.4	2323.9
Total calculated income	4793.8	6809.9	19951.9	11020.2	8461.9
Household income per capita measures					
per household size	1425.7	1908.9	6178.1	2825.3	2279.3
per family MDE	1733.7	2460.3	6339.8	4046.7	2977.2

Source: IRTG (2005).

Results are shown in Table 7.23. The overall Gini coefficient of income inequality is with 0.51 much higher than expected and than the 0.35 for 2002 as reported by Yu et al. (2007, p. 45). This is very likely attributable to the purposive nature of the data, which sought heterogeneity between the villages, and the accuracy of the survey information. As expected, inequality in off-farm income is even higher (0.78). Furthermore, the decomposition of income inequality into the sources crop production, livestock and off-farm activities using equation 9 resulted in 16%, 28% and 57% contributions, respectively.

Table 7.23   Decomposition of inequality in income and land endowment

	Gini	Theil		CV[1]		MLD	
Allocated land per family size							
Total inequality	0.24	0.10	(100%)	0.10	(100%)	0.15	(100%)
Intra-county	-	0.09	(90%)	0.09	(90%)	0.14	(93%)
Inter-county	-	0.01	(10%)	0.01	(10%)	0.01	(7%)
Off-farm income p.c.							
Total inequality	0.78	1.28	(100%)	2.76	(100%)	7.59	(100%)
Intra-county	-	1.02	(80%)	2.45	(89%)	7.33	(97%)
Inter-county	-	0.26	(20%)	0.29	(11%)	0.26	(3%)
Total income p.c.							
Total inequality	0.51	0.46	(100%)	0.60	(100%)	1.19	(100%)
Intra-county	-	0.37	(80%)	0.51	(85%)	1.11	(93%)
Inter-county	-	0.09	(20%)	0.09	(15%)	0.08	(7%)

[1] Expressed as half the squared coefficient of variation. CV = Coefficient of variation. MLD = Mean logarithmic deviation.
Source: IRTG (2005).

Inequality in land endowment can be decomposed analogously to the decomposition of income inequality. As said above, land allocation is typically based either on family or labor size. It is therefore of interest to test how inequality in land endowment changes when different measures are used as the basis. In Table 7.24, inequality in land endowment is evaluated based on family size, household size, family labor (Family MDE) and farm labor (Farm MDE). Furthermore, a differentiation can be made between the cultivated farm area at the time of the survey (Farm size) and the initially allocated area (Allocated land), which adds the area currently rented out and subtracts the area rented in. However, as shown above, there are only few such cases in the sample. Therefore, the Gini coefficients hardly differ whether the currently cultivated area or the allocated area is used.

Under the assumption that administrative land allocations seek egalitarian land distribution, it can be concluded from Table 7.24 that these reallocations actually use the total family size as the basis and do not account for residence or occupation of family members, since this measure gives the lowest Gini coefficient of land endowment (0.24). A weighting of family members by gender, giving female members a weight of 0.6 as suggested by Li and Bruce (2005), did not give significantly different results.

Table 7.24   Inequality in land endowment (Gini coefficients)

	Family size	Household size	Family MDE	Farm MDE
Farm size	0.24	0.28	0.27	0.30
Allocated land	0.24	0.28	0.26	0.31

Source: IRTG (2005).

Based on this result, inequality of allocated land per family size is decomposed in Table 7.23 above. The decompositions show that inequality of allocated land, off-farm income and total income within counties contributes much more to overall inequality than inequality between counties. This result is the same for the different indices used and is surprising, given the very different economic conditions of the five survey counties.

7.2 Village level

Microeconomic studies on rural China are mostly conducted at the household level as the basic decision making unit. However, China is also characterized by significant heterogeneity between villages in terms of land tenure arrangements, productivity and efficiency, even within a relatively small administrative area (Rozelle and Li, 1998). While the impact of location on differences in economic development is noted in many household based studies, relatively few studies have actually used larger village samples (e.g. Li et al., 2006; Zhu and Jiang, 1993). The household survey for the present study can also not adequately capture the variation between villages. For this reason, one of the survey counties was chosen as the site of a larger village level case study. Before this case study is presented and discussed, the following section summarizes results of other village level studies conducted in China.

7.2.1 Summary of village level studies in rural China

In the course of institutional reforms outlined in section 4.2.1, the role of the village as the basic administrative unit in rural China has been strengthened. The resurgence of traditional norms and culture since the reform period has already been noted above and the way in which village culture and social structure may influence economic performance has sparked some academic interest.

Perkins (2003) studied inequality between villages in a rural township in Tianjin (see Appendix) and suggested that the structure of village surnames (clans) impact on overall village development in the sense that a more fragmented structure of clans would cause villagers to be less inclined to work and cooperate for the overall village well-being. Furthermore, the distance to market centers played an important role for shaping a village's level of commercialization. Although the physical distance to a market may not be a constraint anymore today, the existence of such constraints in the past created path-dependencies between villages (Perkins, 2003, p. 733).

Equally important for village well-being is, according to Perkins (2003, p. 738), strong leadership capable of fostering a sense of solidarity among villagers. Mood (2005) shifts the focus from village characteristics to interactions between village and township leaders and argues that the relation between both largely explains different levels of economic development of villages within a county. This view can better explain different development between townships in one county. According to Mood's study of villages in Tianjin and Shanxi, township leaders can be differentiated by their degree of transmission and enforcement of county policies in their subordinate villages and their commitment to village economic development. Mood (2005) argues that frequent visits of county leaders to township officials are important for strengthening township compliance with county policies and that consequently the distance of a township to the county seat is important for the ability of counties to control townships.

Following the analysis of Mood (2005), the role that village leaders play for village economic development is strongest in townships that are less strict in enforcing county policies but that are nonetheless committed towards promoting the village economy. Mood (2005) distinguishes between village leaders who follow group-oriented economic goals (promoting the development of collective enterprises) and more individual-oriented goals (promoting more private enterprises). This perspective serves to explain different development of otherwise homogeneous villages in one township. In some cases, village leaders may also be more interested in personal enrichment than village development. In the past, village leaders have been criticized for exploiting villagers by levying numerous intransparent fees and taxes, especially fees termed *cun ti liu* which were directly allocated to the village budget (see e.g. Ke et al., 2003). As stated above, such fees, together with grain quotas and agricultural taxes, have been abolished. With the introduction of elections of village leaders, the empowerment of villagers to improve the integrity of their leaders is expected to further increase (Guo and Bernstein, 2004; Hu, 2005; Yao, 2006).

Apart from the capabilities of village leaders and interactions between village leaders and their superiors, Mood (2005) also recognizes that the location of a village within a county may be an important factor determining its economic orientation, i.e. its employment and cropping patterns and also its participation in agricultural factor markets. A number of studies confirm this. Zhu and Luo (2006) used the distance from a village to the site of the township government, the distance to the nearest railway station and the distance to the nearest bus station as variables to explain participation of households in non-farm activities and found all three variables to have a significantly negative impact. The same result is obtained by de Janvry et al. (2005) for data from Hubei Province using the distance of a village to the county center. Li et al. (2006) studied income inequality within and between villages in Guizhou Province and found the distance of a village to the township seat to have a negative impact on income levels. Similarly, Morduch and Sicular (2002) found that the village location within one county is an important factor contributing to income inequality. Remoteness of a village seems to have a number interrelated and reinforcing effects as shown by Zhang et al. (2006) who observed a negative correlation between the distance of a village to the nearest all-weather road and the level of public investments in the rural industry and attributed this also to a "showcasing effect" which favors easily accessible villages.

Market reforms at the beginning of the 1980s appear to have strengthened these negative effects. Nee and Su (1990) studied 30 villages in Fujian Province and found that mean per capita income growth between 1980 and 1984 was negatively associated with the distance to the nearest urban marketing center. Furthermore, in a regression analysis of the determinants of mean per capita income in 1980 and 1984, distance to an urban center had a significantly negative effect on income after market reform (1984) but not before (1980).

7.2.2 Data base for the village-level analysis

Mainly two types of sources are used for the village-level analysis: the county statistical yearbooks (henceforth QSY) from 1996-2006 and a survey of village leaders. Statistical yearbooks of the type available from Quzhou County have also been collected from Huimin (HM) and Liangshan County (LS) for 2003. For the remaining survey counties such yearbooks should, in principle, be also published but could not be obtained for this study. Building on the results of pilot village level surveys in Quzhou in September 2006 and March 2007, a final survey was conducted in September 2007. Focusing on the key research questions, a random sample of 90% of the villages was selected for interviews. Since conducting such a large number of face-to-face interviews would have exceeded time and cost limitations, it was decided to do the interviews with village leaders by phone. The lists with contact persons in the villages, obtained from the respective town and township governments, usually only contained two names: that of the director (*zhu ren*) of the Villagers' Committee and of the secretary (*zhi shu*) of the village Party branch. This confirms the observation, made by Zhou and Yang (2004) and others, that in practice these two persons may be regarded as being in power of village affairs. As found during the field work, both VC directors and Party secretaries regularly hold meetings with township officials.

The variables contained in the QSY are listed in Table 7.26. These village-level data are mainly based on reports by village leaders to the County Statistical Bureau. Since other studies analyzing secondary data mainly make use of more aggregated county or provincial statistics, the following paragraphs introduce this data set and discuss the data quality. Village-level data is available for 11 consecutive years, which may allow conclusions as to the heterogeneity of village development over the years. However, the time span is probably too short to distinguish impacts of structural and market reforms between villages.

Data on cropping areas and yields comprise the three most important crops wheat, maize and cotton and the remaining crops aggregated as oilseeds and vegetables. There are distinct differences in the cropping patterns between different parts of the county, which is also reflected by the fact that the Quzhou Agricultural Bureau (QAB) divides the county into districts (*chan ye qu*) according to the main crops cultivated. However, the QAB could not give further information as to whether these districts are part of rural land use plans as described in Pieke (2005).

These measures of village location were obtained using the map shown in Figure 5.1. A function in the program ArcMap® allows to automatically compute the nearest distance of a village (available only as point-data) to any other object (in this case main roads, surface water channels and township seats) in the map. The output is imprecise in the sense that it only computes airline distances. However, in the preliminary survey of the villages in ST, HNT and HQ, village leaders were directly asked about the distance to the nearest paved road and the correlation between the survey information and the distance as calculated from the map was high and significant (Pearson's correlation coefficient = 0.61, significant at the 0.1% level). Therefore the approach of using the map to compute distances appeared justified and was applied to the remaining villages.

The climate data from the local Quzhou Experimental Station mentioned in section 5.2 (Cui, various years) may be used as an additional source to explain yield differences between years. Temperature and precipitation are recorded from 1980 through 2006 on a daily basis for most days in a month. In principle, temperature accelerates plant growth and too high temperatures in certain months might cause plants to reach a certain growth stage too early, which would cause yields to decrease. Maize needs a minimum germinating temperature of around 8 °C. Winter wheat, on the other hand, needs a certain degree of frost to enter the generative stage. Additional water for irrigation is particularly beneficial for maize during blooming (beginning of August) and the milk-ripe stage (beginning of September) and for wheat during tillering in April and blooming and the milk-ripe stage in May (Binder, 2006).

Table 7.25   Village-level summary statistics (September 2007)

	N =	Mean	Min	Max	St. Dev.	Moran's I	
Plots per household	306	4.6	1	13	1.8	0.25	***
Share of off-farm income in net HH income (%)	306	34.9	3	90	20.1	0.07	**
Share of off-farm income from local employment in total-off farm income (%)	305	17.6	0	90	15.5	0.09	***
Number of TVE operating in the village	306	0.7	0	8	1.4	0.11	***
HHs having exchanged plots since the last large land reallocation (%)	305	6.3	0	70	10.7	0.00	
HHs having rented in any land from other HHs in this village (%)	306	4.9	0	50	6.7	0.03	
HHs having rented out any land to other HHs in this village (%)	306	4.5	0	50	6.5	0.04	*
Village allows renting out land to HHs in other villages (1 = yes, 0 = no)	305	0.8	0	1	0.4	0.08	**
HHs having rented out any land to HHs in another village in Quzhou (%)	306	0.3	0	20	1.3	-0.01	
HHs having rented out any land to HHs in another village outside Quzhou (%)	306	0.002	0	0.5	0.003	-0.01	
HHs having rented in any land from HHs in another village in Quzhou (%)	306	1.1	0	36	3.8	0.05	*
HHs having rented in any land from HHs in another village outside Quzhou (%)	306	0.4	0	25	1.9	0.10	***
Average land rental price between HHs in this village (¥/mu)	257	343.1	50	650	84.6	0.32	***
Village keeps any reserve land (1 = yes, 0 = no)	306	0.2	0	1	0.4	0.00	
Average age of farm labor in this village	305	48.2	30	60	5.8	0.10	***

* (**) [***] Significant at the 5% (1%) [0.1%] level of error probability (one-tailed test). See section 6.3 for an explanation of Moran's I.
Source: Own data (2007).

Table 7.26   Quzhou Statistical Yearbook: Summary statistics (2006)

	N =	Mean	Min.	Max.	St. Dev.	Moran's I	
Population	342	1153.0	86	7791	735.2	0.14	***
Number of households	342	251.9	18	1029	143.1	0.22	***
Labor	342	510.1	27	2058	310.3	0.24	***
Male labor	342	281.1	16	1120	171.7	0.23	***
Arable land (mu)	342	2097.1	135	8190	1232.7	0.24	***
Irrigated land (mu)	342	1770.8	72	7999	1110.2	0.23	***
Number of wells	342	21.5	1	86	16.9	0.40	***
Number of deep wells	342	2.4	0	18	2.3	0.38	***
Wheat area (mu)	342	1097.8	0	4950	739.6	0.30	***
Wheat yield (kg/mu)	341	352.1	249.6	440	25.0	0.58	***
Cotton area (mu)	342	679.6	0	2941	441.7	0.39	***
Cotton yield (kg/mu)	339	72.4	41	85	5.5	0.49	***
Maize area (mu)	342	1122.6	0	4850	729.3	0.26	***
Maize yield (kg/mu)	341	382.9	300	498	48.4	0.66	***
Oilseed area (mu)	342	45.5	0	1000	124.1	0.73	***
Oilseed yield (kg/mu)[1]	181	219.4	100	425	26.8	0.41	***
Vegetable area (mu)	342	296.0	0	3409	359.4	0.39	***
Vegetable yield (kg/mu)	337	3062.9	1181	5575	1027.8	0.76	***
Cattle	342	115.2	4	548	72.9	0.24	***
Horses	342	11.5	0	351	27.8	0.27	***
Pigs	342	772.0	8	7450	587.1	0.21	***
Sheep	342	534.3	1	2043	341.3	0.43	***
Lambs	342	326.4	20	2598	305.5	0.50	***
Poultry	342	36938.5	1348	521364	50025.6	0.17	***
Rabbits	342	823.8	26	4238	743.3	0.52	***

[1] Due to the low number of observations, one village had no neighbor as defined in the text. See section 6.3 for an explanation of Moran's I.
* (**) [***] Significant at the 5% (1%) [0.1%] level of error probability (one-tailed test).
Source: Quzhou County Statistical Bureau (various years).

Figure 7.1 shows the average temperatures and precipitation for the whole period available. Interestingly, this figure reveals on the one hand a trend towards increasing mean annual temperatures and on the other hand strong fluctuations of precipitation between years. 2004 was characterized by exceptionally high precipitation, which might have led to particularly favorable conditions in agriculture. This phenomenon may suggest that only part of yield increases in that year can be attributed to state policy interventions, which has also been noted by Tan (2005, p. 3).

When estimating impacts of institutional variables on production, it is often not possible to control for differences in soil quality. For the study at hand, a georeferenced soil map of Quzhou County has been available. This map is based on a national soil survey from the 1980s and shows the 16 predominant soil types for which the main physical and chemical properties such as soil organic matter, texture and pH-value had been calculated (Liu et al., 2007). As

Liu et al. (2007) note, these parameters need to be updated to better correspond to the changes in farming practices in the last 20 years. Although the parameters may be quite different today, the information on which soil types are located in which parts of the county may still be used for this study. By overlaying the soil map with the topographic map (Figure 5.1), it is possible to identify the soil types dominating in each village. These soil types can therefore be included in a statistical model as dummy variables to explain differences in the production data. Another means to assess the data quality is to compute their spatial correlation (see section 6.3). Variables such as yields and input costs are expected to be highly correlated between adjacent villages due to similar natural conditions.

Figure 7.1   Average temperature and precipitation in Quzhou County, 1980-2006

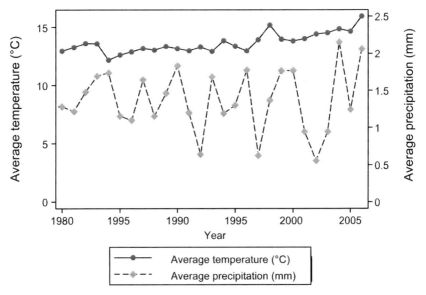

Source: Cui (various years).

The results from the village-level survey are shown in Table 7.25 and Table 7.29. Questions in Table 7.25 mainly relate to land tenure arrangements and income sources, while in Table 7.29 average production costs for the main crops wheat, maize and cotton are shown. Since the newest yearbook available contains data related to the cultivation year 2005/2006 while the survey was conducted in September 2007, there is an obvious inconsistency. Nevertheless, questions on production costs referred to the latest cultivation year 2006/2007. Asking about the situation in the cultivation year before probably would have caused problems of a similar magnitude due to less precise recall by village leaders. Moreover, farmers reported to hardly change their input decisions over the years.

7.2.3 Agricultural production

Village leaders were asked about average production costs for the main crops in their village and this information was combined with the production data from the QSY. Before proceeding in chapter 8 with the estimation of a village-level production function, the following paragraphs aim to provide first insights concerning the data quality.

As is typical for the NCP and China in general, land per capita endowment of rural households is low, ranging from 0.24 mu to 4.40 mu with an average of 1.90 mu in 2006. Figure 7.2 shows the development of the shares of the five types of crops in the total sown area and the development of average yields. The share of winter wheat has decreased significantly since 2000 in favor of cotton, in particular, which corresponds well to the overall development in Hebei Province as demonstrated in section 3.2.2. Since 2000, the price for winter wheat had risen, and farmers began to increase the area sown to winter wheat again since 2003. The area sown to maize dropped sharply in 2003 and declined further in 2006. Area sown to vegetables increased slowly but steadily while the area sown to oilseeds declined slightly.

The importance of wheat for staple food production deserves a closer look at the development of wheat production over the years. The total change in production between years can be expressed as the sum of the contributions due to changes in sown area, yields and an interaction term of changes in both factors (Hazell, 1982). This relation can be found by first stating that average production in a given year ($\overline{P}_1$) equals sown area ($\overline{A}_1$) times yield ($\overline{Y}_1$):

$$\overline{P}_1 = \overline{A}_1 * \overline{Y}_1. \tag{25}$$

The values of each of the two factors in the following year can be expressed as their values in the previous year plus their change between both years. Expanding this equation for the following year then gives:

$$\overline{P}_2 = \overline{A}_1\overline{Y}_1 + \overline{A}_1\Delta\overline{Y}_1 + \Delta\overline{A}_1\overline{Y}_1 + \Delta\overline{A}_1\Delta\overline{Y}_1. \tag{26}$$

**Figure 7.2   Development of sown area and yields in Quzhou County,
1996-2006**

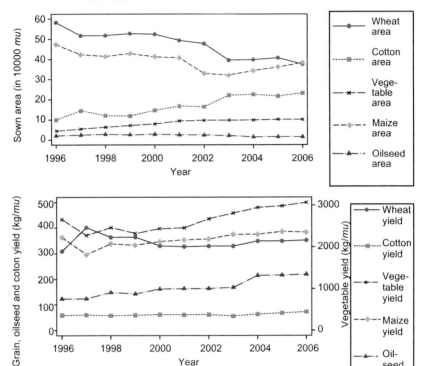

Source: Quzhou County Statistical Bureau (various years).

Table 7.27 shows the decomposition of changes in average wheat production relative to the previous years. Taking 1997 as an example, the figures state that increased yield relative to the previous year contributed 192% to the increase in average production of 16%, whereas the decreased area and the interaction term contributed -92%, i.e. these three factors explain 100% of the total change in production. Increases in yield therefore over-compensated the loss in area. On the other hand, from 2005 to 2006 the average production dropped by 7% which was mainly caused by the loss in area (112%) which could only partly be compensated by increased yield (-13%).

Table 7.27   Decomposition of changes in average wheat production

	Change in average production (%)	Contributions to average change in production (%)		
		Change in yield	Change in area	Interaction between changes in yield and area
1997	16	192	-71	-21
1998	-9	103	-3	0
1999	2	12	87	0
2000	-9	100	0	0
2001	-7	13	88	-1
2002	-3	-28	127	1
2003	-17	0	100	0
2004	7	92	8	0
2005	2	-3	103	0
2006	-7	-13	112	1

Source: Quzhou County Statistical Bureau (various years).

Summing up the area sown with the five groups of crops listed in the QSY and comparing the total sown area with the arable land leads to the multi-cropping index (MCI), which stood on average at 1.60 in 2006. Taking only the irrigated arable land as the basis increases the MCI to 1.97.

Contrary to the expectation suggested above, a comparison between the production and the climate data does not indicate a strong relation between yields and precipitation. This may be attributable to the substantial reliance on groundwater irrigation. The data further shows a positive correlation of yields with average temperature. However, due to the short time span of 11 years, this can not be explored further.

The QSY contain a number of indicators of agricultural infrastructure and input use. At the township level, the statistics list total consumption of chemical fertilizer and use of agricultural machinery power (given in kilowatt). A comparison of the level and development of both indicators between *zhen* and *xiang*, as shown in Figure 7.3, does not indicate clear differences between both administrative units but a much higher level of both fertilizer and machinery use in the county seat (QZ).

Figure 7.3   Fertilizer consumption and agricultural machinery use in Quzhou County

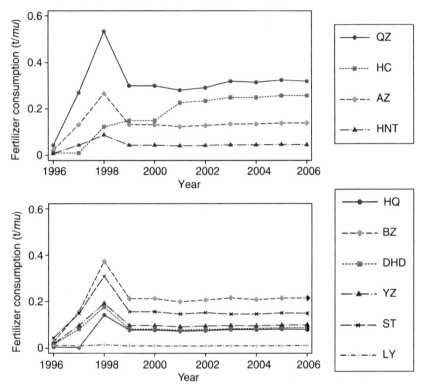

Figure 7.3   Continued

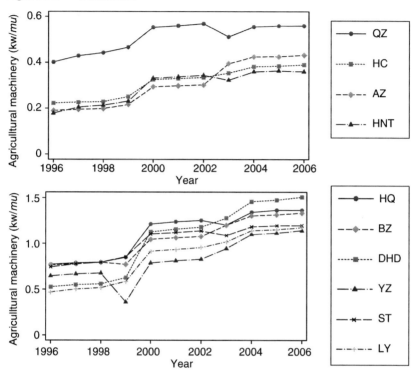

For the final survey in September 2007, it was decided to ask only about production costs rather than input quantities in order to reduce the complexity of the questions. These production costs are shown in Table 7.29 for wheat, maize and cotton. Most of the production costs show high spatial correlation as indicated by the significance of Moran's I in the last column.

Also the total production costs for wheat, maize and cotton are highly correlated, implying that there are indeed systematic differences in production costs between villages and that interviewees did not give answers arbitrarily (Table 7.28).

Table 7.28   Correlations of production costs between villages

	Wheat	Maize	Cotton
Wheat	-	-	-
Maize	0.64***	-	-
Cotton	0.47***	0.58***	-

*** Significant at the 1% level of error probability.
Source: Quzhou County Statistical Bureau (various years).

Table 7.29   Village-level questionnaire (September 2007): Direct
              production costs for wheat, maize and cotton (¥/*mu*)

	N =	Mean	Min.	Max.	St. Dev.	Moran's I	
Wheat							
Seeds	295	32.4	15	100	10.2	0.09	**
Fertilizer	295	118.4	40	300	43.2	0.18	***
Machinery	295	59.3	10	200	22.5	0.18	***
Irrigation	295	84.5	15	180	29.4	0.15	***
Pesticides	295	16.7	0	80	10.5	0.27	***
Others	295	0.6	0	50	4.6	0.03	
Total	295	312.0	143	480	63.2	0.13	***
Maize							
Seeds	295	33.3	8	80	11.2	0.26	***
Fertilizer	295	105.3	10	240	46.9	0.22	***
Machinery	295	32.3	0	120	19.7	0.05	*
Irrigation	295	71.1	0	180	34.5	0.25	***
Pesticides	295	13.4	0	50	7.5	0.07	**
Others	295	0.4	0	50	3.4	-0.01	
Total	295	255.8	70	430	75.2	0.31	***
Cotton							
Seeds	290	57.9	4	200	22.9	0.06	*
Fertilizer	290	118.0	22	240	37.6	0.06	*
Machinery	290	36.3	0	100	17.3	0.07	**
Irrigation	290	58.3	0	180	32.3	0.22	***
Pesticides	290	87.9	10	200	29.4	0.01	
Others	290	31.7	0	100	10.9	0.15	***
Total	290	390.2	163	630	80.7	0.17	***

* (**) [***] Significant at the 5% (1%) [0.1%] level of error probability (one-tailed test).
Source: Own data (2007).

In the preliminary village survey in March 2007, village leaders were also asked about typical fertilizer input in terms of quantities in their villages. Additionally, the QSY records total nitrogen fertilizer consumption at the township level as shown in Table 7.30 (without information as to what types of N-fertilizers or to which crops they are applied) and a different publication by the Quzhou Agricultural Bureau (QAB) lists township-level soil N-contents for the year 2002. These different sources are combined in Table 7.30, which leads to some interesting conclusions. The center of the county, Quzhou town (QZ), is characterized by the highest quantity of N-fertilizer, highest soil N-content and second highest fertilizer costs. This result is in line with Hu et al. (2005) who took samples of shallow groundwater wells at 139 different locations in Quzhou County in 1999 and measured groundwater depth, nitrate content and electrical conductivity. Nitrate contents were found to be highest in QZ and HNT, which Hu et al. (2005) attributed to runoff of domestic sewage and wastewater and excessive fertilizer use in vegetable production.

Table 7.30   Fertilizer consumption in Quzhou County

	Total amount of N-fertilizer consumed (kg/mu; QSY, 2006)	Pure nitrogen applied to winter wheat (kg N/mu; preliminary village survey, March 2007)	Soil N-content (%; QAB, 2006)	Typical fertilizer costs for winter wheat (¥/mu; village survey, Sept. 2007)
Zhen:				
QZ	539.3	22.0	1.01	133.4
AZ	185.7	14.0	0.98	151.8
HC	394.0	20.0	0.94	116.9
HNT	36.7	21.3	0.94	107.0
Xiang:				
ST	141.3	19.5	0.99	127.0
HQ	82.0	21.3	0.94	111.1
BZ	320.7	15.9	0.98	101.4
DHD	50.0	15.3	0.91	115.6
YZ	47.3	16.1	0.87	93.6
LY	10.7	10.8	0.78	95.2

The different sources shown in Table 7.30 are also consistent in that YZ and LY township can be found at the lower end in terms of fertilizer use. Whether these differences have indeed to do with the distinction between *zhen* and *xiang* – possibly in the relatively better-off but labor scarce villages in *zhen*, higher income from off-farm employment finances agricultural working capital which leads to excessive fertilizer use – is a question that can not be satisfyingly answered from this. This would require a larger sample of both *zhen* and *xiang*. In the September 2007 survey, use of farmyard manure and other sources of organic fertilizer in crop production was not explicitly assessed. However, the aggregate quantity of organic fertilizer produced in a village is likely to be used by some, if not all households in production. Kueh (1984, p. 221) presents calculations of nutrient contents for different livestock in China as well as for other sources of organic fertilizer including night soil. If the proposition is correct, that these sources of organic fertilizer will somehow be utilized within a village, it is expected that this should contribute to lower costs for chemical fertilizer.

Table 7.31   Nitrogen excretion from organic fertilizer sources in China (kg/capita/year)

Human	4.25	Horses	43.55
Pigs	8.47	Donkeys	21.78
Goats and sheep	5.89		
Cattle	38.22		

Source: Kueh (1984).

Net income from agriculture was calculated by multiplying the output as recorded in the statistics with average producer prices, which were obtained from the Quzhou Agricultural Bureau (Table 7.32), and subtracting production costs according to the village-leader survey.

Table 7.32   Producer prices of agricultural products in Quzhou County

	Average selling price, (¥/kg), QAB		Average selling price, (¥/head), QAB
Wheat	1.46	Goats	235
Maize	1.15	Sheep	350
Cotton	5.28	Cows	3000
Vegetables	1.19	Pigs	870
Oilseeds	3.36	Chicken	15
		Horses	900

As can be seen from Table 7.29, in some cases production costs for wheat, maize and cotton are missing. Furthermore, very few villages provided production costs for vegetables and oilseeds, which is why these are not reported in Table 7.29. The reason for these missing values is that interviewers began asking about the main crops wheat, maize and cotton and then, at the end of the questionnaire, about the quantitatively less important oilseeds and vegetables. Apparently, most village leaders became impatient and were unwilling to answer the questions. While this is unfortunate, it clearly demonstrates the limitations of phone interviews as compared to face-to-face interviews. For the calculation of net income, these missing values were replaced by average production costs at the township level.

Additionally, livestock production has not been considered in the survey. Income from livestock was calculated taking typical costs and producer prices, using the QAB as well as data from the 2005 household survey conducted by the IRTG as sources. Since animal husbandry is done very extensively in the study region, the resulting error is probably not as significant as in the case of vegetables and oilseeds.

Assuming that in Quzhou, income from agriculture, livestock production and income from off-farm employment approximately add up to total household income allows calculating total income from the production data and the reported shares of off-farm income (Table 7.33). This approach of asking village leaders only about typical costs and shares of off-farm income rather than asking directly about total income seemed less sensitive to over- or underreporting.

The QSY themselves do not contain any data on household income for recent years, only for 1996 and 1997. For these years, average per capita income is reported to be 2051 ¥ and 2325 ¥, respectively. The average income per capita across all townships of 3588 ¥ as calculated in Table 7.33 is surprisingly close to the 3552 ¥ as reported for Quzhou County in provincial statistics (Hebei Province Statistical Bureau, 2006).

Table 7.33   Calculation of net income per capita

	QZ	HQ	BZ	AZ	DHD	HC	YZ	HNT	ST	LY
N =	41	27	39	37	17	39	11	32	35	24
Crop production										
Gross value of output (¥/*mu*)	3468	794	1655	1021	1098	1067	802	833	1032	878
Total costs (¥/*mu*)	1003	500	650	635	525	608	529	455	580	463
Net income (¥/capita)	3613	621	1314	760	1057	831	472	819	984	786
Net income from livestock production (¥/capita)	907	967	1172	1117	828	860	733	737	582	1029
Off-farm employment										
Share in total income (%)	32	35	41	27	39	43	39	32	32	28
Net off-farm income (¥/capita)	2227	1058	2037	830	1777	1760	894	1154	938	882
Total net income (¥/capita)	**6748**	**2647**	**4523**	**2707**	**3662**	**3451**	**2100**	**2710**	**2504**	**2697**

Note: Calculations in this table are based on 302 villages from the sample. Four villages with extreme values are dropped.
Source: Own data (2007).

7.2.4 Socio-demographic analysis

The QSY records population, number of households, total labor force and male labor force for all villages. Especially the share of male labor is an interesting variable. As stated above, there is disagreement whether a "feminization of agriculture" takes place in China and whether this has had an impact on agricultural productivity. The household survey has shown that women indeed participate less in off-farm work. The village-level survey asked about the typical share of off-farm income in total income and the share of off-farm income from local employment (defined as jobs where employees return home every day after work). Grouping all villages in the sample according to their shares of off-farm income as stated by village leaders and plotting the development of the percentage of male labor force for each group (Figure 7.4) leads to the following conclusion. Overall, the share of male labor has indeed declined by about 5%, which is mainly caused by a sharp decline between 1996 and 1998. The decline is slightly more pronounced in the villages of group 1, which are characterized by a share of off-farm income in total income above the median of 30% but a share of local sources in total off-farm income below its median of 12%. One plausible interpretation of this result is that off-farm income in these villages is mainly earned by migrating male household members, which leads to the decline of male labor force in the villages (Li and Bruce, 2005).

Figure 7.4   Development of male labor force in Quzhou County

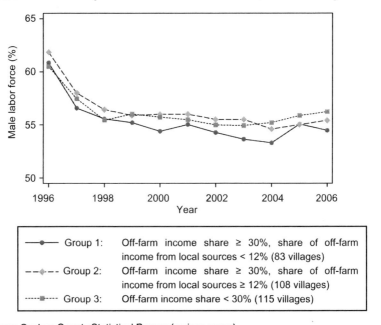

Source: Quzhou County Statistical Bureau (various years).

A few other measures are available to characterize the socio-economic situation of the villages. The share of labor force in the total population could allow conclusions as to the average dependency ratio in the villages. At the township level, the QSY also differentiates between rural and non-rural population, which probably refers to the *hukou* although this is not clear. Additionally, the survey asked about the average age of the labor force working in agriculture (Table 7.34). First, recalling from section 4.2.1 that *zhen* are characterized by a certain share of non-agrarian population, the result in Table 7.34 that the share of rural population is lowest in the four *zhen* (QZ, AZ, HC, HNT), and particularly low in the county seat, is in line with expectation. Second, although not apparent from Table 7.34, the average age of farm labor is in fact positively correlated with the share of off-farm income (Pearson's correlation coefficient = 0.17, significant at the 1% level), which confirms that in a situation of good off-farm income opportunities, agriculture is left to the elderly. Third, the differences in the share of labor in the total population can not be plausibly explained from the data.

Table 7.34   Demographic variables by townships

	QZ	HQ	BZ	AZ	DHD	HC	YZ	HNT	ST	LY
Share of rural population (%)	67	100	100	96	100	96	100	98	99	100
Age of farm labor (N = 305 villages)	48	51	48	49	51	50	48	47	44	46
Share of labor force (%)	39	48	50	47	49	49	45	46	43	39
Share of male labor (%)	56	55	50	57	57	54	57	56	60	53

Sources: Quzhou County Statistical Bureau (various years), own data (2007).

Furthermore, as suggested by Perkins (2003), the preliminary village survey in September 2006 contained questions regarding the structure of village surnames. Although large differences were found, ranging from six villages with only one surname to eight villages with more than ten different surnames, this variable showed no correlation with available indicators of village development as observed by Perkins (2003). This irrelevance of clan structures in Quzhou County was confirmed by informal discussions with villagers.

7.2.5 Off-farm employment and inequality

Across all villages, on average 35% of net household income is derived from off-farm sources, from which 18% are from local sources defined as above. As expected (see section 3.2.1.2), there is a clear relation between cropping patterns and off-farm employment. The share of labor intensive vegetables per sown area is significantly lower in villages with a high share of off-farm employment. Likewise, the share of labor extensive wheat per sown area is significantly higher in these villages (Table 7.35).

Table 7.35   Correlation between cropping patterns and off-farm
              employment

	Share of wheat per sown area (%)	Share of cotton per sown area (%)	Share of vegetables per sown area (%)
Share of off-farm income (%)	0.12*	0.01	-0.17**

* (**) Pearson's correlation coefficients significant at the 5% (1%) level of error probability.
Sources: Quzhou County Statistical Bureau (various years), own data (2007).

Table 7.36 displays descriptive evidence that the location of a village within the county indeed appears to have impacts on some economic indicators. On the one hand, population density decreases with the distance of a village from the township seat and the nearest large road, which leads to significantly higher land per capita endowment in these villages. Interestingly, the share of off-farm income in total household income does not differ significantly between villages depending on the locational variables used. However, the share of off-farm income derived from local sources is significantly lower in villages further away from the township seat or the nearest large road. This can be explained by a lower number of Township and Village Enterprises (TVE) operating in more remote villages. This confirms the results of studies on spatial heterogeneity in Chinese counties discussed above.

Table 7.36   Correlation between the village location and socioeconomic
              variables

	Arable land per capita (2006)	Share of off-farm income (%)	Share of local off-farm income (%)
N =	341	306	305
Distance to township (km)	0.34***	-0.09	-0.17**
Distance to large road (km)	0.27***	-0.04	-0.14*

* (**) [***] Pearson's correlation coefficients significant at the 5% (1%) [0.1%] level of error probability.
Sources: Quzhou County Statistical Bureau (various years), own data (2007).

It should be noted that the mere traveling distance to places in the county with better employment opportunities is unlikely to be the decisive factor for the low share of local off-farm income of households in more remote villages – the average distance between two villages being 16 km and the maximum distance between two villages 43 km. It is more likely that such local off-farm jobs are first provided to inhabitants of the village in which the TVE is located and that households from other villages lack the social connections to enter this sector. This is confirmed by the Quzhou Agricultural Bureau, which stated that job seekers from more distant villages are more likely to temporarily migrate, e.g. to the neighboring provinces Shandong, Tianjin or Jiangsu.

Since access to land and local off-farm employment are unequally distributed within the county, the decisive question is what impact this has on the distribution of total income. This question is dealt with in section 8.1.2. For the Quzhou case study, inequality in terms of land endowment and income can only be broken down into intra-township and inter-township inequality. Results are shown in Table 7.37, which displays Gini coefficients of inequality in land per capita endowment, off-farm income and total income as well as the Theil-Index, the CV and the MLD together with their decomposition into their intra- and inter-township components.

Table 7.37   Inequality decomposition in Quzhou County

	Gini	Theil		CV[1]		MLD	
Land per capita							
(p.c.)							
Total inequality	0.17	0.05	(100%)	0.05	(100%)	0.06	(100%)
Intra-township	-	0.04	(80%)	0.04	(80%)	0.05	(83%)
Inter-township	-	0.01	(20%)	0.01	(20%)	0.01	(17%)
Off-farm income							
p.c.							
Total inequality	0.50	0.46	(100%)	0.70	(100%)	0.47	(100%)
Intra-township	-	0.36	(78%)	0.58	(83%)	0.37	(79%)
Inter-township	-	0.10	(22%)	0.12	(17%)	0.10	(21%)
Total income							
p.c.							
Total inequality	0.34	0.20	(100%)	0.27	(100%)	0.18	(100%)
Intra-township	-	0.11	(55%)	0.16	(59%)	0.10	(56%)
Inter-township	-	0.09	(45%)	0.11	(41%)	0.08	(44%)

[1] Expressed as half the squared coefficient of variation. CV = Coefficient of variation, MLD = Mean logarithmic deviation.
Source: Own data (2007).

Despite the significant differences in land endowment discussed above, inequality in land is much lower than income inequality while inequality in off-farm income is higher than overall income inequality. However, the proportionate contributions of agricultural production (including livestock) and off-farm employment to income inequality show with 48% and 52%, respectively, only a slightly higher contribution of off-farm income. The Gini coefficient of income inequality is with 0.34 much more in line with the 0.35 as reported by Yu et al. (2007). Contrary to findings of Yu et al. (2007), inequality seems to be predominantly caused by inequality within rather than between townships, although the importance of inter-township factors increases when looking at inequality in total income. Table 7.38 further shows how inequality in land, off-farm income and total income relate to each other by showing their Gini coefficients at the township level.

Table 7.38   Gini coefficients in Quzhou County by townships

	QZ	HQ	BZ	AZ	DHD	HC	YZ	HNT	ST	LY
Land per capita	0.25	0.12	0.15	0.14	0.08	0.12	0.10	0.14	0.11	0.13
Off-farm income p.c.	0.49	0.41	0.38	0.43	0.52	0.40	0.31	0.53	0.51	0.45
Total income p.c.	0.29	0.25	0.25	0.19	0.33	0.22	0.14	0.25	0.31	0.19

Source: Own data (2007).

7.2.6 Land transfers and land use rights

Concerning land tenure, the survey asked about the percentage of households renting land within their village and between other villages. For the case of land renting within a village, interviewees were asked about the average land rental price (see Table 7.25). Noteworthy is the strong positive spatial correlation of land rental prices, which may suggest that current land prices are indeed related to the value of land. Other questions pertained to the percentage of households having exchanged plots with other households (a practice that is expected to reduce land fragmentation) and whether the village has currently set aside any of its arable land as "reserve land" (*jidong di*).

The preliminary survey in September 2006 covering the villages in HNT, ST and HQ asked about restrictions in land transfers and revealed that mainly the right to rent out land to households in other villages was prohibited by some villages. Renting between households in the same village and renting from households in other villages was allowed in all cases. Some village leaders required written contracts or previous notification. However, since outright prohibition of land leases to non-villagers more directly limits the scope for land transfers, the subsequent survey (September 2007) only asked about this type of restriction. It turned out that almost 20% of the villages in the sample do not allow renting out of land to households in other villages. Although inter-village land use transfers are very infrequent also in those villages which allow such transfers, Wang (2005), in discussing options for land reform in China, suggests that there should be an explicit policy allowing land renting to non-villagers. This shows that this issue is in fact not a trivial one for Chinese policy makers. Intuitively, one would expect that the decision to allow or deny the right to rent out land to non-villagers is mainly dependent on the relative scarcity of land in a village. This is confirmed by the data and qualitative interviews with village leaders. A comparison of average land per capita endowment between villages allowing (1.95 *mu*) and not allowing transfers to non-villagers (1.76 *mu*) confirms this, although the difference is not large. Furthermore, public investments in land quality could motivate the village community to restrict transfers. A high share of irrigated farm land could be seen as an indicator of such investments. Indeed, the average percentage of irrigated farm land is significantly lower in villages that allow inter-village transfers (84%) than in villages that do not (88%). Both mean comparison tests are significant at the 5% level of error probability using the non-parametric Mann-Whitney U test.

The following paragraphs show descriptive results concerning the characteristics of intra- and inter-village land transfers. Based on these results, hypotheses on the determinants of land transfers and land transfer restrictions are formulated. It is often claimed that land use transfers take place mostly between friends and relatives (Chen and Brown, 2001). Lohmar et al. (2001, p. 2) found that land transfers do occur mainly between members of the same collective organization, but not necessarily confined to friends and relatives. In the September 2006 survey among 101 villages, this was quantitatively assessed. Figure 7.5 shows that less than 50% of land rental transfers take place between households that do not either belong to the same clan, family or *xiaozu*, which is a group of 30 to 40 households equivalent to the former production team (Lohmar et al., 2002). Almost 50% of plot exchanges occur between households belonging to the same *xiaozu* because plots of one *xiaozu* are typically located in one part of the village, thus making plot exchanges convenient.

Figure 7.5   Between which groups land transfers take place (N = 101 villages)

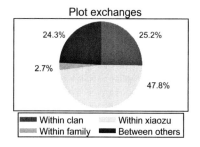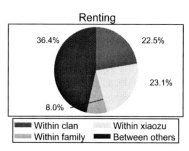

Source: Own data (2006).

While a lot of research has been conducted on the development of land rental markets as commonly understood, the direct exchange of plots between households (*hu huan*) as a means to improve land allocation has been largely neglected, although Kung (1995, p. 84), concludes that this practice is widespread and has indeed contributed to land consolidation. Wan and Cheng (2001) argue that as long as the land rental market remains narrow, Chinese policy makers should emphasize plot exchanges as a means to consolidate land holdings. It is interesting to note that this practice has been advocated by the government of the Socialist Republic of Vietnam, which has issued a policy in 1998 to promote exchanges of plots to encourage larger plot sizes (Hung et al., 2007).

On average, 6% of HHs have engaged in plot exchanges. There is a strikingly strong correlation between the percentage of households having exchanged plots and the share of off-farm income from local sources (Pearson's correlation coefficient = 0.40, significant at the 0.1% level). One explanation could be that risk aversion, which is hypothesized to keep farmers from consolidating their plots (Fleisher and Liu, 1992, p. 114) plays less of a role when local off-farm opportunities are plentiful.

Repeatedly, village leaders stated that a good, trustful relationship between households is the most important determinant for deciding to rent or exchange plots. Farmers are found to be concerned about differences in soil quality when considering exchanging plots. Apart from the importance of trust, this concern is less pronounced when soil quality is relatively less important, as it is the case when mainly cotton is cultivated. The latter statement suggests that a beneficial effect of plot exchanges may be more recognizable in villages with a high share of cotton the cropping pattern.

Since a good, cooperative culture in a village might in itself be beneficial for village development it is hypothesized that a productivity or efficiency enhancing effect can be observed in villages with a high share of households engaged in land transfers also due to this cooperative environment. However, if such a causal relation in fact exists, it is likely to be only observable if a sufficiently large share of households in a village engages in land transfers.

Only 46 of the 306 sampled villages reported no rental activities at all. On average close to 5% of all households participate in land rentals, which is again very close to the number given in other studies. In 3 cases village leaders reported land rental activities but were not able to give average rental fees, so that the survey contains 257 observations of rental prices.

Village leaders were asked about both the percentage of households having rented *in* any land as well as the percentage of households having rented *out* any land to other households. The two numbers can differ to some extent if, for example, only a few households have rented out larger shares of land which are then rented in by a higher number of households. However, the data is in some cases inconsistent because the question on renting in was asked in the March 2007 survey round, while the survey asked about renting out only in September that year. It was not expected to find larger discrepancies between the two points in time and the fact that the data is partly inconsistent may reveal that village leaders are actually only able to give rough estimates of land rental activities in their village.

Land transfers between villages are less frequent, but do occur. Some rental arrangements also cross county-borders and it was reported that in few cases households even rent in land from neighboring provinces. This shows that there is in fact some scope for such transfers and the question is whether demand is fully satisfied or whether some households feel rationed in their decision to participate in the land rental market.

An institutionalized "land bank" (see section 4.2) does not exist in Quzhou, but village leaders confirmed that households that wish to rent in land from outside their village often depend on some mediating person (who could be a friend or relative) who has relations to another household willing to rent out. Lack of market information can therefore be seen as one reason for the low level of inter-village land transfers.

The discrepancies between villages renting in from other villages within and outside Quzhou (30.5% and 13.1%) and those renting out (13.5% and 0.7%) may be due to an underreporting of renting out. In either case, the percentage of households involved in such transfers is on average below 5%.

This observation confirms the result of Bowlus and Sicular (2003) that inter-village land markets are underdeveloped. In their study of Zouping County (Shandong Province) this situation had led to labor surplus existing side by side with labor scarcity within the county and hence to nonseparability of labor input decisions. Bowlus and Sicular (2003) found separability present for households in villages with average land endowment, but rejected separability in villages with very high and very low land endowment. Separability was also rejected in villages with no or very little off-farm employment within the village and high off-farm employment within the village but not outside, i.e. within the township. Only in villages with access to off-farm employment within the township, the null hypothesis of separability was not rejected. The data from Quzhou County does not allow to directly identify such villages with good off-farm opportunities outside the village but within the township. However, these may be villages that reported a high share of local off-farm income but with no TVEs on their own.

Bowlus and Sicular (2003) conclude that exchange of land and labor between villages within one county could achieve separability of production and consumption decisions. Thus, policies are needed that promote between-village factor markets. An important question is whether inter-village land transfers can in fact reduce intra-county income inequality by providing access to more land for those villages with poor access to off-farm employment.

Furthermore, the village survey asked about the year of the last small and large reallocation and when villages consider conducting the next reallocations. Most villages have conducted the last large reallocation in 1992, 15 years after the initial issuance of land use rights to individual households, following the policy at that time. Only 25 villages in the sample (8%) reported to have conducted the last large reallocation after 1992 while 17 villages (6%) have conducted the last reallocation before 1992. This situation was confirmed by the Quzhou Agricultural Bureau. This low variation is surprising insofar as the local heterogeneity in terms of land reallocations has been frequently noted in the literature. On the other hand, Kung (2000) had also found in a survey of 80 villages that reallocations were in fact less frequent than expected.

The question, when the village leaders consider conducting the next reallocation was, in general, not answered. This has two main reasons: first, the topic is politically sensitive (village leaders are aware, that the official policy requires them to keep land use contracts stable for 30 years after the initial use right period of 15 years) and, second, the village leaders may simply not anticipate themselves, when the appropriate time to conduct a reallocation may have come (Jacoby et al., 2002). Small reallocations are also infrequent and most village leaders stated that newly established households do not receive any land shares in the village. If such households wish to acquire land use rights, they are forced to either rent from other households or rent reserve land from the collective.

8 Econometric Results

This chapter presents results of different econometric models at the plot level, household level and village level. These models were estimated in Stata, except the stochastic frontier models. Influential observations in the models were detected by making use of Cook's D influence statistic which computes the effect of removing an observation on the estimated coefficient vector (Long, 1997, p. 128). Observations with a Cook's D larger than 1 were examined and if identified as outliers dropped from the regressions (Field, 2005, p. 165). Multicollinearity of regressors was tested using their variance inflation factor (VIF). The value 1/VIF indicates the proportion of a regressor's variance that is independent of the other regressors in the model. Multicollinearity is considered not to be a serious problem if the largest VIF is below 10 and the mean VIF is not larger than 1 (Hamilton, 2004, p. 212). For testing the assumption of constant error variance (homoskedasticity) the Breusch-Pagan/Cook-Weisberg test for heteroskedasticity was employed, and if the null hypothesis of constant error variance was rejected, the regression was performed with robust standard errors (Hamilton, 2004, p. 196).

In models with dummy variables for the village location, the omitted township category is Liyue (LY) in the case of the Quzhou County study. In models that use the household data, the omitted county category is Kaifeng (KF) and the omitted village category is village 20. Estimated coefficients for village dummy variables are not reported to save space.

The analysis can be broadly subdivided into six sets of models, each looking at a particular part of the overall research question of the link between land property rights and natural resource use. The first part (8.1) asks what factors determine the land endowment of a household, i.e. the land allocated to a household by the village. These models aim to test the results of Burgess (2001), that household characteristics apart from family size also influence the share of land allotted to a household. Results of these models may allow conclusions as to which types of households are favored in the administrative allocation process.

Next is an analysis of the determinants of the intensity of input use, namely nitrogenous chemical fertilizer, followed by regression models to explain restrictions of farmers' land use rights. What factors influence the decision to participate in land rental markets is then explored in section 8.4. The agricultural production process at the household and village level is modeled in section 0, which also includes a discussion of the results on the spatial correlation of the data from Quzhou County. Finally, the relation between the estimated MVP of land and current rental prices is then explored in section 8.6.

8.1 Land endowment and land fragmentation

8.1.1 Household level

In spite of the highly egalitarian system of land allocation there may be more locational and idiosyncratic factors determining land endowment other than the family size (Burgess, 2001). The following Table 8.2 shows the results of an OLS regression of allocated land (*alloc_land*), on household demographic variables. Since the land allocation process is village-specific, village-level dummy variables are included in the model. The dependent variable *alloc_land* is regressed on family size (*f_size*) and family size squared, because it is likely that larger families will in fact receive less land per capita. A high share of the household labor working in agriculture (*mde_ratio*) may lead to granting households more land. Furthermore, 18% (61 households) of the HHs in the first household survey reported to have at least one family member who currently holds or has held in the past an administrative position in the village (*pos*). As Jia (2007) showed, HHs with a present or former village cadre are less likely to be constrained in the formal credit market. Given that local cadres and personal ties are attributed great importance in rural China, families with a former or present village cadre may also be given priority in land allocations. The share of female family members is captured by the variable *sh_fem*. It is hypothesized to negatively affect land endowment. *age_flabor* is the average age of those household members working full-time on-farm. Furthermore, *any_title* is a dummy variable which equals 1 if HHs claimed to hold a land right certificate and 0 otherwise. The number of years the currently held plots have been on average cultivated is captured with the variable *cult_since* and it is hypothesized that HHs are able to hold on longer to their land rights if they have smaller farm sizes. Finally, *rented_in* is a dummy variable which equals 1 for HHs having rented in any land at the time of the survey.

Furthermore, other studies and discussions with farmers and village leaders suggest that land quality is taken into account in the allocation process (Lohmar, 2006). This implies that HHs with more land are endowed with land of poorer quality. To test this hypothesis, the average winter wheat yield potential (*avwheat_pot*), which was intended to serve as an indicator of land quality, is included in the regression. Additionally, Table 8.2 shows regressions of the number of plots allocated to a household (*plots_hh*), the Simpson Index (SI) of allocated plots (*si_alloc*) and of cultivated plots (*si_cult*) on the same variables. Summary statistics of the variables in the regressions are presented in Table 8.1.

**Table 8.1   Determinants of land endowment and fragmentation:
Summary statistics**

	Mean	Min.	Max.	St. Dev.
alloc_land (*mu*)	7.7	1.0	28.0	3.9
plots_hh	3.2	0.0	8.0	1.7
f_size	4.4	1.0	9.0	1.4
si_alloc	0.5	0.0	0.9	0.3
si_cult	0.5	0.0	0.8	0.3
mde_ratio	0.8	0.0	1.2	0.2
pos (1 = yes, 0 = no)	0.2	0.0	1.0	0.4
age_flabor	42.6	24.0	77.5	9.3
sh_fem (%)	46.1	0.0	85.7	15.4
any_title (1 = yes, 0 = no)	0.6	0.0	1.0	0.5
cult_since (years)	8.6	0.0	26.0	6.4
avwheat_pot (kg/*mu*)	355.6	150.0	550.0	64.3
rented_in (1 = yes, 0 = no)	0.1	0.0	1.0	0.3

Source: IRTG (2005).

The results in Table 8.2 imply the following. Total allocated land appears to be mainly determined by the family size. HHs having rented any land have indeed been allocated less land, which suggests that the decision to rent in land is actually motivated by land scarcity and land demand. However, the regression of the number of plots allocated (*plots_hh*) shows a slightly different picture. As it was expected, the number of plots per capita decreases with increasing family size, as indicated by the significant negative coefficient of the squared term of *f_size*. Furthermore, HHs with older farm labor force (*age_flabor*) cultivate less plots. Lastly, and rather surprisingly, holding a land title is highly significant in this regression. One explanation for the different outcome in both regressions could be that HHs underestimated their actual farm size, while they were more capable of reporting the number of allocated plots. The SI of both allocated and cultivated land also increases with family size, since larger families are more likely to have multiple plots. What is noteworthy in the last regression of *si_cult* is that this land fragmentation index is actually significantly higher for renting-in HHs, because HHs regard their rented plots still as separate parcels. A fragmentation reducing effect of the land rental market can therefore not be confirmed from this data. The variable *avwheat_pot* is insignificant in all regressions. Possibly, this variable is in fact not a suitable proxy for land quality.

Apart from the determinants of land fragmentation, it is interesting to explore how farmers perceive the effects of fragmentation and whether fragmentation has any influence on their input use decisions. An indication that HHs indeed realize negative effects of fragmentation comes from the second household survey, in which respondents were asked to rate the quality of their plots as being less, equal or higher than average village quality.

Table 8.2   Determinants of household land endowment and fragmentation (OLS)

	Farm size (alloc_land)		Number of allocated plots (plots_hh)		Simpson Index			
					si_alloc		si_cult	
Constant	9.275	(2.243) ***	-0.116	(1.158)	0.048	(0.187)	0.057	(0.179)
f_size	1.412	(0.518) ***	1.047	(0.268) ***	0.108	(0.043) **	0.102	(0.041) **
f_size²	-0.022	(0.053)	-0.084	(0.027) ***	-0.007	(0.004) *	-0.007	(0.004)
mde_ratio	-0.073	(0.735)	-0.194	(0.379)	-0.075	(0.061)	-0.086	(0.059)
pos	0.528	(0.405)	-0.156	(0.209)	-0.019	(0.034)	-0.016	(0.032)
age_flabor	-0.014	(0.017)	-0.016	(0.009) *	0.000	(0.001)	0.000	(0.001)
sh_fem	0.004	(0.009)	0.001	(0.005)	0.000	(0.001)	0.000	(0.001)
any_title	0.129	(0.383)	0.546	(0.198) ***	0.057	(0.032) *	0.056	(0.030) *
cult_since	0.011	(0.032)	0.017	(0.017)	0.004	(0.003)	0.004	(0.003) *
avwheat_pot	-0.001	(0.002)	0.000	(0.001)	0.000	(0.000)	0.000	(0.000)
rented_in	-1.818	(0.543) ***	-0.237	(0.280)	0.029	(0.046)	0.149	(0.043) ***
Observations	303		303		302		303	
R²	0.637		0.490		0.415		0.441	

Notes: Standard errors in parentheses. Village dummy variables included in the model.
* (**) [***] Significant at the 10% (5%) [1%] level of error probability.
Source: IRTG (2005).

A multinomial logit model is used to analyze the factors determining the plot categorization into less, equal or higher than average quality (Table 8.4). The dependent variables and plot characteristics which may explain their subjective categorization are summarized in Table 8.3.

While the coefficients for the category "higher than average" are all insignificant, small, distant plots on which no winter wheat is cultivated are considered to be of inferior quality. This may be regarded as evidence for the existence of adverse effects of land fragmentation. It is not clear, however, whether respondents took ease of cultivation into consideration when evaluating the "quality" of a plot or whether this result actually has to do with soil properties. If this were so, it would be in opposition to Nguyen and Cheng (1996) who claimed that in the course of reallocations, plots of better quality had been divided up into smaller fields.

Table 8.3   Categorization of plot qualities: Summary statistics

	Mean	Min.	Max.	St. Dev.
Plot quality "below average"	0.19	0.00	1.00	0.39
Plot quality "average"	0.58	0.00	1.00	0.49
Plot quality "above average"	0.23	0.00	1.00	0.42
Plot size (mu)	3.04	0.10	13.00	2.10
If the plot is rented (1 = yes, 0 = no)	0.03	0.00	1.00	0.18
If wheat is planted (1 = yes, 0 = no)	0.70	0.00	1.00	0.46
Cultivated since (years)	7.76	0.00	19.00	5.63
Distance House – plot (m)	820.61	10.00	5000.00	742.06
Distance plot – water source (m)	124.94	0.00	1500.00	202.35

Source: IRTG (2005).

Table 8.4   Categorization of plot qualities (Multinomial logistic regression)

	Category "Less than average"			Category "higher than average"	
Constant	1.78	(0.49)	***	-0.78	(0.43)
Plot size	-0.41	(0.09)	***	0.03	(0.05)
If the plot is rented	-0.76	(1.09)		0.34	(0.55)
If wheat is planted	-1.65	(0.33)	**	0.21	(0.32)
Cultivated since	0.06	(0.05)		-0.04	(0.04)
Distance House – plot	5E-4	(0.00)	***	3E-5	(0.00)
Distance plot – water source	-2E4	(0.00)		3E-4	(0.00)
Observations	557				
Pseudo-R^2	0.10				
Log likelihood	-483.90				

Notes: Standard errors in parentheses. Village dummy variables included in the model. The comparison group is the category "equal to village quality". * (**) [***] Significant at the 10% (5%) [1%] level of error probability.
Source: IRTG (2005).

8.1.2 Village level

The following regression table attempts to explain differences in plots per household and average plot size between villages in Quzhou County. First, higher land endowment per household (*lp_household*) is likely to go along with both a larger number of plots and larger plot sizes. Second, following the argument that an active land rental market within a village (*rent_within*) reduces land fragmentation, this effect may also be recognizable at the village level. Third, the practice of plot exchanges (*plot_exch*) should have a strong effect on reducing fragmentation, since this is its very purpose. Finally, the number of wells per arable land (*wells_pa*) is included to account for differences in land quality and irrigation infrastructure and the percentage of wheat per sown area (*perc_wheat*) since the household survey showed that wheat is mainly cultivated on larger plots (Table 8.5 and Table 8.6).

The hypothesized relationship between land fragmentation and the land rental market can not be confirmed. However, this is in line with discussions with local experts who indicated that consolidating landholdings is not the main motivation behind renting land. More surprising is that the percentage of HHs engaging in plot exchanges seems to be related with an increase in the number of plots per household and a decrease in the average plot size. As one explanation, discussions with interviewers about this result revealed that village leaders apparently sometimes reported the original number of plots allocated to HHs and not the number of plots after plot exchanges had taken place.

Table 8.5   Determinants of plots per household and average plot size: Summary statistics

	Mean	Min.	Max.	St. Dev.
Plots per household	4.58	1.00	13.00	1.78
average plot size (*mu*)	2.08	0.21	8.39	1.09
lp_household (*mu*)	8.60	0.64	83.86	4.96
rent_within (%)	4.86	0.00	50.00	6.70
plot_exch (%)	6.32	0.00	70.00	10.67
wells_pa	0.01	0.00	0.04	0.01
perc_wheat (%)	0.33	0.00	0.52	0.07

Source: Own data (2007).

Furthermore, if this was not the case, it could be that the number of plots still remained high in some villages in spite of a number of HHs having exchanged their plots. Unfortunately, this can not be clearly disentangled from the survey data.

There is a strong negative relation between irrigation facilities, measured by the number of wells per arable land (*wells_pa*), and the number of plots cultivated by a household. This seems plausible, since better irrigation infrastructure will allow HHs to cultivate larger, contiguous fields.

Table 8.6   Determinants of plots per household and average plot size:
             Findings for Quzhou County (OLS)

	Plots per household			Average plot size		
Constant	5.81	(0.67)	***	0.52	(0.43)	*
lp_household	0.06	(0.01)	***	0.12	(0.02)	***
rent_within	-0.01	(0.01)		0.00	(0.01)	
plot_exch	0.02	(0.01)	**	-0.01	(0.00)	***
wells_pa	-42.71	(13.07)	***	16.01	(8.41)	**
perc_wheat	-4.22	(1.47)	***	1.88	(0.71)	***
QZ	-0.55	(0.40)	*	-0.25	(0.27)	*
BZ	0.86	(0.46)		-0.50	(0.25)	*
HQ	0.14	(0.36)	**	-0.39	(0.24)	**
AZ	0.38	(0.47)	*	-0.15	(0.27)	
DHD	0.50	(0.62)	*	-0.26	(0.31)	*
HC	-0.55	(0.38)	*	0.39	(0.30)	*
YZ	-0.31	(0.41)	*	-0.25	(0.26)	*
HNT	-0.13	(0.42)		-0.05	(0.26)	
ST	0.98	(0.44)	**	-0.59	(0.24)	**
Observations	305			305		
R²	0.23			0.39		

Note: Numbers in parentheses are robust standard errors.
* (**) [***] Significant at the 10% (5%) [1%] level of error probability.
Source: Own data (2007).

In section 7.2.5 it was stated that households in more remote areas have fewer opportunities for local off-farm income but more land than their counterparts in the more densely populated centers of the county and the question was raised what this implies for total income inequality. From the available data, only few other variables could be used to explain income differences between villages, most of which are highly collinear or endogenous, which is why regressions shown in Table 8.7 only include the distance of a village to the respective township seat and township dummy variables as explanatory variables. While the statistical data on incomes in 1996 and 1997 generally do not seem to be very trustworthy (they show signs of censoring at an upper value of around 3000 ¥), the distance had a significantly negative impact on income in both years (columns 1 and 2 in Table 8.7) Also according to the survey data, villages further away from the township seat are characterized by a lower level of off-farm income and a lower share of local sources in total off-farm income (columns 4 and 5). Total income per capita in 2006 does, however, not decline with increasing distance from the respective township seat (column 7). Apparently, more remote villages with poorer access to local off-farm income sources are able to compensate this deficit due to their higher land endowment (column 3). Especially in comparison to the statistical data from the mid-1990s, this is an encouraging result.

Table 8.7 Regression analysis on the impact of village location (OLS)

	QSY data			Processed survey data			
	1	2	3	4	5	6	7
DV =	Income p.c. (1996)	Income p.c. (1997)	Arable land per capita (2006)	Off-farm income p.c.	Share of local off-farm income	TVE per 1000 in-habitants	Total income p.c. (2006)
Distance to township seat (km)	-29.78 (7.29)**	-26.35 (6.20)**	0.05 (0.01)**	-62.68 (26.90)*	-0.60 (0.25)*	-0.05 (0.02)**	-2.16 (33.87)
QZ	925.34 (109.79)**	156.91 (93.46)	-0.48 (0.11)**	1325.74 (418.19)**	2.69 (3.87)	0.40 (0.32)	4050.47 (526.43)**
HQ	-0.88 (126.21)	-687.03 (107.43)**	0.26 (0.13)*	210.81 (456.61)	-3.01 (4.28)	0.53 (0.35)	-49.13 (574.80)
BZ	101.28 (116.00)	-255.31 (98.72)*	-0.56 (0.11)**	1290.30 (425.98)**	-5.34 (4.00)	0.10 (0.33)	1831.22 (536.24)**
AZ	310.10 (117.63)**	-47.88 (100.13)	-0.09 (0.12)	147.13 (434.81)	0.18 (4.08)	0.40 (0.34)	16.61 (547.36)
DHD	-59.99 (142.17)	-983.74 (121.02)**	-0.03 (0.15)	881.57 (515.72)	-5.94 (4.83)	0.15 (0.40)	964.60 (649.21)
HC	282.35 (119.93)*	-462.29 (102.09)**	-0.14 (0.12)	1153.53 (438.36)**	-1.91 (4.10)	0.12 (0.34)	763.41 (551.83)
YZ	198.61 (162.20)	239.60 (138.06)	-0.16 (0.17)	67.97 (592.80)	-0.21 (5.54)	0.62 (0.46)	-595.17 (746.24)
HNT	289.19 (120.59)*	-81.09 (102.65)	0.30 (0.12)*	303.31 (439.48)	5.78 (4.13)	0.86 (0.34)*	14.10 (553.24)
ST	275.00 (118.13)*	-333.13 (100.56)**	0.17 (0.12)	240.53 (438.31)	1.86 (4.11)	0.14 (0.34)	-186.73 (551.76)
Constant	1937.92 (95.66)**	2707.55 (81.43)**	1.68 (0.10)**	1179.44 (355.80)**	21.76 (3.37)**	0.61 (0.27)*	2707.10 (447.90)**
Obs.	342	342	342	302	305	306	302
R^2	0.34	0.43	0.36	0.11	0.08	0.08	0.33

Notes: Standard errors in parentheses. * (**) Significant at the 5% (1%) level of error probability.
Sources: Quzhou County Statistical Bureau (various years) and own data (2007).

8.2 Determinants of input use

For reasons given above, the analysis of input use focuses on nitrogenous fertilizer. There are two competing propositions to be tested. First, fertilizer input decisions are determined by property rights and tenure insecurity. Second, fertilizer use is determined by off-farm employment and the resulting changes in the availability of labor and capital.

8.2.1 Household level

As stated above, the variable *mde_ratio*, which is the share of family labor working in agriculture weighted as shown in section 7.1.1, appears to be an appropriate measure to characterize a household as predominantly agriculturally or off-farm oriented. To test the influence of off-farm employment, this variable is therefore included in the Ordinary Least Squares regression model explaining input of pure nitrogen per hectare of winter wheat. Furthermore, in an exploratory analysis of the possible determinants of nitrogen fertilizer use, it was found that the share of produced winter wheat consumed within the household (*w_own_cons*) is highly correlated with nitrogen input. A plausible explanation for this observation is that wheat plays a more important role for sustaining food security for these households, which in turn provides the incentive to overuse fertilizer in order to guarantee stable yields.

Ye and Rozelle (1994) find in their simulation of a representative farm model that in a situation of other policy restrictions such as mandatory grain quotas and the lack of a market for hired labor, easing constraints to engage in off-farm employment leads to an increased use of chemical fertilizer. They conclude that farmers use chemical fertilizer directly to substitute labor. This result can not be confirmed in the present study and also does not seem plausible for the case of the North China Plain, which is, as shown above, characterized by high labor surplus. In fact, 80% of all fertilizer applications in the household survey are done manually.

Furthermore, the regression output shown in Table 8.9 includes the dummy variable *rented_in* to control for HHs who stated to have rented any land, the average age (*age_flabor*) and years of education (*ed_flabor*) of the farm labor force as well as dummy variables for the surveyed villages (see Table 8.8 for summary statistics). If renting-in HHs were in fact better, more efficient producers, one would expect a negative effect on the amount of fertilizer applied, which is not asserted in the regression shown in Table 8.9. However, both *w_own_cons* and *mde_ratio* increase the amount of applied nitrogen. While the impact of *w_own_cons* was expected, the second result is worrying, since it implies that management capabilities in agriculture and the off-farm sector are indeed positively correlated, as Wu (2006) and Zhu et al. (1993) have argued.

Table 8.8   Determinants of nitrogen fertilizer use in winter wheat: Summary statistics

	Mean	Min.	Max.	St. Dev.
Applied Nitrogen (kg/ha)	358.18	0.00	1380.00	219.12
w_own_cons (%)	53.19	0.00	100.00	33.09
mde_ratio	0.68	0.00	1.00	0.24
rented_in (1 = yes, 0 = no)	0.10	0.00	1.00	0.29
ed_flabor (years)	6.40	0.00	11.33	2.21
age_flabor (years)	42.21	24.00	77.50	9.04

Source: IRTG (2005).

Table 8.9   Determinants of nitrogen fertilizer use in winter wheat (OLS)

	kg N/ha applied to winter wheat		
Constant	232.89	(97.05)	*
w_own_cons	1.13	(44.49)	*
mde_ratio	98.94	(49.54)	*
rented_in	-8.00	(47.77)	
ed_flabor	-0.58	(1.35)	
age_flabor	-4.06	(5.04)	
Observations	315		
R^2	0.21		

Notes: Robust standard errors in parentheses. Village dummy variables included in the model.
* Significant at the 5% level of error probability.
Source: IRTG (2005).

8.2.2 Village level

From the village survey, only average production costs are known, not quantities. The analysis here therefore only looks at what determines differences in capital intensity between villages. From the different cost components, mainly fertilizer and irrigation costs are expected to differ significantly between the villages, so that the linear regressions shown in Table 8.11 only regress these cost components and total direct production costs for wheat on village specific variables. These include the average plot size (plot_size), the amount of nitrogen from organic sources accumulated in a year as calculated from Table 7.31 and Table 7.26 (nexcr), the distance to the nearest large road (dist_road) and surface water channel (dist_channel), the percentage of irrigated land (perc_irrig) and the number of wells per arable land (wells_pa). In particular nexcr is expected to reduce fertilizer costs. The distance to a road and the nearest water channel may increase production costs, while good irrigation infrastructure (proxied by perc_irrig and wells_pa) may result in lower irrigation costs. Furthermore, dummy variables for whether 10% or more of the HHs have rented (rent10) or exchanged plots (exch10) are included and also whether the village keeps reserve land (reserve) and whether any land rental transfers between villages take place (*outstrans*). Summary statistics for the variables in the models are shown in Table 8.10 and results in Table 8.11 below.

Table 8.10   Determinants of wheat production costs: Summary statistics

	Mean	Min.	Max.	St. Dev.
Fertilizer costs (¥/*mu*)	118.15	40.00	300.00	43.02
Irrigation costs (¥/*mu*)	84.56	15.00	180.00	29.42
Total direct costs (¥/*mu*)	311.77	143.00	480.00	63.18
plot_size (*mu*)	2.08	0.21	8.39	1.05
nexcr (calculated organic fertilizer per arable land in kg N/*mu*)	25.46	6.72	404.95	29.97
dist_road (km)	1.37	0.00	4.93	1.03
dist_channel (km)	1.03	0.01	3.70	0.80
perc_irrig (% of irrigated land)	0.85	0.34	1.00	0.13
wells_pa (number of wells per arable land)	0.01	0.00	0.04	0.01
rent10 (1 = yes, 0 = no)	0.12	0.00	1.00	0.32
exch10 (1 = yes, 0 = no)	0.26	0.00	1.00	0.44
reserve (1 = yes, 0 = no)	0.20	0.00	1.00	0.40
outstrans (1 = yes, 0 = no)	0.43	0.00	1.00	0.50

Source: Own data (2007).

As expected, *nexcr* significantly reduces fertilizer costs, which also leads to lower total costs. The distance variables *dist_road* and *dist_channel* as well as the variables measuring irrigation infrastructure show no effect. Also whether or not a village keeps reserve land (*reserve*) is not related to differences in production costs. Surprisingly, fertilizer costs and total costs for wheat are higher in villages with an active land market (*rent10*) while irrigation costs are lower where 10% or more of the HHs have engaged in plot exchanges. The latter result conforms to discussions with farmers in Quzhou who indicated that one significant benefit of rearranging their plots is to make access to wells easier and thus improve irrigation efficiency. Finally, whether village leaders reported that some HHs transfer land use rights between HHs in other villages apparently has a positive effect on both irrigation costs and total costs. It has been stated above that HHs that wish to rent in (out) land from (to) other villages depend on some kind of network or middlemen to provide them with information on land demand or supply in other villages. The incidence of inter-village land transfers may therefore be correlated with good information networks. Possibly, households in these villages not only have better access to information regarding the land rental market, but, due to the same unobservable characteristics, also better access to markets and production knowledge.

Table 8.11   Determinants of wheat production costs (OLS)

	Fertilizer costs (¥/mu)			Irrigation costs (¥/mu)			Total direct costs (¥/mu)		
Constant	114.10	(20.90)	***	76.20	(16.31)	***	306.20	(35.20)	***
plot_size	1.13	(2.21)		-1.61	(1.46)		-0.61	(3.26)	
nexcr	-0.13	(0.06)	**	-0.03	(0.05)		-0.17	(0.09)	*
dist_road	3.85	(2.39)		0.31	(1.62)		5.14	(3.70)	
dist_channel	-2.77	(3.31)		1.02	(2.78)		-2.62	(5.25)	
perc_irrig	-17.47	(19.42)		-3.28	(11.90)		-25.38	(29.49)	
wells_pa	-201.71	(372.50)		152.77	(290.11)		53.59	(672.86)	
rent10	16.34	(8.75)	*	4.52	(5.07)		25.40	(10.67)	**
exch10	-6.83	(5.40)		-7.43	(3.68)	**	-11.63	(8.56)	
reserve	3.31	(5.61)		2.85	(4.32)		6.12	(8.51)	
outstrans	-6.56	(5.14)		-11.18	(3.50)	***	-17.74	(7.91)	**
QZ	38.76	(11.06)	***	27.22	(9.01)	***	57.61	(18.77)	***
HQ	12.06	(9.71)		14.14	(9.07)		28.09	(18.16)	
BZ	8.87	(10.98)		3.66	(10.16)		13.62	(18.60)	
AZ	59.55	(10.80)	***	24.94	(8.39)	***	69.33	(18.78)	***
DHD	26.61	(12.92)	**	13.22	(11.49)		24.90	(27.54)	
HC	15.35	(10.32)		15.37	(8.69)	*	20.36	(18.36)	
YZ	-10.92	(10.58)		23.97	(9.02)	***	2.83	(18.30)	
HNT	5.93	(10.63)		24.40	(9.77)	**	37.87	(19.05)	**
ST	28.16	(11.48)	**	26.36	(9.82)	***	47.47	(21.26)	**
Obs.	294			294			294		
R^2	0.20			0.14			0.15		

Note: Robust standard errors in parentheses.
* (**) [***] Significant at the 10% (5%) [1%] level of error probability.
Source: Own data (2007).

8.3 Determinants of land use right restrictions

8.3.1 Household level

The descriptive part of this study has shown that there are a number of ways in which farmers' land use rights can be restricted. However, the extent of restrictions observed in the household survey was not as high as expected. For example, according to their answers, none of the sample HHs are denied the right to rent in or rent out land (questions on renting between villages were not included in the household survey). Furthermore, the survey asked whether HHs had been affected by any land requisitions, for instance due to construction activities. Although there were in total 16 reported cases, the extent of such requisitions was small and all HHs apparently received adequate compensation. This leaves the issuance or otherwise of land use right certificates as a restriction which may have an effect on HHs decision making. It is known, however, that rural land use rights are not allowed to be used as collateral to access credit. Therefore, any link between credit access and land titles seems unlikely. Nevertheless, in the two logistic regression models shown in Table 8.13, with the dependent variables being whether or not a household applied for a credit in the formal or informal credit market, holding a land title (*any_title*) significantly increased the probability of an application (for a more in-depth analysis of actual credit rationing see Jia, 2007). If this has in fact a causal explanation, it may be that holding such land use right certificates increases the perceived creditworthiness of borrowers, since such households may be more likely to be able to pay back a credit with the earnings from their land. However, there is no more qualitative information available to substantiate this hypothesis.

Further household specific variables in the models include the average age of the labor force (*age_labor*), the household size (*h_size*), the share of the family labor force working in agriculture as defined above (*mde_ratio*), whether the HH operates an own small side-line business (*sbusiness*) and whether there is any present or former village cadre (*pos*) in the family (see Table 8.12 for the summary statistics). In particular the sign and significance of *sbusiness* in both models is in line with the expectation that HHs with such side-line businesses will be more active in the formal as well as the informal credit market.

8.3.2 Village level

Not many variables are available to explain differences in land tenure arrangements between villages. Nevertheless, the conception that maintaining egalitarian land allocation in view of land scarcity is the main motivation to undertake a reallocation can be confirmed (Rozelle and Li, 1998). The variables used in the logistic regression model (Table 8.14) to explain whether a village has conducted any land reallocation after 1992 include the average land per capita endowment in the village in 2006 (*lpc*), a dummy variable that equals 1 if the village allows renting out to nonvillagers and 0 otherwise (*allow*), the average age of the farm labor force (*age*) and the variables *rent10*, *exch10* and *perc_irrig* as defined above. Furthermore, a dummy variable for the location of the village in a *zhen* is included. The model on the right side of Table 8.14 explaining whether the village restricts land rental to within-village transfers includes the same variables except *allow*.

Those 30 villages having conducted any large or small land reallocation since 1992 are indeed characterized by higher land scarcity as indicated by the negative and significant coefficient on land per capita endowment (Table 8.14). Other control variables that were hypothesized to be explanatory variables for the decision to conduct a reallocation are not significant except *perc_irrig* and *age*, however. By the same token, land scarcity motivates the restriction to intra-village land transfers. Furthermore, villages located in *zhen* are more likely to allow inter-village transfers.

Table 8.12 Determinants of credit applications: Summary statistics

	Mean	Min.	Max.	St. Dev.
Formal credit (1 = yes, 0 = no)	0.12	0.00	1.00	0.33
Informal credit (1 = yes, 0 = no)	0.29	0.00	1.00	0.46
age_labor (years)	40.19	24.00	77.50	8.77
any_title (1 = yes, 0 = no)	0.61	0.00	1.00	0.49
h_size	3.78	1.00	9.00	1.37
mde_ratio	0.68	0.00	1.00	0.24
sbusiness (1 = yes, 0 = no)	0.16	0.00	1.00	0.37
pos (1 = yes, 0 = no)	0.18	0.00	1.00	0.39
dist_town (km)	3.49	0.50	10.00	2.43

Source: IRTG (2005).

Table 8.13 Determinants of credit applications (Logistic regression)

	Any application for formal credit in 2004			Any application for informal credit in 2004		
	Coefficient		dy/dx	Coefficient		dy/dx
Constant	-4.562	(1.969)	**	-1.928	(1.088)	*	
any_title	0.816	(0.479)	*	0.036	0.546	(0.313)	*	0.099
age_labor	-0.048	(0.025)	*	-0.002	0.009	(0.015)		0.002
h_size	-0.173	(0.163)		-0.008	0.216	(0.100)	**	0.040
mde_ratio	-0.082	(0.902)		-0.004	-1.043	(0.602)	*	-0.195
sbusiness	2.227	(0.476)	***	0.218	1.028	(0.344)	***	0.221
pos	1.150	(0.515)	**	0.078	-0.778	(0.381)	**	-0.127
dist_town	0.386	(0.195)	**	0.018	-0.021	(0.075)		-0.004
town1	3.747	(1.284)		0.567	0.529	(0.624)		0.109
town2	1.489	(1.280)		0.124	0.605	(0.608)		0.126
town3	1.548	(1.114)		0.131	0.064	(0.638)		0.012
town4	1.570	(1.282)		0.134	-0.464	(0.666)		-0.078
town5[1]	-	-		-	0.095	(0.623)		0.018
town6	4.741	(1.241)	***	0.759	-2.602	(1.151)	**	-0.268
town7	4.512	(1.196)	***	0.716	1.219	(0.599)	**	0.271
town8	-1.659	(1.466)		-0.046	0.326	(0.612)		0.065
town9	2.514	(1.355)	*	0.295	0.581	(0.651)		0.120
Observations	332			332			
Pseudo-R²	0.30			0.11			
Log likelihood	-82.21			-173.85			

Notes: Standard errors in parentheses. * (**) [***] Significant at the 10% (5%) [1%] level of error probability. [1] town5 predicted the outcome perfectly in the case of formal credit applications, i.e. no formal credit application was reported in town5.
Source: IRTG (2005).

Table 8.14   Land right restrictions (Logistic regressions)

	Reallocation after 1992[1]			Restricting land transfers[2]		
	Coefficient		dy/dx	Coefficient		dy/dx
Constant	-0.38	(2.00)		0.87	(2.12)	
lpc	-0.70	(0.31)	** -0.06	-0.65	(0.34)	* -0.09
allow	-0.23	(0.54)	-0.02			
age	-0.06	(0.03)	* 0.00	-0.04	(0.03)	-0.01
reserve	-0.13	(0.52)	-0.01	-0.44	(0.41)	-0.05
rent10	0.44	(0.59)	0.04	-0.75	(0.69)	-0.08
exch10	0.16	(0.45)	0.01	0.29	(0.36)	0.04
perc_irrig	2.24	(1.27)	* 0.18	1.71	(1.65)	0.22
zhen	0.53	(0.45)	0.04	-1.13	(0.34)	*** -0.15
Observations	298			303		
Pseudo-R²	0.05			0.10		
Log likelihood	-92.46			-		

[1] Dependent variable is a dummy variable with 1 = village has conducted a large reallocation since 1992 and 0 = otherwise. [2] Dependent variable is a dummy variable with 1 = village does not allow renting out of land to non-villagers and 0 = otherwise. Robust standard errors in parentheses.
* (**) [***] Significant at the 10% (5%) [1%] level of error probability.
Source: Own data (2007).

8.4 Determinants of the participation in land transfers

8.4.1 Household level

The literature review above has shown that there are divergent arguments concerning the characteristics of lessees in the rural land rental market in China. Some authors have argued that lessees are indeed more productive in agriculture (de Janvry et al., 2005), while others have come to the conclusion that renting-in households are in fact those that have not succeeded in entering the off-farm labor market and that ability in both sectors are positively correlated (Wu, 2006). Given these divergent arguments, it is questionable whether renting-in households do at all have certain characteristics in common that can be tested in econometric models. It is more plausible that there are very different reasons for renting in, just as there are different reasons for non-participation in the market as has been shown in the descriptive part of this study. This concern is even more relevant since there are only 32 renting-in HHs in the sample. Unfortunately, no additional qualitative information for these HHs was gathered as to their motivation for renting in. At the aggregated, regional level, the determinants for a land rental market are more discernable. The descriptive analysis confirmed the expectation that a more developed rental market would be found in the more prosperous counties of Shandong Province. Beyond this observation, however, reasons for participation of individual HHs in the land rental market are difficult to explain with the available data. Table 8.15 compares two logistic models. In the first model, the dependent variable is the dummy variable for having rented any land (*rented_in*). In the second model, the dependent variable equals one if the interviewee responded to not rent in additional land because no land is offered in the market (*no_land*, see Table 7.18). This answer may be seen as a motivation or willingness to rent in land. It turns out that farm labor in this group of HHs is significantly younger (*age_flabor*) and these HHs have been allocated less land per family member (*alp_fsize*). This confirms that these HHs have a propensity to enlarge their farm sizes if more land was offered to them. In the case of HHs having rented land, these two variables have the same sign, but only *age_flabor* is significant at the 10% level. Using manure in crop production (*any_manure*) increases the probability of belonging to the renting-in group of HHs, but whether this indicates higher managerial abilities of renting-in HHs is questionable.

Table 8.15   Determinants of land market participation (Logistic regression)

Variables	If HH has rented any land (*rented_in*)			"No land available" (*no_land*)		
	Coefficient		dy/dx[a]	Coefficient		dy/dx[a]
Constant	-0.64	(1.57)		-0.63	(0.21) *	
alp_fsize	-0.30	(0.34)	-0.02	-0.03	(0.02) ***	-0.14
age_flabor	-0.04	(0.03) *	0.00	-0.20	(0.28) **	-0.01
any_manure	1.16	(0.49) **	0.06	-0.04	(0.28)	-0.05
any_off	0.33	(0.45)	0.02	-0.20	(0.31)	-0.01
any_title	-0.82	(0.49) *	-0.05	-0.20	(0.29)	-0.05
any_asset	0.31	(0.44)	0.02	-1.60	(0.40)	-0.05
QZ	-0.83	(0.83)	-0.04	-2.28	(0.48) ***	-0.30
LS	-0.79	(0.79)	-0.04	-0.73	(0.45) ***	-0.39
HM	1.51	(0.60) **	0.13	-0.16	(0.44)	-0.15
YJ	-0.80	(0.82)	-0.04	3.32	(0.99)	-0.04
Observations	331			297		
Pseudo-R²	0.16			0.14		
Log likelihood	-88.17			-170.61		

Note: Robust standard errors in parentheses.
* (**) [***] Significant at the 10% (5%) [1%] level of error probability.
[a] Marginal effects on probabilities evaluated at sample means (for dummy variables discrete change from 0 to 1).
Source: IRTG (2005).

HHs holding a land title (*any_title*) are less likely to rent in, possibly because they have been allocated sufficient land with secure use rights as is suggested by the results in Table 8.2. Two other control variables, whether any family member has an off-farm job (*any_off*) and whether the HH owns any of the agricultural assets listed in Table 7.9 (*any_asset*) did not have any influence.

8.4.2 Village level

For the Quzhou study, the extent of land rental activities within villages can be analyzed. In a model with the percentage of HHs renting land within a village as the dependent variable, a tobit regression model is suitable due to the 46 villages which reported no rental activity at all. As the results of the tobit model in Table 8.16 show, the relation between the average share of off-farm income (sh_off) and land rental activities seems to be quadratic rather than linear as is indicated by the significantly negative coefficient of its squared term (sh_off²). One possible explanation is that in a situation of a very high average share of off-farm income, the land per capita endowment is too low to permit households to rent out any land and other households also may not be willing to rent in any land because they also already have a high share of off-farm income.

Table 8.16   Determinants of land market activity at the village level (tobit model)

	% renting within same village		
Constant	-7.973	(4.459)	
sh_off	0.184	(0.082)	*
sh_off²	-0.002	(0.001)	*
allow	0.305	(1.166)	
lpc	0.460	(0.838)	
reserve	-1.110	(1.078)	
plot_exch	0.043	(0.039)	
perc_irrig	5.811	(4.079)	
QZ	2.174	(1.977)	
HQ	2.543	(2.057)	
BZ	-0.627	(1.988)	
AZ	2.138	(1.963)	
DHD	0.348	(2.333)	
HC	4.280	(1.956)	*
YZ	6.981	(2.667)	**
HNT	6.607	(2.126)	**
ST	4.988	(1.978)	*
Observations	304		
Pseudo-R²	0.020		
Log likelihood	-910.58		

Note: Standard errors in parentheses.
* (**) Significant at the 5% (1%) level of error probability.
Source: Own data (2007).

However, other variables possibly related to an active land rental market are not significant and the model therefore shows a very low fit. This either suggests that other important variables explaining rental activity are omitted or that village leaders could not accurately state the extent of rental transfers.

8.5 Results of the production function models

8.5.1 Household level

At the household level, the survey data allows to estimate crop-specific production functions as well as aggregated production functions with the total value of agricultural production as the dependent variable. Since winter wheat is the main crop in the study region and is grown by almost all farmers, one production function for the total amount of wheat harvested by a HH in 2004 (*w_harvest*) and one for the total value of crop output produced by a HH (*gvao*) are estimated in this section. Due to problems of multicollinearity with the translog function, the Cobb-Douglas functional form is used in both cases. The variables used for these functions are summarized in Table 8.17. Due to a few missing values, the production function for wheat is estimated with 306 observations and the one for the total value of output with 326.

As the land input variables (*land*), the size of plots planted with wheat and the total planted area by the HH are used. For labor input, the variable *mde_farm* as defined above is used for both functions because the specific labor input for wheat as stated by the HHs did not seem very reliable and contained many missing values. As further inputs, the amount of fertilizer applied (*fert*) as well as costs for seed (*c_seed*) and other costs (*c_oth*) are used. In order to account for natural conditions of production, township dummy variables are included in both models.

Table 8.17 Variables used in the stochastic frontier models at the household level

Variables	Description	Wheat production				Total production (GVAO)			
		Mean	St. Dev.	Min.	Max.	Mean	St. Dev.	Min.	Max.
Dependent var.									
w_harvest	Logged total amount of winter wheat harvested by a HH in 2004 (kg)	2102.1	1526.4	350.0	10500.0				
gvao	Logged total value of HH production (¥)					7679.0	5949.5	760.0	55990.0
Input variables									
land	Logged area of land planted with wheat (logged total area planted by a HH))	6.0	3.9	1.0	25.0	8.5	5.2	1.0	36.5
mde_farm	Logged available farm labor (see above)	2.0	0.8	0.3	5.0	2.1	0.8	0.3	5.5
fert	Logged fertilizer input in wheat (logged total fertilizer input) in kg	140.8	135.4	8.1	1313.2	222.1	234.9	0.1	2414.0
c_seed	Logged seed costs for wheat (logged total seed costs) in ¥	212.4	215.9	7.5	1687.5	572.3	561.2	42.9	4864.0
c_oth	Logged other costs for wheat (logged other costs for total production) in ¥	563.0	401.7	37.7	2340.0	1316.8	1929.9	26.0	31035.4
Dummy var. (DV)									
town1-town9	Dummy variables for the townships; the omitted category is town10								
Inefficiency effects									
w_plots	Number of plots planted with wheat	2.1	1.2	1.0	6.0				
si	Simpson Index (see above)					0.5	0.3	0.0	0.8
perc_wheat	% wheat per sown area					0.4	0.2	0.0	1.0
rented_in	DV if HH has rented in any land (= 1, else = 0)	0.1	0.3	0.0	1.0	0.1	0.3	0.0	1.0
mde_ratio	Share of farm labor to total labor	0.7	0.2	0.1	1.0	0.7	0.2	0.0	1.0
ed_flabor	Average years of education attained by farm labor	6.3	2.2	0.0	11.3	6.4	2.2	0.0	11.3
dist_town	Distance of village to township (km)	3.6	2.5	0.5	10.0	3.5	2.4	0.5	10.0
QZ, LS, HM, YJ	DV for the counties								

Note: Summary statistics are shown for the unlogged variables. Source: Own data (2007)

The following variables explaining technical efficiency (TE) are included in the wheat model. The number of plots on which wheat is cultivated (*w_plots*) may be an indicator of land fragmentation and therefore be detrimental to TE. A dummy variable which equals 1 if the HH has rented in any land (*rented_in*) is included in order to test the hypothesis that renting-in HHs are better, i.e. more efficient producers. The share of full labor units working on-farm (*mde_ratio*) reflects the degree to which household members earn additional income off-farm. The effect on TE is unclear. As discussed above, both arguments, that of an increasing as well as a decreasing impact of off-farm employment on TE can be found in the literature. The possibly positive influence of education is captured by *ed_flabor* which are the average years of education attained by the farm labor force. Finally, the distance of a village to the township (*dist_town*) is likely to correlate with poorer infrastructure and market access and hence lower TE.

For the total production model, the same variables are included except that the Simpson Index (*si*) is measuring land fragmentation and the percentage of sown area planted with wheat (*perc_wheat*) is used to account for specialization in wheat. On the one hand, wheat is a low value crop which would probably decrease TE if the total value of production is used as the dependent variable. On the other hand, a high share of wheat may also indicate a low level of commercialization which may as well go along with lower TE.

Table 8.18   **Maximum likelihood estimates of the stochastic frontier functions for winter wheat and GVAO (Cobb-Douglas)**

Variable	Parameter	ML estimate		Parameter	ML estimate	
		Wheat production			**Total production (GVAO)**	
Constant	β_0	6.987	(0.251) ***	β_0	6.807	(0.399) ***
land	β_1	0.569	(0.059) ***	β_1	0.486	(0.078) ***
mde_farm	β_2	0.121	(0.047) **	β_2	0.012	(0.078)
fert	β_3	0.035	(0.032)	β_3	0.122	(0.035) ***
c_seed	β_4	0.079	(0.026) ***	β_4	0.087	(0.039) **
c_oth	β_5	0.087	(0.032) ***	β_5	0.074	(0.040) *
town1	β_6	-0.466	(0.238) *	β_6	-1.268	(0.235) ***
town2	β_7	-0.298	(0.257)	β_7	-0.714	(0.260) ***
town3	β_8	2.128	(0.862) **	β_8	-0.645	(0.225) ***
town4	β_9	2.221	(0.865) **	β_9	-0.454	(0.227) **
town5	β_{10}	-0.889	(0.122) ***	β_{10}	-0.358	(0.253)
town6	β_{11}	-0.647	(0.119) ***	β_{11}	-0.636	(0.246) **
town7	β_{12}	-0.948	(0.119) ***	β_{12}	-0.820	(0.233) ***
town8	β_{13}	-0.968	(0.126) ***	β_{13}	-0.736	(0.234) ***
town9	β_{14}	-0.363	(0.106) ***	β_{14}	-0.290	(0.173) *
Returns to scale		**0.855**	**(0.052)**		**0.769**	**(0.073)**

* (**) [***] Significant at the 10% (5%) and [1%] level of error probability. Standard errors in parentheses.
Source: IRTG (2005).

The results for both functions are shown in Table 8.18. The parameter estimates of the input factors can be directly interpreted as partial production elasticities which should add up to unity in order to satisfy the constant returns to scale assumption. In both models this assumption is violated which is surprising but would support the results of Chen et al. (2003) and Chen and Huffman (2006). The partial production elasticity of land is with 0.57 and 0.49 below those found in the studies cited above, which lie around 0.60. The labor input variable is positive and significant in the wheat model but insignificant in the total production model, which may have to do with measurement errors. Interestingly, fertilizer input is insignificant in the wheat model but positive and significant in the total production model. One possible explanation is that fertilizer is particularly overused in wheat, but not so much in other crops. Table 8.19 presents the results for the inefficiency effects models. For the interpretation of the parameter estimates it needs to be noted that a positive sign indicates a positive contribution to the one-sided error term, which means a contribution to inefficiency. The variables measuring land fragmentation, w_plots and si, do not show the expected results. While w_plots is insignificant, si has a significantly positive effect on TE in the second model. The reason for this unexpected result may be that HHs with multiple, scattered plots are more likely to have a more diverse cropping pattern which allows them to grow high value crops besides grain. With the same reasoning it can be explained that the share of wheat (perc_wheat) in the cropping pattern has a negative effect on TE, although both variables are not significantly correlated. The significance of a HH having rented any land (rented_in) is inconclusive. While it is in fact positive in the wheat model, it is insignificant in the total production model. Which of these results more adequately reflects the effect of the land rental market cannot be answered from the data. As said above, this would require a larger sample of renting-in HHs.

The only two variables which have the same effect in both models are mde_ratio and dist_town. Both are efficiency reducing. While the negative effect of remoteness of a village is as expected, the effect of a high share of the labor force working in agriculture deserves more attention. It is in line with the finding above that these HHs overuse nitrogen fertilizer and suggests that indeed capabilities in the off-farm sector and agriculture are positively related.

Mean technical efficiency in wheat production is with 0.63 much lower then those estimates shown Table 6.1. An inspection of the mean efficiency scores across provinces (Table 8.20) reveals that this is mainly due to a mean technical efficiency of only 0.30 in Shandong which seems unreasonably low, while those for Hebei and Henan conform much better with those estimated by Tian and Wan (2000). Also the mean technical efficiency scores for the GVAO are in line with Tian and Wan (2000) who reported a slightly lower TE in wheat and maize production for Henan Province compared to Hebei and Shandong Province.

Table 8.19   Maximum likelihood estimates of the parameters in the inefficiency model for winter wheat and GVAO

Variable	Parameter	ML estimate		Parameter	ML estimate	
		Wheat production			**Total production (GVAO)**	
Constant	δ_0	-2.066	(0.433) ***	δ_0	-0.976	(0.460) **
w_plots	δ_1	0.033	(0.028)			
si				δ_1	-0.485	(0.245) **
perc_wheat				δ_2	1.153	(0.389) ***
rented_in	δ_2	-0.202	(0.101) **	δ_3	0.240	(0.200)
mde_ratio	δ_3	0.317	(0.162) *	δ_4	0.387	(0.231) *
ed_flabor	δ_4	-0.003	(0.016)	δ_5	0.020	(0.022)
dist_town	δ_5	0.133	(0.022) ***	δ_6	0.124	(0.035) ***
QZ	δ_6	-0.179	(0.206)	δ_7	-1.367	(0.443) ***
LS	δ_7	2.131	(0.603) ***	δ_8	-0.264	(0.341)
HM	δ_8	4.664	(1.259) ***	δ_9	-0.526	(0.317) *
YJ	δ_9	1.903	(0.422) ***	δ_{10}	-0.448	(0.370)
Variance parameters						
σ^2		0.118	(0.014) ***		0.248	(0.024) ***
γ		0.457	(0.097) ***		0.226	(0.097) **
Mean efficiency		**0.63**			**0.87**	

* (**) [***] Significant at the 10% (5%) and [1%] level of error probability. Standard errors in parentheses.
Source: IRTG (2005).

Table 8.20   Mean efficiency scores by provinces

	Hebei	Shandong	Henan
Wheat	0.96	0.30	0.78
GVAO	0.96	0.92	0.78

Source: IRTG (2005).

Several hypotheses of model applicability can be tested by likelihood ratio tests. First, a likelihood ratio test (see section 6.2.1) can be used to test whether any inefficiency is actually present in the sample. For this test, $LL(H_0)$ becomes the log likelihood function when imposing that all δ's and γ be zero and $LL(H_1)$ the log likelihood function without these restrictions. The null hypothesis H_0: $\gamma = 0$ is rejected when λ exceeds the critical value as derived from a table of a mixed χ^2 distribution (Coelli et al., 2005; Kodde and Palm, 1986). The degrees of freedom for this test are the number of parameters δ in the inefficiency equation plus one for the part of the overall variance attributed to inefficiency (γ). The null hypothesis of no inefficiency is strongly rejected (for a total of 11 restrictions) in the case of the wheat production function but only at the 10% level (for 12 restrictions) in the case of the total value production function.

Additionally, a LR-test can be performed to test whether the inefficiency determinants are jointly zero. For this test, the number of restrictions is equal to the number of inefficiency determinants in the model, i.e. 9 for the wheat model and 10 for the GVAO model. Again, the rejection of the null hypothesis is much stronger for the former than for the latter model (Table 8.21).

Table 8.21 Likelihood ratio tests of hypotheses related to the specification of the stochastic frontier models at the household level

	Wheat production		Total production	
	Crit. χ^2 value	Test value λ	Crit. χ^2 value	Test value λ
H_0: $\gamma = 0$	30.54^1	60.87^{***}	17.95^2	18.30^*
H_0: $\delta_1 = ... = \delta_n = 0$	27.88	60.87^{***}	18.31	22.51^{**}

^{1,2} Critical mixed χ^2 values for 11 and 12 restrictions as taken from Kodde and Palm (1986).
* (**) [***] The null hypothesis is rejected at the 10% (5%) and [1%] level of error probability.
Source: IRTG (2005).

8.5.2 Village level

This section aims to estimate a village-level production function using the aggregate production data from the QSY and the village survey data. Referring to the study of Chen and Huffman (2006), such an approach should generally be possible. Originally it was intended to use a stochastic frontier model also for the village data. However, all model specifications proved to be very unstable and almost all of the variation was attributed to the symmetric error term. Moreover, the interpretation of technical efficiency with such aggregated production data is problematic, since in fact very different production systems and cropping patterns are compared and not producers with a homogeneous production technology. For example, Chen and Huffman (2006) used the amount of geomembrane (i.e. plastic sheets to cover the soil) consumption in a county as a TE determinant, although a high amount of geomembrane simply indicates a high share of cash crops, for which geomembrane is mainly used. These reflections cast doubt on the suitability of a stochastic frontier function approach for such aggregated data. Therefore it was decided to simplify the analysis to a deterministic Cobb-Douglas function.

The variables used in the agricultural production function for Quzhou County are summarized in Table 8.22. As the dependent variable, the calculated gross value of total village agricultural production (*vlg_gvao*) is chosen since this will allow at a later stage to compare the total MVP of land with current land rental prices.

As discussed above, different approaches have been used in other studies to construct the land input variable. For the case of the Quzhou model, either the total arable land, the sown area or only the irrigated land (*irrigarable*) as defined in the QSY could be used. While taking arable land instead of the sown area as the land input variable is preferred due to the endogeneity of sown area, the irrigated area may still be more appropriate since all of agriculture in the county is dependent on irrigation.

Table 8.22   **Variables used in the deterministic production function for Quzhou County**

Variables	Description	Mean	St. Dev.	Min.	Max.
Dependent variable					
vlg_gvao	Logged value of total village agricultural production (in 1000 ¥)	2598.3	2197.4	136.4	22900.0
Input variables					
irrigarable	Logged total irrigated land (*mu*)	1837.2	1130.3	72.0	7999.0
wells	Logged number of operating wells in a village	22.2	17.2	2.0	86.0
labor	Logged weighted total labor force (male labor = 1, female labor = 0.75)	471.1	285.8	25.8	1823.5
Dummy variables (DV)					
QZ-ST	DV for townships; the omitted township category is LY				
reserve	DV if village keeps reserve land (= 1, else = 0)	0.2	0.4	0.0	1.0
outstrans	DV if any land transfers with other villages have been reported (= 1, else = 0)	0.4	0.5	0.0	1.0

Note: Summary statistics are shown for the unlogged variables.
Source: Own data (2007).

The use of total village-level production costs as an input variable, as initially intended, led to a partial production elasticity for land of only 0.12 which seemed much lower than expected. Most likely, total production costs are in fact not an appropriate proxy for actual input quantities, also because of the large number of missing values for vegetables and oilseeds. A variable that could be used instead in order to proxy for actual input intensity is the number of wells in a village (*wells*), which indicates good irrigation infrastructure.

Finally, for the labor input variable, the total labor force in a village is used, weighted with 0.75 for female labor (*labor*). This is likely to overstate the labor input, but the share of the village labor force actually working in agriculture cannot be extracted from the statistical data. Alternatively, assumptions could be made about the actual share of labor working in agriculture by using the share of off-farm income in total income. However, the income share does not necessarily correspond closely to the time available for farm work. Therefore, this approach is not taken. Another alternative could be to impute average labor demand for the five crops as stated by the QSB. These are 8 days/*mu* for wheat and maize, 30 days for cotton, 23 days for vegetables and 5 days for oilseeds.

A problem that could not be completely resolved in the function is that of multicollinearity of the input variables. Also for this reason, a specification with interaction terms such as the translog function, which would further increase multicollinearity (Keil, 2004), was not preferred. Although multicollinearity was reduced by weighting total labor force and using the irrigated land instead of total arable land, it still remains high.

While the use of land, labor and the number of wells likely ignores other important production factors, the estimation of a deterministic production function with these three input variables leads to much more reasonable results (Table 8.23). The first model in Table 8.23 shows the estimated function without spatial autocorrelation being accounted for. As can be seen, the partial production elasticity for irrigated land is with 0.61 much closer to those presented in Table 6.1. The computations of Moran's I (Table 7.25, Table 7.26 and Table 7.29) confirm that most of the production data and survey questions from Quzhou in fact show signs of spatial correlation. Interesting is for example the strong positive correlation of land rental prices. First, since most of the data was expected to show such correlations, this result implies that the collected data is of reasonable quality. Second, the question arises whether the spatial correlation of production costs mainly stems from correlation of natural conditions, for example soil quality and water availability, or from underlying preferences for higher inputs.

Furthermore, it needs to be tested how the estimated coefficients in the production function change when the spatial autocorrelation is incorporated in the model. As described in section 6.3, spatial autocorrelation can take the form of correlation in error terms or correlation of the dependent variables. The spatial error model can be written as

$$Y = X\beta + \varepsilon \tag{27}$$

$$\varepsilon = \lambda W\varepsilon + \mu, \tag{28}$$

where ε is an error term composed of the spatial autoregressive parameter λ, the spatial weights matrix W and the homoskedastic and uncorrelated error term μ (Pisati, 2001). In the spatial lag model, the spatially lagged dependent variable together with the autoregressive parameter ρ enters the model on the right hand side of the equation:

$$Y = \rho WY + X\beta + \mu. \tag{29}$$

Table 8.23   Deterministic production function for Quzhou County (Cobb-Douglas)

	Gross value of agricultural output (vlg_gvao)								
	Linear regression without spatial correlation			Spatial lag dependence model			Spatial error dependence model		
Constant	8.17	(0.30)	***	1.41	(0.82)	*	8.46	(0.28)	***
irrigarable	0.61	(0.07)	***	0.56	(0.06)	***	0.54	(0.06)	***
labor	0.23	(0.07)	***	0.29	(0.06)	***	0.28	(0.07)	***
wells	0.11	(0.04)	***	0.06	(0.04)		0.09	(0.04)	**
reserve	-0.11	(0.06)	*	-0.06	(0.05)		-0.04	(0.05)	
outstrans	0.11	(0.05)	**	0.08	(0.04)	*	0.07	(0.04)	*
QZ	1.12	(0.11)	***	0.84	(0.10)	***	0.77	(0.18)	***
HQ	-0.23	(0.11)	**	-0.15	(0.10)		-0.24	(0.16)	
BZ	0.28	(0.11)	***	0.15	(0.09)	*	0.13	(0.18)	
AZ	-0.01	(0.10)		-0.08	(0.09)		0.00	(0.17)	
DHD	0.06	(0.13)		-0.07	(0.11)		0.18	(0.23)	
HC	0.12	(0.10)		-0.01	(0.09)		0.08	(0.18)	
YZ	-0.01	(0.15)		-0.28	(0.13)	**	-0.19	(0.32)	
HNT	0.20	(0.12)	*	0.07	(0.10)		-0.01	(0.23)	
ST	0.16	(0.11)		0.18	(0.09)	**	0.09	(0.18)	
Observations	306			306			306		
R²	0.70			0.75			0.61		
Log likelihood				-105.62			-102.90		
ρ, λ				0.48	(0.06)	***	0.71	(0.07)	***
Returns to scale	**0.94**	**(0.04)**		**0.90**	**(0.04)**		**0.91**	**(0.04)**	

Notes: Standard errors in parentheses. For the two models with spatial autocorrelation, the R² values are ratios of the variance of predicted values to the variance of observed values of the dependent variable (Pisati, 2001). Lagrange multiplier test for ρ = 0: 82.94*** and for λ = 0: 87.55***.
* (**) [***] Significant at the 10% (5%) and [1%] level of error probability.
Source: Own data (2007).

The null hypothesis that ρ and λ are zero can be tested using a Lagrange multiplier test as described by Anselin et al. (1996). For the Quzhou production function, the null hypotheses are rejected at the 1% level in both cases. Therefore, the production function is estimated also with the spatial lag and spatial error model. As can be seen from the output in Table 8.23, some of the coefficients change substantially and the question is, which model should be preferred. According to Anselin (1988) and Minot et al. (2006), the model with the larger spatial autoregressive parameter is likely to reflect the spatial dependence more appropriately. This would favor the spatial error dependence model (since λ is larger than ρ) and would result in a partial production elasticity for land of 0.54.

8.6 Allocative efficiency in the land rental market

For the Quzhou County case study, the gap between land rental prices and the estimated MVP for land is examined in this section. A comparison of actual land rental prices and marginal value products for the factor land can provide an indication for whether land rental prices are actually competitively determined, i.e. based on the value of land, and whether land allocation between villages is allocatively efficient. Compared to other topics related to China's rural economy, few studies look explicitly at how land rental prices are formed. Kuiper and van Tongeren (2005) found for a rice producing village in Jiangxi Province, that land rental prices are generally below the MVP and explained this with the notion that migrating households are willing to forego some of the income from renting out their land as a kind of insurance to maintain use rights to their land. This implies an indirect transfer of the benefits of migration to non-migrating, renting-in households.

This example shows that the interpretation of a gap between rental prices and the MVP is difficult because rental prices are endogenously determined within the villages. This situation is different from the analysis of price inefficiency in input markets, where it is hypothesized that households adjust their MVP for a factor to its unobserved shadow price instead of the exogenously given market price (Ali et al., 1993). Conversely, for the case of Quzhou, high average rental prices compared to the MVP could be an indicator of high demand for land which is not accounted for in the MVP. Possibly, HHs in such villages would also wish to rent in land from other villages, which would improve allocative efficiency.

Because of the difficulties in interpreting a positive or negative gap between the MVP and land rental prices, Vranken and Mathijs (2001) explain allocative inefficiency in the land rental market in Hungary by taking the absolute value of the allocative inefficiency score AI, defined by the authors as

$$AI = \ln\left(MVP_L / w_{rental}\right), \tag{30}$$

where MVP_L is the marginal value product for land and w_{rental} is the observed land rental price farmers pay or receive. This score is bounded at zero and any positive score indicates deviation from the equality of the MVP and land rental prices. Since none of the AI scores were left-censored at zero, Vranken and Mathijs (2001) then regressed the AI scores on household and regional characteristics to explain allocative efficiency.

For the calculation of the MVP in the present study, the average value product (AVP) is multiplied with the partial production elasticity for land. Since the total irrigated area was used as the land input variable for the production function estimated above, the AVP equals the GVAO divided by the total irrigated area. Given an average AVP for the villages in the sample of 1747 ¥ and the estimated partial production elasticity of 0.54 for land, land rental prices lie in almost all cases below the marginal value product for land. Only in 19 villages the land rental price was above the MVP. One explanation for this is that the estimated output elasticity for land is too high. A partial production elasticity of 0.2 would result in an MVP of 349 ¥, which would more closely relate to the average land rental price of 344 ¥.

Before analyzing the gaps between the MVP and rental fees, it needs to be shown that both are at all related to each other. This is done in this section by estimating the determinants of rental prices. Estimating land rental prices when not all units have reported rental prices because a land rental market is nonexistent causes sample selection bias when those observations are omitted. The solution is the Heckman two-step procedure. As described above, in the first step of this approach a probit model is estimated explaining whether an active land rental market exists in a village. In the second step, an OLS-regression is fitted to explain land rental prices. In this equation, the Inverse Mill's Ratio (IMR) accounts for the non-randomness of the sample.

Since 3 villages reported rental activity but could not give any rental price, these were dropped from the model together with 1 village with a missing value in the explanatory variables. The model thus contains 302 observations. Of these, 46 are censored, meaning that no rental activity takes place. The following variables are included in the model (Table 8.24). In the probit model, the dependent variable is a binary variable which takes the value of 1 if the observation is uncensored (i.e. an active land rental market exists) and 0 otherwise. Three independent variables may have an impact on whether a land rental market exists. First, villages with a high share of HHs having exchanged plots (*plot_exch*) may also have a tendency to have an active land rental market. Second, similar to the model explaining the percentage of HHs renting within their village, the share of off-farm income (*sh_off*) and its squared term are expected to have a positive and negative effect, respectively, on the probability that a land rental market exists. Third, the occurrence of land transfers between villages (*outstrans*) is very likely to correlate with a land rental market within a village.

The dependent variable in the OLS model is the reported average land rental price which is explained by the estimated marginal value product (*mvp*). Other variables which could influence the rental price are whether the village keeps reserve land (*reserve*), the percentage of HHs renting in a village (*rent_within*) and the average plot size (*psize*). Reserve land seems to imply land of lower quality, while the percentage of HHs renting could be an indicator of high demand for land and thus high rental fees. Larger plots are expected to increase the value of land, which would be consistent with the negative coefficient of plot size on the probability that a plot is categorized as below average quality as shown in Table 8.4 above. Finally, township dummy variables are included.

The results in Table 8.24 confirm that rental prices are mainly based on the MVP and location specific factors. The variables *rent* and *psize* have the expected signs but are not significant.

Table 8.24   Land rental prices (Heckman two-step procedure)

Variables	Land rental market activity (Probit)			Land rental prices (OLS)		
Constant	0.743	(0.307)	*	333.919	(20.184)	***
plot_exch	0.065	(0.024)	**			
sh_off	-0.003	(0.016)				
sh_off²	-0.000	(0.000)				
outstrans	0.598	(0.188)	**			
mvp				0.147	(0.031)	***
reserve				1.163	(11.040)	
rent_within				0.656	(0.661)	
psize				6.156	(4.340)	
QZ				-105.343	(23.991)	***
IIQ				22.917	(21.238)	
BZ				-69.452	(21.040)	***
AZ				-7.737	(20.237)	
DHD				-59.566	(24.186)	*
HC				-26.659	(20.811)	
YZ				-85.671	(26.575)	**
HNT				-19.930	(20.795)	
ST				63.533	(20.904)	**
Observations	302					
Censored	46					
Uncensored	256					
Wald χ^2 (13)	111.69					
Prob > χ^2	0.00					

Note: Standard errors in parentheses.
* (**) [***] Significant at the 5% (1%) [0.1%] level of error probability.
Source: Own data (2007).

The absolute value of the AI is on average 0.78. Concerning the factors which determine the allocative inefficiency score AI as defined by Vranken and Mathijs (2001), the available data is inconclusive. The score is significantly lower (at the 5% level) in villages with a very active land rental market (≥10% of HHs), which is in line with the expectation that a more active market leads to more competitive prices. The significance disappears, however, when including township dummy variables and other control variables. This indicates that the gap between the productive value of land and rental prices is influenced by other factors which have not been covered in the survey. Furthermore, the inefficiency score AI is very sensitive to the estimated partial production elasticity of land, which may be faulty since few variables could be used in the village-level production function.

9 Main results, policy recommendations and suggestions for further research

9.1 Main results

Agriculture in China is dominated by extremely small, scattered household farms. Land use rights allocated to households by the village collective are contingent on maintaining some level of agricultural production. Since returns from agriculture are not sufficient to support livelihoods, most families earn some kind of off-farm income from sideline activities or migratory employment. Due to their social security function, very few households are willing give up their land use rights and move out of agriculture completely. This situation inhibits a structural change towards larger, more competitive farms. With this background, the objective of this study was to assess the allocative effects of the emerging rural land rental market and other local tenure arrangements.

To this important issue, this study made the following contributions. First, it highlighted both regional and local heterogeneity in terms of land tenure, agricultural production systems and income opportunities. The household survey in three different provinces in the North China Plain confirmed the expectation that the off-farm labor market and the rural land rental market are closely interlinked. Both off-farm employment and land rental activities were found to be more developed in the prosperous Shandong Province. The labor surplus in agriculture was calculated by comparing the labor demand in the production process with the available labor on-farm. Using secondary data for the calculation of labor demand, the labor surplus was lowest (54%) in Shandong, since in this province the off-farm labor market has already transferred larger shares of the labor force out of agriculture.

At the local level, the Quzhou County case study showed as well that land rental activities increased with increasing shares of off-farm income but decreased again at very high levels of off-farm employment. This was explained by the notion that at very high average levels of off-farm income in a village, the supply as well as the demand for more land again decreases. The rural land rental market in the study region therefore seems to be mainly driven by the off-farm labor market. Given this situation, the question was raised which households mainly specialize in off-farm employment and which households continue working predominantly in agriculture. The descriptive analysis showed that mainly younger, better educated, male family members engage in off-farm employment. The tendency of a higher share of female family members working predominantly in agriculture supports the hypothesis of a "feminization of agriculture". Furthermore, households with higher shares of their labor force working in agriculture are found to overuse nitrogen fertilizer. Also the analysis in a stochastic frontier production framework showed that these households are characterized by lower technical efficiency. This suggested that the off-farm labor market is in fact transferring the more capable labor force out of agriculture, while farming is done predominantly by the elderly, less educated.

Off-farm income contributes slightly more to total income inequality than income from crop and livestock production. However, the analysis of the village-level data suggested that households in villages with poorer access to local off-farm employment are able to compensate this deficit due to their higher land endowment. Villages already seem to be very much specialized into off-farm oriented and agriculturally oriented villages, which could also explain the low level of rental arrangements that transcend villages in Quzhou County. Local off-farm employment was defined in the Quzhou County case study as employment where workers return home daily and such employment was found to mainly depend on the existence of Township and Village Enterprises in the village. Access to such local off-farm employment therefore seems to be given with priority to inhabitants of the village in question, which further suggests that not only imperfections in the land, but also the labor market exist.

The first household survey confirmed that the main constraint for a more developed land rental market is the supply side, but 15% of HHs also responded that agriculture is not profitable enough for renting in additional land, with marked differences between the survey counties. This highlights that not only the supply side needs to be activated but also the incentives to specialize in agriculture. A step in this direction has been made with the abolishment of agricultural taxes and the introduction of direct payments in 2004.

Several indications in this study pointed to the relevance of "village culture" for development and well-being in rural China. Traditional culture and clan ties are being revived. Visits to villages in Quzhou County clearly demonstrated that villages without the fortune of a cooperative culture and good leadership lag behind in the development process. This is an interesting phenomenon that further studies could focus on, but that external policies can hardly influence.

The adverse effects of land fragmentation on resource use and technical efficiency have been difficult to substantiate in this study, which is probably due to the data quality. Nevertheless, farmers have been shown to clearly favor larger plots closer to their homesteads. Also a negative effect of tenure insecurity could not be clearly identified. The use of organic fertilizer in crop production seems to be mainly determined by the availability of manure and not by considerations of long-term effects on soil properties. However, holding a land use right certificate appears to be more relevant than expected. On average, 61% of HHs claimed to possess such certificates. First, the probability of having applied for a credit in the formal or informal credit market was significantly higher for these HHs. Second, these HHs have been allocated more plots and they are less likely to have rented in any land. The underlying effect that holding a certificate has on these outcomes would require further qualitative research.

While the land rental market can play a central role in, first, facilitating an enlargement of farm sizes and, second, guaranteeing a long-term revenue for renting-out households in the form of rental payments, the rural land rental market in China currently does not live up to its potential. In the study area, land rentals are infrequent, small-scale and confined to transfers within villages and often to transfers between relatives or clan members.

A unique contribution of this study is the comparison of current land rental prices across villages. These are found to be correlated with the productive values of land, but are consistently below the estimated MVP. Probably, returns from renting-out can therefore not adequately substitute for own cultivation, also because rental contracts are short-term and insecure. How exactly land rental prices are formed, for example whether lessors or lessees have more power in determining the fee is not known and would require further research.

9.2 Policy recommendations

Based on the findings of this study, this section reflects on the options for China out of the current situation of rural-urban inequality and under-development of agriculture.

In a way, the dichotomy between the thriving Chinese economy in urban areas and the lagging rural sector may seem like a transitory phenomenon which could be expected to resolve over time through the kind of structural change that takes place in other parts of the world. This would be true to the extent that China continues moving from a developing country to an industrialized country. The question is therefore whether any policy interventions are at all needed to facilitate these processes.

In order to encourage the more productive, enterprising households to engage in full-time agriculture, sufficient land needs to be available to establish adequate farm sizes. However, it is unrealistic that in the near future, the off-farm labor market will transfer substantial amounts of households permanently out of agriculture. Even though the largest part of their labor force may already be absorbed by the off-farm sector, land still exerts its basic social security function. Due to the dimensions of the PRC, the establishment of an alternative social security system for the rural population would be extremely costly. Attempts to introduce a rural pension system began in 1990, but the coverage remained with 10% of the rural population low (Zhang, 2005). In its 2004 White Paper on social security, the central government emphasized the separation between social security in rural and urban China: "*In rural areas, the land, as a means of production and livelihood, is owned collectively where the contractual household output-related responsibility system is practiced. Under the influence of China's traditional culture, there is a time-honored tradition of provision by the family, security coming from self-reliance and help from the clan. In accordance with the characteristics of rural socio-economic development, the state's social security measures in rural areas are different from those practiced in cities*" (Anonymous, 2005).

Any policies to promote larger farm sizes should be introduced cautiously and must not ignore the continued dependence of rural households on a minimum amount of land for subsistence. The practice of reserving a part of the village land for rental contracts through a bidding process has been described in this study as a means for providing land to households willing to expand agriculture and generating revenue for the village budget. However, without strict regulations on the contract fees, this practice can lead to exploitation of peasants as the experience with the TFS has shown (Chen and Brown, 2001). Furthermore, it is only appropriate where land is relatively abundant. Moreover, in view of rising global energy costs, the scenario of larger, commercially oriented, mechanized farms in China also has its drawbacks, especially in light of the results of Hu et al. (2004) that there is no cost advantage of North American as compared to Chinese wheat producers.

The heterogeneity of land tenure arrangements as described in this study should not be dismissed prematurely. In fact, allowing this heterogeneity is an interesting feature of Chinese policy making. The "legalization of successful local practice" (Heberer and Schubert, 2006) has led to the establishment of the Household Responsibility System (HRS) as well as the Two-Farmland System (TFS). Another example are the land trusts established in Zhejiang Province. This ability of the Chinese state to adopt what has been proven to work at the local level is remarkable and also underlines the necessity to conduct micro-level studies in order to identify such successful institutional arrangements. Heberer and Schubert (2006) further illustrate that this experimental approach to policy making also takes place in the opposite direction, i.e. from upper to lower levels of the political hierarchy. For example, the Organic Law of the Villagers' Committees was first introduced "for trial implementation" in certain areas before it was adopted nationwide. This approach of piece-wise experimentation with different policies has been quite successful although it is also sometimes criticized as a "muddling through" instead of introducing full-blown, thorough reforms (Heberer and Schubert, 2006; Ho, 2005). However, the concerns about the negative implications of full privatization of rural land rights are probably justified and it seems more promising to further develop and consolidate the local tenure institutions described in this study instead of redefining the whole property paradigm. A benefit of collective land ownership, if practiced properly, that should not be overlooked is that it avoids the problem of landless peasants. In sum, the value of functioning local institutions should not be underestimated although they may appear to be inefficient from a neoclassical perspective (Heidhues et al., 1999).

Moreover, the exclusive focus on tenure insecurity as the main problem of Chinese peasants seems to be too narrow and suffers from preconceptions of what farmers should prefer. The main household survey has shown that frequent land reallocations continue in some parts of the NCP while land allocation remains very stable in others. Furthermore, approval of reallocations is high (64%). In areas with scarce land resources and high dependence on land, reallocaiions are likely to continue to play the important role of guaranteeing equal access to this resource. In other regions where land allocation has become very stable, there seems to be a propensity of parts of the peasantry to enlarge and consolidate their landholdings. This demand is encumbered, however, due to risk aversion, missing market information and imperfections in other factor markets. Policies therefore need to take into account the interlinkages of land, labor and credit markets.

Another concern related to China's agricultural policy is that of the focus on grain self-sufficiency. Although there seem to be no more compulsory planting requirements, Wan and Zhou (2005) state that the Chinese government will probably continue to intervene in grain production whenever this is deemed necessary. However, since Chinese agriculture is generally less competitive in grain production and more competitive in the production of labor intensive crops such as fruits and vegetables (Beghin and Fang, 2000), the currently observed trend of declining grain production may also be desirable from a comparative advantage perspective and this argument would also clearly favor smaller farms (Fan and Chan-Kang, 2005).

As regards farmers' land property rights, further clarification of the individual rights in relation to the rights of the collective is needed. The village collective, as the "management group" governing the common village property has been shown to impose certain restrictions on the use rights of its members, such as the exclusion of nonmembers from access to land. While this narrows the transfer market for land use rights, it is consistent with the definition of common property. A policy towards generally allowing villagers to transfer their land use rights to non-villagers would therefore imply shifting the balance from the *common property regime* towards the *private property regime* – a shift that is not favored by Chinese policy makers (Wang, 2006). Unfortunately, little is known about the decision-making processes within the villages. It would therefore be premature to conclude that such restrictions are imposed on villagers by their leaders against their will. If such restrictions (and other tenure policies such as reallocations) are supported by the majority of the villagers, any intervention by external policies would in fact curtail the status of the collective group as the supreme land owner.

9.3 Suggestions for further research

While there is already a substantial body of literature dealing with the overall topic of this study, the combination of data from various sources with the focus on the situation in a particular county and the explicit modeling of the spatial nature of this data is rare. This approach has been shown to lead to interesting results and the fact that the type of village-level yearbooks as used in this study should in principle be published by all counties in China suggests that similar, comparative studies from other regions of the country could be valuable in order to test the results on village heterogeneity. In particular, the significance of the dichotomy between towns and townships for village development could not be adequately shown in this study since only 4 towns and 6 townships have been compared.

Although a number of studies have attempted to explain the overuse of mineral fertilizer in China, the results are contradictory. A problem that often seems to be overlooked is that of the measurement of nutrient contents in the fertilizer packages applied by farmers. Anecdotal evidence suggests that these are in fact below those indicated on the packages and the overuse may therefore be actually lower than assumed. Studies assessing the perception of fertilizer quality by farmers could substantiate this conjecture.

Some of the reasons for the underdeveloped land rental market resemble very much those found in other transition countries. For example, for the case of Eastern European and Central Asian countries, Swinnen et al. (2006) identify measures that governments should take to support the development of land rental markets. These include safeguarding private property rights, improving access to market information, providing mechanisms for resolving contract disputes and addressing constraints in other markets, for example product, credit and labor markets in order to stimulate both supply of and demand for land. In particular two other socialist countries in transition, Vietnam and Ethiopia, show striking similarities to China with regard to their land tenure system. The government policy of consolidating land holdings through plot exchanges in Vietnam has already been mentioned. Also in Ethiopia, land rentals are restricted to within-village transfers, which is likewise seen as a major obstacle for a more developed land rental market (Berhanu, 2004). These similarities suggest that further studies comparing the situation and possible policy options for these countries could be fruitful.

As a further limitation of this study, the situation of households and villages has only been assessed at one point in time although it is much more informative to look at changes in off-farm activities and land transfers over several years. For further research it is therefore suggested to focus on collecting panel data. This is easier done at the level of villages, due to problems of tracking single households over the years.

References

Admassie, A. (1994). Analysis of production efficiency and the use of modern technology in crop production: A study of smallholders in the central highlands of Ethiopia. Ph.D. thesis. Stuttgart, Germany: University of Hohenheim.

Aigner, D., C. A. K. Lovell, and P. Schmidt. (1977). Formulation and estimation of stochastic frontier production function models. *Journal of Econometrics*, 6, 21-37.

Ali, F., D. Bailey, and A. Parikh. (1993). Price distortions and resource use efficiency in a Pakistani province. *European Review of Agricultural Economics*, 20(1), 35-47.

Alpermann, B. (2001). The post-election administration of Chinese villages. *The China Journal*, 46(July), 45-67.

Anonymous. (2005). Social security in China: Government White Paper (excerpt). *Population and Development Review*, 31(1), 185-189.

Anselin, L. (1988). Spatial econometrics: Methods and models. Dordrecht, The Netherlands: Kluwer.

Anselin, L., A. K. Bera, R. Florax, and M. J. Yoon. (1996). Simple diagnostic tests for spatial dependence. *Regional Science and Urban Economics*, 26(1), 77-104.

Bareth, G. (2003). Möglichkeiten und Grenzen der regionalen agrarumweltrelevanten Modellierung unter Nutzung von GIS in China am Beispiel der Nordchinesischen Tiefebene. Habilitation (postdoctoral lecture qualification). Stuttgart, Germany: University of Hohenheim.

Battese, G. E., and S. S. Broca. (1997). Functional forms of stochastic frontier production functions and models for technical inefficiency effects: A comparative study for wheat farmers in Pakistan. *Journal of Productivity Analysis*, 8, 395-414.

Battese, G. E., and T. J. Coelli. (1995). A model for technical inefficiency effects in a stochastic frontier production function for panel data. *Empirical Economics*, 20(2), 325-332.

Baur, F., J. Baur, and R. Stürmer. (1999). Sachenrecht. München, Germany: C.H. Beck.

Beghin, J. C., and C. Fang. (2000). Competitiveness and protection of Chinese agriculture. *Iowa Ag Review*, 6(4), 9-10.

Benjamin, D. (1995). Can unobserved land quality explain the inverse productivity relationship? *Journal of Development Economics*, 46(1), 51-84.

Benjamin, D., and L. Brandt. (2002). Property rights, labour markets and efficiency in a transition economy: The case of rural China. *Canadian Journal of Economics*, 35(4), 689-716.

Berhanu, A. (2004). Escaping Ethiopia's poverty trap: The case for a second agrarian reform. *The Journal of Modern African Studies*, 42(3), 313-342.

Bichler, B. (2007). Die möglichen Bestimmungsgründe der räumlichen Verteilung des Ökologischen Landbaus in Deutschland. Ph.D. thesis. Stuttgart, Germany: University of Hohenheim.

Binder, J. (2006). Personal communication.

Blarel, B., P. Hazell, F. Place, and J. Quiggin. (1992). The economics of farm fragmentation: Evidence from Ghana and Rwanda. *The World Bank Economic Review*, 6(2), 233-254.

Bowlus, A. J., and T. Sicular. (2003). Moving toward markets? Labor allocation in rural China. *Journal of Development Economics*, 71(2), 561-583.

Brandt, L., J. Huang, and S. Rozelle. (2002). Land rights in rural China: Facts, fictions and issues. *The China Journal*, 47(Jan.), 67-97.

Bromley, D. W. (1989). Property relations and economic development: The other land reform. *World Development*, 17(6), 867-877.

Bromley, D. W. (2005). Property rights and land in ex-socialist states: Lessons of transition for China. In: P. Ho (ed.). Developmental dilemmas: Land reform and institutional change in China. London, UK: Routledge.

Buchenrieder, G. (2005). Non-farm rural employment - review of issues, evidence and policies. *Quarterly Journal of International Agriculture*, 44(1), 3-18.

Burgess, R. (2001). Land and welfare: Theory and evidence from China. Working Paper, London, UK: London School of Economics.

Buschena, D., V. Smith, and H. Di. (2005). Policy reform and farmers' wheat allocation in rural China: A case study. *The Australian Journal of Agricultural and Resource Economics*, 49(2), 143-158.

Cai, Y. (2003). Collective ownership or cadres' ownership? The non-agricultural use of farmland in China. *The China Quarterly*, 175(Sept.), 662-680.

Cao, D. (2001). Fazhi vs/and/or rule of law? A semiotic venture into Chinese law. *International Journal for the Semiotics of Law*, 14(3), 223-247.

Carter, C. A., J. Chen, and B. Chu. (2003). Agricultural productivity growth in China: Farm level versus aggregate measurement. *China Economic Review*, 14(1), 53-71.

Carter, C. A., and A. J. Estrin. (2001). Market reforms versus structural reforms in rural China. *Journal of Comparative Economics*, 29(3), 527-541.

Carter, C. A., and F. Zhong. (1999). Rural wheat consumption in China. *American Journal of Agricultural Economics*, 81(3), 582-592.

Carter, M. R., and Y. Yao. (2002). Local versus global separability in agricultural household models: The factor price equalization effect of land transfer rights. *American Journal of Agricultural Economics*, 84(3), 702-715.

Chakravarty, S. R. (2001). The variance as a subgroup decomposable measure of inequality. *Social Indicators Research*, 53(1), 79-95.

Chambers R. G. (1988). Applied production analysis: A dual approach. Cambridge, UK: Cambridge University Press.

Chan, K. W. (1994). Urbanization and rural-urban migration in China since 1982 - a new baseline. *Modern China*, 20(3), 243-281.

Chen, A. Z., W. E. Huffman, and S. Rozelle. (2003). Technical efficiency of Chinese grain production: A stochastic production frontier approach. Paper presented at the American Agricultural Economics Association Annual Meeting, Montreal, Canada.

Chen, J., C. Tang, Y. Sakura, J. Yu, and Y. Fukushima. (2005). Nitrate pollution from agriculture in different hydrogeological zones of the regional groundwater flow system in the North China Plain. *Hydrogeology Journal*, 13(3), 481-492.

Chen, J., Z. Yu, J. Ouyang, and M. E. F. van Mensvoort. (2006). Factors affecting soil quality changes in the North China Plain: A case study of Quzhou County. *Agricultural Systems*, 91(3), 171-188.

Chen, K., and C. Brown. (2001). Adressing shortcomings in the HRS: Empirical analysis of the Two-Farmland System in Shandong Province. *China Economic Review*, 12(4), 280-292.

Chen, L. (2007). Grain market liberalization and deregulation in China - The mediating role of markets for farm households in Jiangxi Province. Ph.D. thesis. Wageningen: Wageningen University.

Chen, Z., and W. E. Huffman. (2006). County-level agricultural production efficiency in China: A spatial analysis. In: X.-Y. Dong, S. Song, and X. Zhang (eds.). China's agricultural development: Challenges and prospects. Aldershot, UK: Ashgate.

Cheng, E., and Z. Xu. (2004). Rates of interest, credit supply and China's rural development. *Savings and Development*, 2, 131-156.

Cheng, T., and M. Selden. (1994). The origins and social consequences of China's *hukou* system. *The China Quarterly*, 139(Sept.), 644-668.

Cheng, Y.-S. (2006). China's reform of Rural Credit Cooperatives. *The Chinese Economy*, 39(4), 25-40.

Cheng, Y.-S., and S. Tsang. (1994). The changing grain marketing system in China. *The China Quarterly*, 140(Dec.), 1080-1104.

Chin, G. T. (2005). Securing a rural land market: Political economic determinants of institutional change in China's agriculture sector. *Asian Perspective*, 29(4), 209-244.

China Daily. (2004). Grain yield to end decline, June 25, 2004.

China Daily. (2005). Ensuring grain security by setting up "land bank", May 17, 2005.

Choate, A. C. (1997). Local governance in China: An assessment of villagers' committees. Working Paper Series, No. 1. The Asia Foundation.

Chu, N. Y., L. Sung-ko, and T. Shu-ki. (2000). The incidence of surplus labor in rural China: A nonparametric estimation. *Journal of Comparative Economics*, 28(3), 565-580.

Chung, H. (2004). China's rural market development in the reform era. Aldershot, UK: Ashgate.

Cliff, A. D., and J. K. Ord. (1973). Spatial autocorrelation. London, UK: Pion.

Coelli, T. J. (1996). A guide to FRONTIER Version 4.1: A computer program for stochastic frontier production and cost function estimation. CEPA Working Paper, No. 96/07. Armidale, NSW, Australia: Centre for Efficiency and Productivity Analysis, University of New England.

Coelli, T. J., D. S. Prasada Rao, C. J. O'Donnell, and G. E. Battese. (2005). An introduction to efficiency and productivity analysis. 2nd ed. New York, USA: Springer.

Cole, D. H., and P. Z. Grossmann. (2002). The meaning of property rights: Law versus economics? *Land Economics*, 78(3), 317-330.

Colman, D., and T. Young. (1989). Principles of agricultural economics - markets and prices in less developed countries. Wye Studies in Agricultural and Rural Development. Cambridge, UK: Cambridge University Press.

Conning, J. H., and J. A. Robinson. (2007). Property rights and the political organization of agriculture. *Journal of Development Economics*, 82(2), 416-447.

Cui, Z. (various years). Quzhou climate data. Quzhou Experimental Station, Hebei, China.

de Brauw, A. (2003). Are women taking over the farm in China? Working Paper, No. 199. Williamstown, MA, USA: Department of Economics, Williams College.

de Brauw, A., J. Huang, and S. Rozelle. (2000). Responsiveness, flexibility, and market liberalization in China's agriculture. *American Journal of Agricultural Economics*, 82(5), 1133-1139.

de Janvry, A., E. Sadoulet, and Z. Nong. (2005). The role of non-farm incomes in reducing rural poverty and inequality in China. CUDARE Working Paper, No. 1001. Berkeley, CA, USA: Department of Agricultural & Resource Economics, University of California.

Deininger, K. (2003). Land policies for growth and poverty reduction - A World Bank policy research report. Washington, D.C., USA: The World Bank/Oxford University Press.

Deininger, K., and S. Jin. (2002). Land rental markets as an alternative to government reallocation? Equity and efficiency considerations in the Chinese land tenure system. Policy Research Working Paper, No. 2930. Washington, D.C., USA: The World Bank.

Deininger, K., and S. Jin. (2005). The potential of land rental markets in the process of economic development: Evidence from China. *Journal of Development Economics*, 78(1), 241-270.

Deininger, K., and S. Jin. (2006). Securing property rights in transition: Lessons from implementation of China's Rural Land Contracting Law. Paper presented at the American Agricultural Economics Association Annual Meeting, Long Beach, CA, USA.

Deininger, K., and S. Jin. (2007). Land rental markets in the process of rural structural transformation: Productivity and equity impacts from China. Policy Research Working Paper, No. 4454. Washington, D.C., USA: The World Bank.

Deininger, K., S. Jin, and S. Rozelle. (2006). Dynamics of legal change in a decentralized setting: Evidence from China's Rural Land Contracting Law. Paper presented at the Annual Meeting of the Allied Social Science Associations (ASSA), Boston, MA, USA.

Dinh, N. L. (2005). Forest land allocation to households in Northern Vietnam. Ph.D. thesis. Stuttgart, Germany: University of Hohenheim.

Doll, J. P., and F. Orazem. (1984). Production economics: Theory with applications. New York, USA: John Wiley & Sons.

Dougherty, C. (2002). Introduction to econometrics. Oxford, UK: Oxford University Press.

Eggertsson, T. (1990). Economic behavior and institutions. Cambridge, UK: Cambridge University Press.

Epstein, E. J. (1989). The theoretical system of property rights in China's General Principles of Civil Law: Theoretical controversy in the drafting process and beyond. *Law and Contemporary Problems*, 52(2), 177-216.

Fan, J., T. Heberer, and W. Taubmann. (2006). Rural China - Economic and social change in the late twentieth century. London, UK: M.E.Sharpe.

Fan, S. (2000). Technological change, technical and allocative efficiency in Chinese agriculture: The case of rice production in Jiangsu. *Journal of International Development*, 12(1), 1-12.

Fan, S., and C. Chan-Kang. (2005). Is small beautiful? Farm size, productivity, and poverty in Asian agriculture. *Agricultural Economics*, 32(Suppl. 1), 135-146.

Feng, S. (2006). Land rental market and off-farm employment - Rural households in Jiangxi Province, P.R. China. Ph.D. thesis. Wageningen, The Netherlands: Wageningen University.

Fernandez, C., G. Koop, and M. F. J. Steel. (2002). Multiple-output production with undesirable outputs: An application to nitrogen surplus in agriculture. *Journal of the American Statistical Association*, 97(478), 432-442.

Field, A. (2005). Discovering statistics using SPSS for Windows. London, UK: Sage.

Fleisher, B. M., and Y. Liu. (1992). Economies of scale, plot size, human capital, and productivity in Chinese agriculture. *Quarterly Review of Economics and Finance*, 32(3), 112-123.

Fleisher, B. M., and D. T. Yang. (2006). Problems of China's rural labor markets and rural urban migration. *The Chinese Economy*, 39(3), 6-25.

Furubotn, E. G., and S. Pejovich. (1972). Property rights and economic theory: A survey of recent literature. *Journal of Economic Literature*, 10(4), 1137-1162.

Furubotn, E. G., and S. Pejovich. (1974). The economics of property rights. Cambridge, MA, USA: Ballinger.

Gale, F., F. Lohmar, and F. Tuan. (2005). China's new farm subsidies. Electronic Outlook Report from the Economic Research Service, No. WRS-05-01. Washington, D.C., USA: United States Department of Agriculture.

Gray, W., and H. R. Zheng. (1989). General Principles of Civil Law of the People's Republic of China. *Law and Contemporary Problems*, 52(2), 27-57.

Greene, W. H. (2003). Econometric analysis. 5th ed. New Jersey, USA: Prentice Hall.

Guo, S. (2003). The ownership reform in China: What direction and how far? *Journal of Contemporary China*, 12(36), 553-573.

Guo, Z., and T. P. Bernstein. (2004). The impact of elections on the village structure of power: The relations between the village committees and the Party branches. *Journal of Contemporary China*, 13(39), 257–275.

Gustafsson, B., and L. Shi. (2002). Income inequality within and across counties in rural China 1988 and 1995. *Journal of Development Economics*, 69(1), 179-204.

Hamilton, L. C. (2004). Statistics with Stata. Belmont, CA, USA: Brooks/Cole.

Hardin, G. (1968). The tragedy of the commons. *Science*, 162(3859), 1243-1248.

Hazell, P. (1982). Instability in Indian foodgrain production. Research Report, No. 30. Washington D.C., USA: International Food Policy Research Institute.

Healey, J. F. (1999). Statistics - A tool for social research. 5th ed. Belmont, CA, USA: Wadsworth.

Hebei Province Statistical Bureau. (2006). Hebei Statistical Yearbook. Beijing, China: China Statistics Press.

Heberer, T., and G. Schubert. (2006). Political reform and regime legitimacy in contemporary China. *Asien*, 99(Apr.), 9-28.

Heerink, N., M. Kuiper, and X. Shi. (2006). China's new rural income support policy: Impacts on grain production and rural income inequality. *China & World Economy*, 14(6), 58-69.

Heidhues, F., C. Karege, B. Schäfer, and G. Schrieder. (1999). The social dimension of policy reform. Research in Development Economics and Policy, Discussion Paper, No. 02/99. Stuttgart, Germany: University of Hohenheim.

Henan Province Statistical Bureau. (2006). Henan Statistical Yearbook. Beijing, China: China Statistics Press.

Hertel, T., and Z. Fan. (2006). Labor market distortions, rural-urban inequality and the opening of China's economy. *Economic Modelling*, 23(1), 76-109.

Ho, P. (2001). Who owns China's land? Policies, property rights, and deliberate institutional ambiguity. *The China Quarterly*, 166(June), 394-421.

Ho, P. (2005). Institutions in transition - Land ownership, property rights and social conflict in China. Oxford, UK: Oxford University Press.

Holland, L. (2000). Running dry: Northern China's water supply is dwindling fast - but does Beijing have the political will to stop the wastage? *Far Eastern Economic Review*, 3, 18-19.

Honoré, A. M. (1961). Ownership. In: A. G. Guest (ed.). Oxford Essays in Jurisprudence. Oxford, UK: Oxford University Press.

Hsing, Y.-T. (2006). Brokering power and property in China's townships. *The Pacific Review*, 19(1), 103-124.

Hu, K., Y. Huang, H. Li, B. Li, D. Chen, and R. E. White. (2005). Spatial variability of shallow groundwater level, electrical conductivity and nitrate concentration, and risk assessment of nitrate contamination in North China Plain. *Environment International*, 31(6), 896 - 903.

Hu, R. (2005). Economic development and the implementation of village elections in rural China. *Journal of Contemporary China*, 14(44), 427-444.

Hu, X., W. Tu, and X. Fang. (2004). An analysis and comparison of wheat production competitiveness between China and the USA. *Journal of Economic Issues*, 38(4), 1074-1082.

Huang, F. X. (2004). The path to clarity: Development of property rights in China. *Columbia Journal of Asian Law*, 17(2), 191-223.

Hung, P. V., G. MacAulay, and S. P. Marsh. (2007). The economics of land fragmentation in the north of Vietnam. *The Australian Journal of Agricultural and Resource Economics*, 51(2), 195-211.

ILCA. (1990). Livestock systems research manual, Volume 1. ILCA Working paper, No. 1. Addis Ababa, Ethiopia: International Livestock Center for Africa.

IRTG. (2003). International Research Training Group "Modeling material flows and production systems for sustainable resource use in intensified crop production in the North China Plain". Stuttgart, Germany: University of Hohenheim (unpublished).

IRTG. (2005). Household survey.

Jacoby, H. G., G. Li, and S. Rozelle. (2002). Hazards of expropriation: Tenure insecurity and investment in rural China. *American Economic Review*, 92(5), 1420-1447.

Jenkins, S. P. (1999). sg104: Analysis of income distributions. *Stata Technical Bulletin*, 48, 4-18.

Jia, X. (2007). Taking the hands off the rural credit market: An evidence from China. Paper presented at the IAMO Forum 2007, IAMO, Halle (Saale), Germany.

Jia, X., and A. Fock. (2007). Thirty years of agricultural transition in China (1977-2007) and the "New Rural Campaign". Paper presented at the 106th seminar of the European Association of Agricultural Economists, Montpellier, France.

Jia, X., and P. Guo. (2007). Evolution of rural financial market in China: An institutional "Lock in" or gradualism? Paper presented at the 106th seminar of the European Association of Agricultural Economists, Montpellier, France.

Just, R. E., D. Zilberman, E. Hochman, and Z. Bar-Shiva. (1990). Input allocation in multicrop systems. American Journal of Agricultural Economics, 72(1), 200-209.

Kaneko, S., K. Tanaka, and T. Toyota. (2004). Water efficiency of agricultural production in China: Regional comparison from 1999 to 2002. International Journal of Agricultural Resources, Governance and Ecology, 3(3/4), 231-251.

Ke, B., G. Wan, and L. Wu. (2003). China's agriculture after WTO accession: Policy adjustment, trade development and market integration. Paper presented at the international conference "Sharing the prosperity of globalization", Helsinki, Finland.

Keil, A. (2004). The socio-economic impact of ENSO-related drought on farm households in Central Sulawesi, Indonesia. Ph.D. thesis. Göttingen, Germany: University of Göttingen.

Kendy, E., D. J. Molden, T. S. Steenhuis, L. Liu, and J. Wang. (2003). Policies drain the North China Plain - Agricultural policy and groundwater depletion in Luancheng County, 1949-2000. Research Report, No. 71. Colombo, Sri Lanka: International Water Management Institute.

Kodde, D. A., and F. C. Palm. (1986). Wald criteria for jointly testing equality and inequality restrictions. Econometrica, 54(5), 1243-1248.

Kong, X., F. Zhang, Y. Xu, and W. Qi. (2003). Arable land change and its driving forces in intensive agricultural region - the case of Quzhou County in Hebai Province (sic!). Resources Science, 25(3), 57-63.

Kueh, Y. Y. (1984). Fertilizer supplies and foodgrain production in China, 1952-1982. Food Policy, 9(3), 219-231.

Kuiper, M., and F. van Tongeren. (2005). Growing together or growing apart? A village level study of the impact of the Doha round on rural China. Policy Research Working Paper, No. 2696. Washington D.C., USA: The World Bank.

Kumbhakar, S. C., and C. A. K. Lovell. (2000). Stochastic frontier analysis. Cambridge, UK: Cambridge University Press.

Kung, J. K. (1995). Equal entitlement versus tenure security under a regime of collective property rights: Peasants' preference for institutions in post-reform Chinese agriculture. Journal of Comparative Economics, 21(1), 82-111.

Kung, J. K. (2000). Common property rights and land reallocations in rural China: Evidence from a village survey. *World Development*, 28(4), 701-719.

Kung, J. K. (2002a). Chapter 3. The role of property rights in China's rural reforms and development - A review of facts and issues. *The Chinese Economy*, 35(3), 52-70.

Kung, J. K. (2002b). Off-farm labor markets and the emergence of land rental markets in rural China. *Journal of Comparative Economics*, 30(2), 395-414.

Kung, J. K. (2006). Do secure land use rights reduce fertility? The case of Meitan County in China. *Land Economics*, 82(1), 36-55.

Kung, J. K., and Y. Cai. (2000). Property rights and fertilizing practices in rural China - Evidence from Northern Jiangsu. *Modern China*, 26(3), 276-308.

Kung, J. K., and Y. Lee. (2001). So what if there is income inequality? The distributive consequence of nonfarm employment in rural China. *Economic Development and Cultural Change*, 50(1), 19-46.

Kung, J. K., and S. Liu. (1997). Farmers' preferences regarding ownership and land tenure in post-Mao China: Unexpected evidence from eight counties. *The China Journal*, 38(July), 33-63.

Li, G., S. Rozelle, and J. Huang. (2000). Land rights, farmer investment incentives and agricultural production in China. Working Paper, No. 00-024. Davis, CA, USA: University of California Davis.

Li, P. (2003). Rural land tenure reforms in China: Issues, regulations and prospects for additional reform. In: P. Groppo (ed.). Land Reform - Land settlement and cooperatives. Rome, Italy: FAO. pp. 59-72.

Li, X., S. Fan, X. Luo, and X. Zhang. (2006). Village inequality in Western China: Implications for development strategy in lagging regions. DSGD Discussion Paper, No. 31. Washington, D.C., USA: International Food Policy Research Institute.

Li, Y., and Y.-S. Xi. (2006). Married women's rights to land in China's traditional farming areas. *Journal of Contemporary China*, 15(49), 621-636.

Li, Z., and J. Bruce. (2005). Gender, landlessness and equity in rural China. In: P. Ho (ed.). Developmental dilemmas: Land reform and institutional change in China. London, UK: Routledge.

Liang, W., H. Lü, A. Xia, G. Wang, F. Qin, Z. Yang, and Y. Lü. (2006). A preliminary analysis on the yield gap of winter wheat between demonstration plots and farmers' fields. *Journal of Food, Agriculture & Environment*, 4(3/4), 143-146.

Liefert, W. M., B. Gardner, and E. Serova. (2005). Allocative efficiency in Russian agriculture: The case of fertilizer and grain. Working Paper, No. 03-05. College Park, MD, USA: The University of Maryland.

Lin, G. C. S., and P. Ho. (2003). China's land resources and land-use change: Insights from the 1996 land survey. Land Use Policy, 20(2), 87-107.

Lin, J. Y. (1992). Rural reforms and agricultural growth in China. American Economic Review, 82(Mar.), 34-51.

Lin, J. Y. (2004). How did China feed itself in the past? How will China feed itself in the future? In: S. Liu, and D. Luo (eds.). Can China feed itself? Chinese scholars on China's food issue. Beijing, China: Foreign Languages Press.

Lin, Z., and L. Zhang. (2006). Gender, land and local heterogeneity. Journal of Contemporary China, 15(49), 637-650.

Liu, C., X. Yao, W. Lavely et al. (1996). China Administrative Regions GIS Data: 1:1M, County Level, 1990. Published and disseminated by the Center for International Earth Science Information Network (CIESIN). ftp://ftpserver.ciesin.org/pub/data/China/adm_bnd/CTSAR90.bnd90/. November 28, 2007.

Liu, S., and D. Luo. (2004). Can China feed itself? Beijing, China: Foreign Languages Press.

Liu, Y., F. Bode, Z. Yu, and R. Doluschitz. (2007). Land use simulation in the North China Plain under different scenarios - An integrated GIS approach. Paper presented at the Conference on the Science and Education of Land Use, Washington, D.C., USA.

Lohmar, B. (2006). Feeling for stones but not crossing the river: China's rural land tenure after twenty years of reform. The Chinese Economy, 39(4), 85-102.

Lohmar, B., A. Somwaru, and K. Wiebe. (2002). The ongoing reform of land tenure policies in China. Agricultural Outlook, 294, 15-18.

Lohmar, B., Z. Zhang, and A. Somwaru. (2001). Land rental market development and agricultural production in China. Paper presented at the Annual Meeting of the American Agricultural Economics Association, Chicago, IL, USA.

Long, S. J. (1997). Regression models for categorical and limited dependent variables. Thousand Oaks, CA, USA: Sage.

Löw, D. (2003). Crop farming in China - Technology, markets, institutions and the use of pesticides. Ph.D. thesis. Zurich, Switzerland: Eidgenössische Technische Hochschule.

Meeusen, W., and J. van den Broeck. (1977). Efficiency estimation from Cobb-Douglas production functions with composed error. *International Economic Review*, 18(2), 435-444.

Ministry of Agriculture of the People's Republic of China. (2004). China agricultural development report. Beijing, China: China Agriculture Press.

Minot, N., B. Baulch, and M. Epprecht. (2006). Poverty and inequality in Vietnam: Spatial patterns and geographic determinants. Research Report, No. 148. Washington, D.C., USA: International Food Policy Research Institute.

Mood, M. S. (2005). Opportunists, predators and rogues: The role of local state relations in shaping Chinese rural development. *Journal of Agrarian Change*, 5(2), 217-250.

Moran, P. (1948). The interpretation of statistical maps. *Journal of the Royal Statistical Society, Series B*, 10, 243-251.

Morduch, J., and T. Sicular. (2002). Rethinking inequality decomposition, with evidence from rural China. *The Economic Journal*, 112(Jan.), 93-106.

National Bureau of Statistics of China. (2006). China Statistical Yearbook. Beijing, China: China Statistics Press.

National Bureau of Statistics of China. (various years). National compilation of costs and revenues of agricultural products (*Quan guo nong chan pin cheng ben shou yi zi liao hui bian*). Beijing, China: China Statistics Press.

Nee, V., and S. Su. (1990). Institutional change and economic growth in China: The view from the villages. *Journal of Asian Studies*, 49(1), 3-25.

Nguyen, T., and E. Cheng. (1996). Land fragmentation and farm productivity in China in the 1990s. *China Economic Review*, 7(2), 169-180.

Nickum, J. E. (2003). Irrigated area figures as bureaucratic construction of knowledge: The case of China. *Water Resources Development*, 19(2), 249-262.

Ostrom, E., J. Burger, C. B. Field, R. B. Norgaard, and D. Policansky. (1999). Revisiting the commons - Local lessons, global challenges. *Science*, 284(5412), 278-282.

Pang, L., A. de Brauw, and S. Rozelle. (2004). Working until dropping: Employment behavior of the elderly in rural China. Working Paper, No. 201. Williamstown, MA, USA: Williams College.

Pei, X. (1998). Rural industry - Institutional aspects of China's economic transformation. In: F. Christiansen, and J. Zhang (eds.). Village Inc. - Chinese rural society in the 1990s. Richmond, VA, USA: Curzon.

Pemsl, D., H. Waibel, and A. P. Gutierrez. (2005). Why do some Bt-Cotton farmers in China continue to use high levels of pesticides? *International Journal of Agricultural Sustainability*, 3, 44-56.

Perkins, T. (2003). Entrepreneurial fiends and honest farmers: Explaining intravillage inequality in a rural Chinese township. *Economic Development and Cultural Change*, 51(3), 719-751.

Pieke, F. N. (2005). The politics of rural land use planning. In: P. Ho (ed.). Developmental dilemmas: Land reform and institutional change in China. London, UK: Routledge.

Pisati, M. (2001). sg162: Tools for spatial data analysis. *Stata Technical Bulletin*, 60, 21-37.

PRC. (1998). Organic Law of the Villagers' Committees of the People's Republic of China. www.lawinfochina.com. February 16, 2008.

PRC. (2000a). The Guarantee Law of the People's Republic of China. Beijing, China: Foreign Languages Press.

PRC. (2000b). The Land Administration Law of the People's Republic of China. Beijing, China: Foreign Languages Press.

PRC. (2004a). Constitution of the People's Republic of China. Beijing, China: Foreign Languages Press.

PRC. (2004b). Law of the People's Republic of China on Land Contract in Rural Areas. Beijing, China: Law Press China.

Prosterman, R., T. Hanstad, and P. Li. (1998). Large-scale farming in China: An appropriate policy? *Journal of Contemporary Asia*, 28(1), 74-102.

Qaim, M., and D. Zilberman. (2003). Yield effects of genetically modified crops in developing countries. *Science*, 299(5608), 900-902.

Qiao, F., S. Rozelle, B. Lohmar, L. Zhang, and J. Huang. (2003). Producer benefits from input market and trade liberalization: The case of fertilizer in China. *American Journal of Agricultural Economics*, 85(5), 1223-1227.

Quzhou County Agricultural Bureau. (2006). Zong he nongye zi yuan qu hua xin bian. Quzhou, Hebei, China.

Quzhou County Statistical Bureau. (various years). Quzhou Statistical Yearbook. Quzhou, Hebei, China.

Rahman, S. (2003). Profit efficiency among Bangladeshi rice farmers. *Food Policy*, 28(5/6), 487-503.

Reinhard, S., C. A. K. Lovell, and G. Thijssen. (1999). Econometric estimation of technical and environmental efficiency: An application to Dutch dairy farms. *American Journal of Agricultural Economics*, 81(1), 44-60.

Reinhard, S., C. A. K. Lovell, and G. Thijssen. (2000). Environmental efficiency with multiple environmentally detrimental variables; estimated with SFA and DEA. *European Journal of Operational Research*, 121(2), 287-303.

Reisch, E., and E. B. Vermeer. (1992). Land reform policy in China: Political guidelines and tendencies. In: E. B. Vermeer (ed.). From peasant to entrepreneur - growth and change in rural China: Papers originating from the second European conference on agriculture and rural development in China. Wageningen, The Netherlands: Pudoc. pp. 15-20.

Rozelle, S. (1994). Rural industrialization and increasing inequality: Emerging patterns in China's reforming economy. *Journal of Comparative Economics*, 19(3), 362-391.

Rozelle, S., L. Brandt, G. Li, and J. Huang. (2005). Land tenure in China: Facts, fictions and issues. In: P. Ho (ed.). Developmental dilemmas: Land reform and institutional change in China. London, UK: Routledge.

Rozelle, S., and G. Li. (1998). Village leaders and land-rights formation in China. *American Economic Review*, 88(2), 433-438.

Rozelle, S., A. Park, J. Huang, and H. Jin. (1997). Liberalization and rural market integration in China. *American Journal of Agricultural Economics*, 79(2), 635-642.

Schmidt, P., and C. A. K. Lovell. (1979). Estimating technical and allocative inefficiency relative to stochastic production and cost frontiers. *Journal of Econometrics*, 9(3), 343-366.

Schwarzwalder, B., R. Prosterman, J. Ye, J. Riedinger, and P. Li. (2002). An update on China's rural land tenure reforms: Analysis and recommendations based on a seventeen-province survey. *Columbia Journal of Asian Law*, 16(1), 142-225.

Shah, T., M. Giordano, and J. Wang. (2004). Irrigation institutions in a dynamic economy: What is China doing differently from India? *Economic and Political Weekly*, July 31st, 3452-3461.

Shandong Province Statistical Bureau. (2006). Shandong Statistical Yearbook. Beijing, China: China Statistics Press.

Shorrocks, A. F. (1982). Inequality decomposition by factor components. *Econometrica*, 50, 193-212.

Singh, I., L. Squire, and J. Strauss. (1986). Agricultural household models - Extensions, applications and policy. Baltimore, MD, USA: John Hopkins University Press.

Skoufias, E. (1994). Using shadow wages to estimate labor supply of agricultural households. *American Journal of Agricultural Economics*, 76(2), 215-227.

Suresh, A., and T. R. K. Reddy. (2006). Resource-use efficiency of paddy cultivation in Peechi command areas of Thrissur District of Kerala: An economic analysis. *Agricultural Economics Research Review*, 19(Jan.-Jun.), 159-171.

Swinnen, J. F. M., L. Vranken, and V. Stanley. (2006). Emerging challenges of land rental markets: A review of available evidence for the Europe and Central Asia region. Europe and Central Asia Chief Economist's Regional Working Paper Series, No. 1(4). Washington, D.C., USA: The World Bank.

Tan, S. (2005). Land fragmentation and rice production: A case study of small farms in Jiangxi Province, P. R. China. Ph.D. thesis. Wageningen, The Netherlands: Wageningen University.

Tan, S. (2007). Personal communication.

Taubmann, W. (1997). Migration into rural towns (*zhen*) - Some results of a research project on rural urbanization in China. In: T. Scharping (ed.). Floating population and migration in China. The impact of economic reforms. Hamburg, Germany: Mitteilungen des Instituts für Asienkunde, 284.

Tian, W., and G. H. Wan. (2000). Technical efficiency and its determinants in China's grain production. *Journal of Productivity Analysis*, 13(2), 159-174.

Van Banning, T. R. G. (2002). The human right to property. Antwerpen, Belgium: intersentia.

Vermeer, E. B. (2004). Egalitarianism and the land question in China - A survey of three thousand households in industrializing Wuxi and agricultural Baoding. *China Information*, 28(1), 107-140.

von Senger, H. (1996). Einführung in das chinesische Recht. JuS Schriftenreihe Ausländisches Recht. München, Germany: C.H. Beck.

Vranken, L., and E. Mathijs. (2001). The allocative efficiency of land rental markets in transition agriculture. Paper presented at the American Agricultural Economics Association Annual Meeting, Chicago, IL, USA.

Wan, G., and Z. Zhou. (2005). Income inequality in rural China: Regression-based decomposition using household data. *Review of Development Economics*, 9(1), 107-120.

Wan, G. H., and E. Cheng. (2001). Effects of land fragmentation and returns to scale in the Chinese farming sector. *Applied Economics*, 33(2), 183 - 194.

Wang, J., E. J. Wailes, and G. L. Cramer. (1996). A shadow-price frontier measurement of profit efficiency in Chinese agriculture. *American Journal of Agricultural Economics*, 78(1), 146-156.

Wang, J., Z. Xu, J. Huang, and S. Rozelle. (2003). Incentives to managers and participation of farmers: Which one matters for water management reform in China? Working Paper, No. 03-E17. Beijing, China: Center for Chinese Agricultural Policy.

Wang, L. (2006). Rural land ownership reform in China's property law. *Frontiers of Law in China*, 3, 311-328.

Wang, Q., C. Halbrendt, and S. R. Johnson. (1996). Grain production and environmental management in China's fertilizer economy. *Journal of Environmental Management*, 47(3), 283-296.

Wang, W. (2005). Land use rights - Legal perspectives and pitfalls for land reform. In: P. Ho (ed.). Developmental dilemmas: Land reform and institutional change in China. London, UK: Routledge.

Wooldridge, J. (2006). Introductory econometrics - A modern approach. Mason, OH, USA: Thomson South-Western.

World Resources Institute. (2007). Earth Trends: Environmental Information. http://earthtrends.wri.org. November 28, 2007.

Wu, D., Q. Yu, C. Lu, and H. Hengsdijk. (2006). Quantifying production potentials of winter wheat in the North China Plain. *European Journal of Agronomy*, 24(3), 226-235.

Wu, Z. (2005). Does size matter in Chinese farm household production? Paper presented at the Agricultural Economics Society Annual Conference, University of Nottingham, Nottingham, UK.

Wu, Z. (2006). Land distributional and income effects of the Chinese land rental market. Paper presented at the International Association of Agricultural Economists Conference, Gold Coast, Australia.

Yang, X. (2008). Personal communication.

Yang, D. T. (1997). China's land arrangements and rural labor mobility. *China Economic Review*, 8(2), 101-115.

Yang, F. (2004). Chinese government. Beijing, China: Foreign Languages Press.

Yang, H., X. H. Zhang, and A. J. B. Zehnder. (2003). Water scarcity, pricing mechanism and institutional reform in northern China irrigated agriculture. *Agricultural Water Management*, 61(2), 143-161.

Yao, Y. (2006). Village elections, accountability and income distribution in rural China. *China & World Economy*, 14(6), 20-38.

Ye, Q., and S. Rozelle. (1994). Fertilizer demand in China's reforming economy. *Canadian Journal of Agricultural Economics*, 42(2), 191-207.

You, L. (2006). Land use change and sustainability of Chinese grain production. Paper presented at the international conference "Transition towards sustainable rural resource use in rural China", Kunming, China.

Yu, L., R. Luo, and L. Zhang. (2007). Decomposing income inequality and policy implications in rural China. *China & World Economy*, 15(2), 44-58.

Zhang, B., and C. A. Carter. (1997). Reforms, the weather, and productivity growth in China's grain sector. *American Journal of Agricultural Economics*, 79(4), 1266-1277.

Zhang, L., A. de Brauw, and S. Rozelle. (2004). China's rural labor market development and its gender implications. *China Economic Review*, 15(2), 230- 247.

Zhang, L., R. Luo, C. Liu, and S. Rozelle. (2006). Investing in rural China - Tracking China's commitment to modernization. *The Chinese Economy*, 39(4), 57-84.

Zhang, L., S. Rozelle, C. Liu, S. Olivia, A. de Brauw, and Q. Li. (2006). Is feminization of agriculture occurring in China? Debunking the myth and measuring the consequence of women's participation in agriculture. Working Paper. Palo Alto, CA, USA: Stanford University.

Zhang, Q. F., Q. Ma, and X. Xu. (2004). Development of land rental markets in rural Zhejiang: Growth of off-farm jobs and institution building. *The China Quarterly*, 180(Dec.), 1031-1049.

Zhang, W. (2005). Sozialwesen in China. Hamburg, Germany: Dr. Kovač.

Zhang, X., and S. Fan. (2001). Estimating crop-specific production technologies in Chinese agriculture: A generalized maximum entropy approach. *American Journal of Agricultural Economics*, 83(2), 379-388.

Zhao, S. (2006). Township-village relations - Disconnection in the midst of control. *Chinese Sociology and Anthropology*, 39(2), 74-93.

Zhao, Y., and G. J. Wen. (1999). Land holding and social security in rural China. *Homo oeconomicus*, 16(2), 157-176.

Zhen, L., and J. K. Routray. (2002). Groundwater resource use practices and implications for sustainable agricultural development in the North China Plain: A case study in Ningjin County of Shandong Province, PR China. *Water Resources Development*, 18(4), 581-593.

Zhen, L., J. K. Routray, M. A. Zoebisch, G. Chen, G. Xie, and S. Cheng. (2005). Three dimensions of sustainability of farming practices in the North China Plain. A case study from Ningjin County of Shandong Province, PR China. *Agriculture, Ecosystems and Environment*, 105(3), 507-522.

Zhen, L., M. Zoebisch, G. Chen, and Z. Feng. (2006). Sustainability of farmers' soil fertility management practices: A case study in the North China Plain. *Journal of Environmental Management*, 79(4), 409-419.

Zhou, D., and X. Yang. (2004). Power sharing in rural China behind social transformation - traditional culture, town and village enterprises and social transformation. *Chinese Sociology and Anthropology*, 36(4), 5-43.

Zhou, Z.-Y., and W.-M. Tian. (2005). Grains in China - Foodgrain, feedgrain and world trade. Hants, UK: Ashgate.

Zhu, K., R. Prosterman, J. Ye, P. Li, J. Riedinger, and Y. Ouyang. (2006). The rural land question in China: Analysis and recommendations based on a seventeen-province survey. *Journal of International Law and Politics*, 38(4), 761-839.

Zhu, L., and Z. Jiang. (1993). From brigade to village community: The land tenure system and rural development in China. *Cambridge Journal of Economics*, 17(4), 441-461.

Zhu, N., and X. Luo. (2006). Nonfarm activity and rural income inequality: A case study of two provinces in China. Policy Research Working Paper, No. 3811. Washington, D.C., USA: The World Bank.

Zuo, T., X. Li, and X. Xu. (2005). Agricultural science and technology and extension services: Problems and challenges. In: V. Römheld, R. Doluschitz, F. Zhang, R. Jayakumar, and M. Wolff (eds.). Promoting environmentally-friendly agricultural production in China: Resource management for sustainable intensive agriculture systems. Beijing, China: Tsinghua University Press.

Zweig, D. (1992). Urbanizing rural China: Bureaucratic authority and local autonomy. In: K. G. Lieberthal, and D. M. Lampton (eds.). Bureaucracy, politics, and decision making in post-Mao China. Berkeley, CA, USA: University of California Press. pp. 334-363.

Appendix

The People's Republic of China

Source: Adapted from Liu et al. (1996).

The North China Plain (NCP)

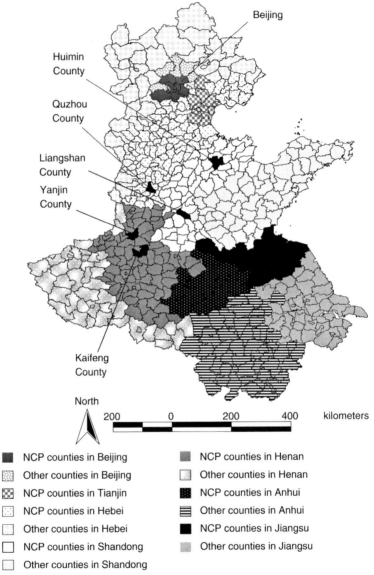

Beijing

Huimin County

Quzhou County

Liangshan County

Yanjin County

Kaifeng County

North

200   0   200   400   kilometers

■ NCP counties in Beijing	▨ NCP counties in Henan
▨ Other counties in Beijing	▧ Other counties in Henan
▨ NCP counties in Tianjin	▦ NCP counties in Anhui
⬚ NCP counties in Hebei	☰ Other counties in Anhui
□ Other counties in Hebei	■ NCP counties in Jiangsu
□ NCP counties in Shandong	▨ Other counties in Jiangsu
□ Other counties in Shandong	

Source: Adapted from Bareth (2003).

Development Economics and Policy

Series edited by Franz Heidhues, Joachim von Braun and Manfred Zeller

Band 1   Andrea Fadani: Agricultural Price Policy and Export and Food Production in Cameroon. A Farming Systems Analysis of Pricing Policies. The Case of Coffee-Based Farming Systems. 1999.

Band 2   Heike Michelsen: Auswirkungen der Währungsunion auf den Strukturanpassungsprozeß der Länder der afrikanischen Franc-Zone. 1995.

Band 3   Stephan Bea: Direktinvestitionen in Entwicklungsländern. Auswirkungen von Stabilisierungsmaßnahmen und Strukturreformen in Mexiko. 1995.

Band 4   Franz Heidhues / François Kamajou: Agricultural Policy Analysis – Proceedings of an International Seminar, held at the University of Dschang, Cameroon on May 26 and 27 1994, funded by the European Union under the Science and Technology Program (STD). 1996.

Band 5   Elke M. Förster: Protection or Liberalization? A Policy Analysis of the Korean Beef Sector. 1996.

Band 6   Gertrud Schrieder: The Role of Rural Finance for Food Security of the Poor in Cameroon. 1996.

Band 7   Nestor R. Ahoyo Adjovi: Economie des Systèmes de Production intégrant la Culture de Riz au Sud du Bénin: Potentialités, Contraintes et Perspectives. 1996.

Band 8   Jenny Müller: Income Distribution in the Agricultural Sector of Thailand. Empirical Analysis and Policy Options. 1996.

Band 9   Michael Brüntrup: Agricultural Price Policy and its Impact on Production, Income, Employment and the Adoption of Innovations. A Farming Systems Based Analysis of Cotton Policy in Northern Benin. 1997.

Band 10   Justin Bomda: Déterminants de l'Epargne et du Crédit, et leurs Implications pour le Développement du Système Financier Rural au Cameroun. 1998.

Band 11   John M. Msuya: Nutrition Improvement Projects in Tanzania: Implementation, Determinants of Performance, and Policy Implications. 1998.

Band 12   Andreas Neef: Auswirkungen von Bodenrechtswandel auf Ressourcennutzung und wirtschaftliches Verhalten von Kleinbauern in Niger und Benin. 1999.

Band 13   Susanna Wolf (ed.): The Future of EU-ACP Relations. 1999.

Band 14   Franz Heidhues / Gertrud Schrieder (eds.): Romania – Rural Finance in Transition Economies. 2000.

Band 15   Katinka Weinberger: Women's Participation. An Economic Analysis in Rural Chad and Pakistan. 2000.

Band 16   Christof Batzlen: Migration and Economic Development. Remittances and Investments in South Asia: A Case Study of Pakistan. 2000.

Band 17   Matin Qaim: Potential Impacts of Crop Biotechnology in Developing Countries. 2000.

Band 18   Jean Senahoun: Programmes d'ajustement structurel, sécurité alimentaire et durabilité agricole. Une approche d'analyse intégrée, appliquée au Bénin. 2001.

Band 19   Torsten Feldbrügge: Economics of Emergency Relief Management in Developing Countries. With Case Studies on Food Relief in Angola and Mozambique. 2001.

Band 20   Claudia Ringler: Optimal Allocation and Use of Water Resources in the Mekong River Basin: Multi-Country and Intersectoral Analyses. 2001.

Band 21   Arnim Kuhn: Handelskosten und regionale (Des-)Integration. Russlands Agrarmärkte in der Transformation. 2001.

Band 22   Ortrun Anne Gronski: Stock Markets and Economic Growth. Evidence from South Africa. 2001.

Band 23   Patrick Webb / Katinka Weinberger (eds.): Women Farmers. Enhancing Rights, Recognition and Productivity. 2001.

Band 24   Mingzhi Sheng: Lebensmittelkonsum und -konsumtrends in China. Eine empirische Analyse auf der Basis ökonometrischer Nachfragemodelle. 2002.

Band 25   Maria Iskandarani: Economics of Household Water Security in Jordan. 2002.

Band 26   Romeo Bertolini: Telecommunication Services in Sub-Saharan Africa. An Analysis of Access and Use in the Southern Volta Region in Ghana. 2002.

Band 27   Dietrich Müller-Falcke: Use and Impact of Information and Communication Technologies in Developing Countries' Small Businesses. Evidence from Indian Small Scale Industry. 2002.

Band 28   Wolfram Erhardt: Financial Markets for Small Enterprises in Urban and Rural Northern Thailand. Empirical Analysis on the Demand for and Supply of Financial Services, with Particular Emphasis on the Determinants of Credit Access and Borrower Transaction Costs. 2002.

Band 29   Wensheng Wang: The Impact of Information and Communication Technologies on Farm Households in China. 2002.

Band 30   Shyamal K. Chowdhury: Institutional and Welfare Aspects of the Provision and Use of Information and Communication Technologies in the Rural Areas of Bangladesh and Peru. 2002.

Band 31   Annette Luibrand: Transition in Vietnam. Impact of the Rural Reform Process on an Ethnic Minority. 2002.

Band 32   Felix Ankomah Asante: Economic Analysis of Decentralisation in Rural Ghana. 2003.

Band 33   Chodechai Suwanaporn: Determinants of Bank Lending in Thailand: An Empirical Examination for the Years 1992 to 1996. 2003.

Band 34   Abay Asfaw: Costs of Illness, Demand for Medical Care, and the Prospect of Community Health Insurance Schemes in the Rural Areas of Ethiopia. 2003.

Band 35   Gi-Soon Song: The Impact of Information and Communication Technologies (ICTs) on Rural Households. A Holistic Approach Applied to the Case of Lao People's Democratic Republic. 2003.

Band 36   Daniela Lohlein: An Economic Analysis of Public Good Provision in Rural Russia. The Case of Education and Health Care. 2003.

Band 37   Johannes Woelcke. Bio-Economics of Sustainable Land Management in Uganda. 2003.

Band 38   Susanne M. Ziemek: The Economics of Volunteer Labor Supply. An Application to Countries of a Different Development Level. 2003.

Band 39   Doris Wiesmann: An International Nutrition Index. Concept and Analyses of Food Insecurity and Undernutrition at Country Levels. 2004.

Band 40   Isaac Osei-Akoto: The Economics of Rural Health Insurance. The Effects of Formal and Informal Risk-Sharing Schemes in Ghana. 2004.

Band 41   Yuansheng Jiang: Health Insurance Demand and Health Risk Management in Rural China. 2004.

Band 42   Roukayatou Zimmermann: Biotechnology and Value-added Traits in Food Crops: Relevance for Developing Countries and Economic Analyses. 2004.

Band 43   F. Markus Kaiser: Incentives in Community-based Health Insurance Schemes. 2004.

Band 44   Thomas Herzfeld: *Corruption begets Corruption*. Zur Dynamik und Persistenz der Korruption. 2004.

Band 45   Edilegnaw Wale Zegeye: The Economics of On-Farm Conservation of Crop Diversity in Ethiopia: Incentives, Attribute Preferences and Opportunity Costs of Maintaining Local Varieties of Crops. 2004.

Band 46   Adama Konseiga: Regional Integration Beyond the Traditional Trade Benefits: Labor Mobility contribution. The Case of Burkina Faso and Côte d'Ivoire. 2005.

Band 47   Beyene Tadesse Ferenji: The Impact of Policy Reform and Institutional Transformation on Agricultural Performance. An Economic Study of Ethiopian Agriculture. 2005.

Band 48   Sabine Daude: Agricultural Trade Liberalization in the WTO and Its Poverty Implications. A Study of Rural Households in Northern Vietnam. 2005.

Band 49   Kadir Osman Gyasi: Determinants of Success of Collective Action on Local Commons. An Empirical Analysis of Community-Based Irrigation Management in Northern Ghana. 2005.

Band 50   Borbala E. Balint: Determinants of Commercial Orientation and Sustainability of Agricultural Production of the Individual Farms in Romania. 2006.

Band 51   Pamela Marinda: Effects of Gender Inequality in Resource Ownership and Access on Household Welfare and Food Security in Kenya. A Case Study of West Pokot District. 2006.

Band 52   Charles Palmer: The Outcomes and their Determinants from Community-Company Contracting over Forest Use in Post-Decentralization Indonesia. 2006.

Band 53   Hardwick Tchale: Agricultural Policy and Soil Fertility Management in the Maize-based Smallholder Farming System in Malawi. 2006.

Band 54   John Kedi Mduma: Rural Off-Farm Employment and its Effects on Adoption of Labor Intensive Soil Conserving Measures in Tanzania. 2006.

Band 55   Mareike Meyn: The Impact of EU Free Trade Agreements on Economic Development and Regional Integration in Southern Africa. The Example of EU-SACU Trade Relations. 2006.

Band 56   Clemens Breisinger: Modelling Infrastructure Investments, Growth and Poverty Impact. A Two-Region Computable General Equilibrium Perspective on Vietnam. 2006.

Band 57   Meike Wollni: Coping with the Coffee Crisis. An Analysis of the Production and Marketing Performance of Coffee Farmers in Costa Rica. 2007.

Band 58   Franklin Simtowe: Performance and Impact of Microfinance. Evidence from Joint Liability Lending Programs in Malawi. 2008.

Band 59   Xiangping Jia: Credit Rationing and Institutional Constraint. Evidence from Rural China. 2008.

Band 60   Holger Seebens: The Economics of Gender and the Household in Developing Countries. 2008.

Band 61   Stephan Piotrowski: Land Property Rights and Natural Resource Use. An Analysis of Household Behavior in Rural China. 2009.

www.peterlang.de

Yaw Osei-Asare

Household Water Security and Water Demand in the Volta Basin of Ghana

Frankfurt am Main, Berlin, Bern, Bruxelles, New York, Oxford, Wien, 2005.
XIII, 151 pp., num. tab. and graf.
European University Studies: Series 5, Economics and Management. Vol. 3152
ISBN 978-3-631-54317-7 · pb. € 36.20*

As water insecurity can threaten the livelihoods of households and economic sectors, especially irrigated agriculture and hydroelectric power generation, this study investigates water security conditions and water demand behaviour in the Ghanaian part of the Volta basin in West Africa. The book examines the extent of household water accessibility, identifies key factors that influence a household's choice for improved water sources, and models household water demand in rural Ghana. A common sampling frame is developed using Principal Component and Cluster Analyses to select observation units for household data collection. The study finds low per capita water consumption and difficult water accessibility with much reliance on unsafe water sources. With water considered as a heterogeneous good and employing the Linearised Almost Ideal Demand System (LAIDS) model, the empirical results indicate that water for drinking and cooking and water for other indoor purposes such as dish washing, bathing and sanitation are normal necessity goods that play complementary roles in achieving complete household water security. Results from a Heckman two-stage procedure indicate that rural households exhibit different water demand behaviour contingent on household size, income levels, type of good and water price.

Contents: Ghana · Volta Basin · Household Water security · Water demand · Consumer demand modelling · Almost Ideal Demand System (AIDS) model

Frankfurt am Main · Berlin · Bern · Bruxelles · New York · Oxford · Wien
Distribution: Verlag Peter Lang AG
Moosstr. 1, CH-2542 Pieterlen
Telefax 00 41 (0) 32 / 376 17 27

*The €-price includes German tax rate
Prices are subject to change without notice
Homepage http://www.peterlang.de

Peter Lang · Internationaler Verlag der Wissenschaften